The Struggle for Greek Independence

The Struggle for Greek Independence

Essays to mark the 150th anniversary of the Greek War of Independence

Edited by
RICHARD CLOGG

Lecturer in Modern Greek History, School of Slavonic and East European Studies and King's College, University of London

Archon Books
1973

Library of Congress Cataloging in Publication Data

Main entry under title:

The Struggle for Greek Independence; essays to mark the 150th
anniversary of the Greek War of Independence.

"With two exceptions the essays printed in this collection
are based on papers read at a seminar organised under the
auspices of the History Department of the School of Slavonic
and East European Studies and the Department of Byzantine
and Modern Greek Studies, King's College, University of London. The seminar was held during the winter term 1971."
   Includes bibliographical references.
   1. Greece, Modern—History—War of Independence,
1821–1829—Addresses, essays, lectures.   I. Clogg, Richard,
1939– ed.
DF804.7.S8   949.5′06   73–12073
ISBN 0–208–01303–2

© The Macmillan Press Ltd 1973

First published 1973 by
THE MACMILLAN PRESS, LTD
London and Basingstoke
and in the United States of America
as an Archon Book, an imprint of
THE SHOE STRING PRESS, INC.
Hamden, Connecticut 06514

Printed in Great Britain

Contents

Preface

With two exceptions the essays printed in this collection are based on papers read at a seminar organised under the auspices of the History Department of the School of Slavonic and East European Studies and the Department of Byzantine and Modern Greek Studies, King's College, University of London. The seminar was held during the winter term 1971, to mark the 150th anniversary of the outbreak of the Greek War of Independence in 1821. The two additional contributions are those of Professors Cyril Mango and George Frangos. Regrettably, one of the papers given at the seminar, that of Professor Bernard Lewis on the Ottoman background to 1821, is not included. I have tried to give some account of this Ottoman background in my introductory chapter, which accounts for its greater length.

I should like to thank the contributors to this volume for the readiness with which they agreed to prepare their papers for publication, and also those who attended the seminar and whose participation in the discussion greatly contributed to its liveliness. Thanks are also due to Anne Pilcher of King's College and to Mary Jo Clogg for help in the preparation of this book.

Richard Clogg

January 1973

I Aspects of the Movement for Greek Independence

RICHARD CLOGG

This introductory chapter does not seek to provide a comprehensive analysis of the movement for Greek independence, but rather to sketch in some features of the movement not covered in subsequent chapters and to give some indication of the nature of Greek society during the pre-independence period. For the period of the *Tourkokratia* remains the least studied and least understood period of Greek history and is likely to remain so for as long as the Ottoman sources relating to this period remain inaccessible, for linguistic and other reasons, to most historians (including myself). This neglect of the Ottoman background has inevitably led to a somewhat one-sided picture. For the growth of the movement for Greek independence, a nationalist movement which has a number of distinctively modern features,[1] can only be properly understood within the overall Ottoman imperial context, and more particularly within the context of Ottoman decline.

During the four centuries of Ottoman rule, the preservation of a sense of corporate identity among the Greeks was materially assisted by the general policy adopted by the Ottomans towards their non-Muslim subjects. All the Orthodox Christians within the Empire, irrespective of ethnic origin, constituted the Orthodox *millet*. The head (*millet başı*) of this *Rum milleti* was the Ecumenical Patriarch, who was always a Greek, as indeed were the members of the Holy Synod.[2] In addition to his spiritual jurisdiction over the Orthodox *pliroma*, the Patriarch, together with the Orthodox hierarchy, exercised a considerable jurisdiction in civil affairs, and more particularly in marital and testamentary matters. As Bishop Theophilos of Kampania observed in his *Nomikon* of 1788:

In the days of the Christian kingdom (alas) [i.e., the Byzantine Empire] prelates had jurisdiction only over the priesthood
and ecclesiastical matters and did not meddle in civil matters
. . . now prelates must have experience not only in ecclesiastical law . . . but also in civil law so as not to make illegal
and stupid judgements.[3]

At the same time the Orthodox subjects of the Empire
suffered from certain disabilities. The Christian, among other
obligations, was liable to the *cizye* (poll-tax) and *harac* (a tax
levied in lieu of military service); his evidence in the Muslim
kadi's court was not accepted against that of a Muslim; he could
not marry a Muslim woman; he had to wear distinctive clothing; he was forbidden to bear arms and to ride horses, although
these latter prohibitions were honoured more in the breach than
in the observance (see also Chapter 7).

In the early centuries of the *Tourkokratia*, the most onerous
imposition to which the Balkan Orthodox Christians were subject was the *devşirme* or *paidomazoma*. This was the obligation,
imposed at regular intervals, to hand over a certain proportion
of Christian children, who were to be raised in the Muslim
faith and serve the Ottoman state either in a civilian or in a
military capacity as janissaries. This forced tribute was, of
course, often bitterly resented, but there is also evidence that
Christian, and indeed Muslim, parents actively sought enrolment in the janissary corps for their children, as this was seen as
an important means of worldly advancement. This system,
however, seems to have lapsed into almost complete abeyance
by the end of the seventeenth century, although there are indications that it lingered on in isolated areas until the early years of
the eighteenth century.[4]

Moreover, in certain areas of the Empire the Greeks enjoyed
virtual autonomy and a high degree of self-government, often
combined with special tax privileges. Among these areas were
the *Dervenokhoria* (seven villages in the Megarid plain), the
Eleftherokhoria (three confederations of villages in Khalkidiki),
Zagora, Sphakia, Mani, Ayvalık (Kydonies), Chios and the
Peloponnese.[5]

Of major relevance to the growth of the Greek national movement was the protracted process of Ottoman decline. This had

begun, of course, long before the first stirrings of the movement for Greek independence began to manifest themselves in the middle of the eighteenth century. But the process of decline gained momentum during the course of the eighteenth century, under the impetus of external and internal pressures, so that by the decades immediately before 1821 the Ottoman Empire had ceased in a number of significant respects to function as a unitary state. This, of course, was of inestimable benefit to the Greeks when hostilities did eventually break out, for the impotence and disorganisation of the central government enabled them to prolong their struggle until the Powers were reluctantly, and against their natural inclination, forced to intervene in the struggle, thereby assuming the role of guarantors of Greek independence.

Already by the early seventeenth century Ottoman observers were pondering the reasons for the decline of the Ottoman Empire. Koçu Bey, 'the Turkish Montesquieu', in a memorandum drawn up for Sultan Murad IV in 1630 pointed to the deleterious consequences of the Sultan's withdrawal from direct supervision of the affairs of state and to the debasement of the office of Grand Vizir, with a resulting growth in corruption, place-seeking and intrigue of all kinds. In the mid-seventeenth century Hacı Halifa even called for a man of the sword to take dictatorial action to restore the declining fortunes of the Ottoman Empire, while in 1669 Hüseyin Hezarfenn stressed the need for efficient and just governors.[6] By the eighteenth century, however, provincial governorships were often held for as little as a year, as competition for such lucrative posts increased among those anxious to amass private fortunes from the fruits of office.[7]

The halting of the Empire's westward expansion into Europe and indeed the beginning of the slow but steady retreat of the Empire in Europe, signified in the treaties of Karlowitz (1699), Pruth (1711), Passarowitz (1718) and Belgrade (1739), cut at the very roots of an imperial system predicated on military expansion and colonisation. The loss of territory in Europe resulted in a serious loss of manpower and tax revenues which aggravated the already serious economic problems facing the Empire. These were also compounded by massive inflation, which the Porte vainly tried to check by the introduction of new types of coinage. It was the Porte's chronic shortage of money that contributed to the institutionalisation of extortion and rapacity at all levels of society.

This was reflected in the provinces by the decline of the system of military fief-holders, the *sipahis*, who had provided the Ottoman armies with cavalry. Gradually their fiefs or *timars* were taken over by tax-farmers or *mültezims*, or were transformed into heritable *çiftliks*. The *mültezims* were principally interested in maximising the returns from landed property regardless of peasant hardship, while, as Professor Stoianovich has put it, 'the çiftlik marks the transition from a social and economic structure founded upon a system of moderate land rent and few labor services to one of excessive land rent and exaggerated service.' One consequence of this development was that the proprietor of a *çiftlik* village often received as much as one half of the produce of his peasants after they had paid the land tax to the state.[8]

The collapse of the *devşirme* system was paralleled by the decline of the janissaries from a military *corps d'élite* to an armed and largely hereditary faction which was to remain an actual or potential threat to imperial authority until its destruction by Mahmud II in 1826. It is worth noting in this context that the Serbian revolt of 1804 was essentially a response to intolerable oppression by the janissaries.

Moreover, the Ottoman imperial structure was threatened from without, as well as from within, during the late seventeenth and eighteenth centuries, both on its western and northern flanks and on its eastern flank. For the Austrian push into the Balkans was matched, during the early eighteenth century at least, by the power of Nadir Shah in Persia. But much the most serious external threat to the Empire was represented by the expansionist ambitions of Russia (see below).

Probably the one factor in the decline of the Ottoman Empire which most directly assisted the Greek cause was the virtual collapse of the Ottoman Empire as a unitary state in the course of the eighteenth century, with the growth of provincial autonomies in many regions of the Empire, characterised by the emergence of a new provincial élite, composed of the Anatolian *derebeys* (valley lords) and the Rumeliot *ayans* (notables), who developed strong local roots in the territories over which they ruled.[9] The *ayans* and *derebeys* built up dynasties which were frequently *de facto*, if not necessarily *de jure*,[10] independent of the

Ottoman central government, and these dynasties had effective control over large areas of the Empire.[11] According to the Ottoman historian Ahmed Cevdet Paşa, during the first decade of the nineteenth century three great families, those of Canikli Ali Paşa, Çapanoğlu and Karaosmanoğlu, controlled virtually the whole of Asia Minor, with the exception of the unimportant *eyalets* of Kütahya and Karaman.[12]

Moreover, the rise to power of powerful provincial warlords such as Tepedelenli Ali Paşa,[13] whose power base was Ioannina and Epirus, and Pasvanoğlu of Vidin afforded the Greeks a suggestive example of successful and prolonged defiance of the Porte. Significantly, the Greek revolutionary Rigas Velestinlis in his *Thourios* of 1797 wrote:

> Pasvanoğlu, why do you remain so impassive
> Throw yourself on the Balkans, nest there like an eagle
> . . .
> Join with the *rayas* if you wish to conquer.[14]

Significantly it was the Porte's attempt, launched in 1820, to destroy Ali Paşa as an independent power that was to prove a factor of crucial importance to the timing of the outbreak of the Greek revolt in 1821.[15]

Many observers, too, favourably contrasted the rule of the *ayans* and *derebeys* with that of officials who remained loyal to the Porte, and stressed particularly their ability to supply the conditions of law and order of which the central government was so manifestly incapable.[16] The Anatolian *derebeys*, in particular, seem to have gone out of their way to encourage the settlement of Greeks within their territories,[17] and particularly of Greeks who fled from the Peloponnese to escape the reprisals consequent on the collapse of the *Orloffika* in 1770 (see below). One of these was the future Ecumenical Patriarch Grigorios V, who was to be executed in 1821 following the outbreak of hostilities in the Danubian Principalities and in the Peloponnese. In 1776, Grigorios, a native of Dimitsana, wrote from Smyrna an enthusiastic account of conditions on the western littoral of Asia Minor:

> And daily there disembark here countless men with their wives and children . . . for the *ağas* of Anatolia are jealous as to

who should first take them to their own district and build
churches for them, in separate Greek villages, with exemption
from the *harac* for ten years.[18]

This virtual collapse in the authority of the central government in the provinces was paralleled by an increasing loss of
control of the provincial cities of the Empire, a loss of control
directly linked to the decline of the janissaries into what
amounted to an 'armed political party'.[19] The incorrigible
indiscipline of the janissary regiments in the provincial cities is
strikingly illustrated in what is known as the Smyrna 'rebellion'
of March 1797, which the British Minister to the Porte, Spencer
Smith, quite mistakenly linked with French influence: 'a
contagious consequence of the destructive doctrines so progressive in the present day'. Following a minor incident involving some Austrian-protected tumblers and rope dancers visiting
the city, the janissaries ran amok in an orgy of violence and
destruction, directed in the first instance against the Greek *raya*
and then more generally at the Frank merchant community.
It has been estimated that about 1500 Greeks were massacred
while much of the property of the Frank merchant community
was destroyed. The British community alone suffered losses to
the value of 1,130,346 piastres, with a single merchant, Joseph
Franel, losing property worth 409,129 piastres.[20] It was un-
predictable and arbitrary outbursts of this kind that led the
Greek merchants to contrast the uncertain conditions prevailing
within the Empire with the ordered societies of Western Europe,
where property rights were given their proper respect.

During the course of the eighteenth century, efforts were
made to stem and reverse this process of decline. Attempts were
made to introduce the superior military technology of the West
by the employment of French military experts or European
renegades, such as the Hungarian Baron de Tott, the Frenchman
Count Alexander de Bonneval, and a Scotsman called Campbell
who, as Mustafa Ağa or Ingiliz Mustafa, became *kumbaracı
başı*,[21] or commander of artillery. Printing in Turkish was
introduced into the Empire, again by a renegade, the Transyl-
vanian Hungarian Ibrahim Müteferrika, in 1727 and in the
course of the eighteenth century a number of books on scientific
and military matters were printed.[22]

In an effort to modernise the army a school of geometry, the *Hendeshane*, was opened in Üsküdar in 1734, while a new naval academy was created at Aynalıkavak, under the impetus of the disastrous naval defeat at the hands of the Russians at Çeşme in 1770. A number of similar efforts were made during the century, but much the most sustained and coherent effort to modernise the institutions of the Ottoman Empire, and in particular the army and navy, was that of Selim III (1789–1807) in his *Nizam-i Cedid*, or New Order.[23] The primary objective of Selim's reforms was, of course, to strengthen the military power of the state, but he also made concerted efforts to tackle some of the other problems facing the Empire. He sought, for instance, to check the relentless drift to the cities, particularly on the part of the Christian *raya*, which was one of the consequences of endemic rural disorder. He tried to reimpose the dress regulations to which the *raya* were subject, and to stamp out the widespread abuses associated with the *berats* or *firmans* granted to the interpreters of foreign diplomatic missions and their servants.[24] These afforded considerable privileges, particularly with regard to taxation, and rendered their holders virtually immune to Ottoman jurisdiction. For this reason they were much sought after by *raya* merchants, who were willing to pay high prices for them.[25]

Selim had scarcely any more success in imposing his will in these matters than in carrying out lasting reforms in the military sphere. He was able by the end of his reign to build up a *Nizam-i Cedid* army of some 20,000 men, trained and equipped along Western lines, but this constituted only a small fraction of the total armed forces of the Empire. Moreover, these troops were bitterly resented by the janissary corps, which not only managed to resist attempts to curb its numbers but succeeded in almost doubling in size between 1794 and 1806.[26] In the end the united opposition of the janissaries and the reactionary *ulema* of theologians and judges combined to overthrow Selim III. This failure by Selim to modernise the Ottoman armies meant that when the Greeks revolted in 1821 they were confronted for the most part by ill-disciplined, ill-equipped and inefficient troops. Had Selim's reforms succeeded, the situation facing the Greeks, both politically and militarily, might have been very different.

Directly linked with the virtual collapse of Ottoman control
in the provinces was the phenomenon of *armatoloi* and *klephts*
(see also Chapter 7). These were an important element in
Greek society, for it was from the ranks of the *armatoloi* and
klephts that much of the fighting capability of the Greeks during
the War of Independence derived. The *armatoloi* were bodies of
irregular troops, for the most part Christians, employed by the
Porte in European Turkey for the maintenance of local order,
the suppression of brigandage, and the guarding of the important mountain passes of Rumeli. There is some controversy as to
the origins of this system, but it appears, in Rumeli at least,
to have assumed its classic form by the seventeenth century.

A firman of Sultan Mustafa II issued in 1699, for instance,
and addressed to Hasan Paşa, *mutassarıf* of the *sancak* of Thessaloniki, directed that 'for the guarding of the mountain passes,
bridges and dangerous points in the region of Ioannina, Larissa,
Servia, Grevena, Gennitsa, Doiran, Stromnitsa, Monastir,
Prilep and Köprülü and for the protection of travellers and
merchants in these regions, *armatoloi* are to be appointed by the
notables of the *vilayet*, and they are to be paid by the inhabitants,
both *raya* and *non-raya* . . .'[27] Rumeli seems to have been divided
into between 14 and 18 *armatoliks*, some of which became with
the passage of time hereditary, their leaders being known as
kapetanioi. In the Peloponnese the functions of the *armatoloi* in
Rumeli were carried out by the *kapoi*, who constituted virtual
private armies in the pay of the Greek primates.[28] Although
they owed allegiance to the Porte, the *armatoloi* did on occasion
rise up against their masters. At the time of the Russian
expedition to the Peloponnese in 1770, for example, *armatoloi* in
Macedonia, at the instigation of Georgios Papazolis of Siatista,
an emissary of Catherine II and the author of a book on military
strategy,[29] rose up against the Turks.

One of the ostensible duties of the *armatoloi* was to hold in
check that other great body of Greek irregulars, the *klephts*. The
klephts were essentially bandits, who had taken to the mountains
for a number of reasons, usually to avoid the payment of taxes
or to escape pursuit by the authorities. As their attacks tended
principally to be directed against Ottoman officials and tax
collectors, and members of the Greek élite, namely wealthy
merchants, primates, clerics and monasteries, they acquired

among the Greek population at large something of a Robin
Hood image. The *klephts* were organised in bands up to 200 or
300 strong, although 50 was a more normal figure.

The distinction between *armatolos* and *klepht* should not be
overstressed. The dividing line between the two was often very
narrow – the *armatolos*, for instance, if his pay was not forthcoming, might easily slip into banditry while the *klepht*, if the
proceeds of banditry were showing signs of dropping off, and if
the *armatoloi* were being paid, might, temporarily at least,
transfer his allegiance. In the words of one of the klephtic
ballads, which provide the best insight into the klephtic
Weltanschauung,

> For twelve years long I lived a cleft on Chasia and Olympos;
> At Luros and Xeromeros I served as armatolos.[30]

The phenomenon of the *klephtouria* was, of course, by no means
confined to the Greek lands. Similar formations existed in the
Bulgarian (*haiduts*), Serbian (*haiduks*) and Rumanian (*haiduci*)
provinces. Indeed, Professor T. Stoianovich has estimated that
'by the end of the eighteenth or beginning of the nineteenth
century, perhaps 10 per cent or more of the Balkan Christian
population, at least in some of the frontier areas, was organized
militarily for the purpose of transforming or abolishing rather
than defending the Empire'.[31]

A much smaller, élite group within pre-revolutionary Greek
society, the nearest thing to a 'noblesse de robe', and a group
whose rise to power and influence was a function of Ottoman
decline, were the Phanariots, who are the subject of Cyril
Mango's Chapter 2. For as the Ottoman Empire was forced on
to the defensive towards the end of the seventeenth century, the
Porte was forced to treat with, rather than dictate to, the
Christian powers of the West. For the conduct of their diplomacy
they were forced increasingly to rely on the Phanariots. During
the eighteenth and first two decades of the nineteenth century
the Phanariots came to monopolise the office of *megas diermenefs*
(*tercüman başı* or principal interpreter) to the Ottoman Porte. In
this office they were frequently able to exercise a considerable
influence over the conduct of Ottoman diplomacy. It is no
mere coincidence that the greatest achievement of the first
Phanariot of significance, Alexandros Mavrokordatos o ex

Aporriton, was the negotiation of the treaty of Karlowitz in 1699.[32]

The tightly-knit group of Phanariots, drawn from eleven families, came, during the course of the eighteenth century, to monopolise not only the post of *megas dierminefs* but also that of *dierminefs tou stolou*, principal interpreter to the *kaptan paşa* of the Ottoman fleet and effective governor of the islands of the Archipelago, and the posts of *hospodar*, or prince, of Moldavia and Wallachia. Arnold Toynbee has advanced the view that the Phanariots may well have imagined that they had within their grasp the kind of ascendancy for the Greeks within the Ottoman Empire that Joseph II had been working to secure for the Germans within the Hapsburg monarchy. But this idea that the Phanariots were working to subvert the Empire from within in the interest of the Greeks as a whole is scarcely tenable. Certainly their contemporaries regarded the Phanariots as instruments of Turkish oppression, indifferent to the plight of the Greeks. In the popular satirical poem *Rossanglogallos*, which appears to have enjoyed a wide manuscript circulation during the first decade or so of the nineteenth century, the 'vlakhbey' of Wallachia declares that:

> The freedom of Hellas
> Implies poverty for me
> . . .
> As a slave I am glorified
> Beloved by the Turks.[33]

The rise to positions of power and influence during the eighteenth century of the Phanariots was paralleled by the growth of a substantial Greek merchant class, both within the Greek lands and, more significantly, without. The development of this Greek merchant diaspora had the paradoxical result that the Greeks controlled a commercial empire before they had gained political independence.[34] George Frangos, in Chapter 4, provides a survey of growth of this merchant diaspora, while T. Stoianovich has isolated the factors which he believes to have been instrumental in contributing to the growth of a Balkan Orthodox merchant class.[35] Stoianovich has warned against assuming that all the Orthodox merchants trading in Central Europe were 'Greeks', as the Hapsburg authorities tended indiscriminately to classify them. Greek was the *lingua franca* of Balkan commerce and for this reason Vlachs, Orthodox Albanians, Macedonian slavs, Bulgarians and Serbs were often indiscriminately lumped together as 'Greeks'. But it is undeniable that Greeks and hellenised Vlachs constituted the largest single element in this Balkan Orthodox merchant class. In the words of Henry Holland:

> The active spirit of the Greeks, deprived in great measure of political or national objects, has taken a general direction towards commerce. But, fettered in this respect also, by their condition on the continent of Greece, they emigrate in considerable numbers to adjacent countries, where their activity can have more scope in the nature of the government . . . by far the greater part of the exterior trade of Turkey, in the exchange of commodities, is carried on by Greek houses, which have residents at home, and branches in various cities of Europe, mutually aiding each other . . . Many of the merchants here [Ioannina] have extensive continental connections, which are often family ones likewise. An instance at this time occurs to me of a Greek family, with which I was intimate, where, of four brothers, one was settled at Ioannina, another at Moscow, a third at Constantinople, and the fourth in some part of Germany; all connected together in their concerns.[36]

Substantial Greek merchant colonies were to be found throughout Central Europe and Southern Russia, particularly in lands that had recently been won from the Ottoman Empire, such as Hungary[37] and the Crimea. Newly created towns on the Black Sea and the sea of Azov, such as Odessa, Mariupol and Taganrog, contained large Greek colonies, while Greeks were able to trade under the Russian flag in the Black Sea after the Treaty of Küçük Kaynarca (1774). The bulk of the commerce of the principal seaports of the Ottoman Empire, such as Constantinople, Thessaloniki, Patras, Smyrna and Alexandria,[38] was shared between Ottoman Greeks and foreign merchants. During the seventeenth and eighteenth centuries, flourishing Greek communities developed throughout the Mediterranean in Venice, Trieste,[39] Livorno, Marseilles, Naples, etc. One of the most interesting and least known Greek merchant communities established during the course of the eighteenth century was the small but flourishing community established in Bengal, at Calcutta and Dacca, and which was mainly composed of Greeks from Plovdiv (Philippopolis). On the outbreak of the Greek War of Independence a philhellenic society to raise funds for the prosecution of the war was set up, in which the Anglican bishop of Calcutta played a leading part and to which Chinese merchants in the city are reported to have contributed.[40]

A prime factor in the growth of the Mediterranean diaspora was the growth of the Greek merchant marine, which grew at a very rapid rate during the last decades of the eighteenth century, and the first of the nineteenth century, particularly under the impetus of the French revolutionary and Napoleonic wars. Greek sea captains made large fortunes out of blockade running and the Greeks eclipsed the French in the commerce of the Eastern Mediterranean. Islands such as Hydra, Spetsai and Psara built up large merchant fleets. By 1806, for instance, that of Hydra totalled 73 large and 26 small ships, with a combined tonnage of some 15,000 tons. By the eve of the War of Independence the Hydriot fleet had risen to 186 (totalling some 27,716 tons), while it has been estimated that the overall size of the Greek merchant marine had risen to almost 1000 vessels by the end of the Napoleonic wars. These fleets, and the expertise of Greek seamen and privateers, were, of course, to prove an invaluable asset to the Greeks in 1821. Moreover, the slump that followed the ending of the Napoleonic wars hit Greece's seaborne commerce very hard. The aggregate profits of Hydriot merchants, for instance, fell from 7,749,510 piastres in 1816 to 1,375,039 in 1820. This was undoubtedly a factor in precipitating the wealthy shipowners and sea captains of the islands to throw in their lot, if reluctantly at first, with the insurgents.[41]

Much of the considerable wealth of the Greek merchant bourgeoisie was gained in the export of goods and raw materials from the Ottoman Empire. For the general arbitrariness of life under Ottoman rule disinclined Greek entrepreneurs to risk their capital in industrial or semi-industrial enterprises, the physical assets of which would, of course, have been particularly vulnerable to the depredations of local Ottoman officials. Commercial activity on the other hand offered numerous opportunities to salt away money out of the reach of the Ottoman tax collector. There were some exceptions, however, to this general rule and, of these, the Thessalian town of Ambelakia is probably the most significant. Ambelakia, in the closing years of the eighteenth century, according to the French consul in Thessaloniki, Felix Beaujour, 'by the activity of its inhabitants, resembles rather a city of Holland than a Turkish village'. The German traveller, J. L. S. Bartholdy, even came across a small amateur theatre in the town, in which, 'as throughout the civilized world', the audience wept over a performance of Kotzebue's *Menschenhass und Reue.*[42]

During the last three decades of the eighteenth century the population of Ambelakia tripled, and the twenty-four manufactories in the town produced annually some 2000 bales of spun red cotton, each weighing approximately 312 lbs. This output was wholly exported to Central Europe and particularly to Pest, Vienna, Leipzig, Dresden, Anspach and Bayreuth, where the Ambelakiots maintained agents. After 1777 an elaborate cooperative enterprise was created out of hitherto competitive enterprises, and returns of 60, 80 or even 100 per cent on capital invested were not unknown. But the system eventually collapsed into factional dispute in which 'everyone wished to command' and in which 'all those petty shuffling passions, which enter into the composition of the Greek character', manifested themselves.[43]

This massive upsurge in Greek commercial activity in the eighteenth century, then, is an established fact. But what was the political significance of the emergence of this Greek commercial bourgeoisie scattered throughout the Mediterranean, Central Europe and Southern Russia? Historians have too often simply assumed a direct and necessary link between the growth of this merchant bourgeoisie and the flowering of the independence movement. How revolutionary in fact was this merchant class and what was its precise contribution to the movement for liberation?

The first point to emphasise, of course, is the obvious one that the term 'merchant' can embrace anyone from an itinerant pedlar to a wealthy entrepreneur. In this context the term merchant is employed in the sense of the more prosperous members of this merchant class. On one level, of course, these merchants, or some of them, did make a contribution to the

Greek national revival by financing the educational revival
which is so pronounced a feature of the pre-independence
decades. Adamantios Korais, for instance, in his *Mémoire sur
l'état actuel de la civilisation dans la Grèce*, the text of a lecture
delivered in Paris in 1803 and perhaps the most remarkable
literary document of the Greek national movement, makes the
point that the need of Greek merchants of the diaspora to
acquire the languages of the countries in which they were
settled led them to acquire 'a tincture of erudition and belles
lettres'.[44]

Hence their patronage of schools and libraries in their own
native communities and their patronage of young Greeks who
wished to study abroad (see also Chapter 3).[45] Some, notably
the brothers Zosimas of Ioannina, extended their patronage of
learning to the subsidy of books printed in Greek for free
distribution among Greek schools, notably, of course, Korais'
Elliniki Vivliothiki, an extended series of editions of classical texts
with improving introductions, discussing the cultural problems
of contemporary Greece. Moreover, Korais, the foremost
ideologist of Greece's national revival, was himself, it should be
remembered, the son of a silk merchant in the *bezesten* of Smyrna,
and began his career with an unhappy stint as a merchant in
Amsterdam, but, as a friend pointed out, he was 'not cut out for
commerce' ('Touto dia negotzio den einai').

It has also been suggested that, in addition to acting as
patrons of learning, the merchants themselves acted as vehicles
for the collection and dissemination of Western ideas in the
Orthodox world.[46] But there is little tangible evidence for this,
although there are indications that some merchants, at least,
may have been enthused by French revolutionary principles. In
a despatch of 15 October 1793, for instance, the French consul in
Bucharest, Hortolan, reported to his ambassador in Constantinople, Descorches, that 'presque tous les négociants de Janina et
de l'Albanie, établis ici, sont des sans-culottes. Ils ont traduit les
Droits de l'Homme; tous les savent par coeur.'[47]

More plausibly, it has been suggested that the merchants as a
class were moved to throw their weight behind the struggle for
independence by their increasing impatience with the arbitrariness and uncertainty that characterised Ottoman rule, and
which obviously stood in the way of the maximisation of

profits.[48] The classic and often quoted statement of this view on the part of one of these merchants is that of Ioannis Pringos, a native of Zagora and for many years established in Amsterdam as a prosperous merchant.[49] Pringos was a fervent admirer of the order and commercial freedom that prevailed in the Dutch republic. Amsterdam he described as 'a great place for trade' and he spoke with awed respect of the Amsterdam stock exchange and of the system of commercial companies established in Holland. He wrote:

All these things . . . cannot be supported under the Turk, nor cannot they come about, for he is without order and justice, and when the capital (*sermaye*) amounts to one thousand, he deems it ten times as much, so as to confiscate it, to impoverish the others, not appreciating that the wealth of his subjects is the wealth of his Empire. They (the Dutch) maintain justice but he (the Turk) is wholly unjust and cannot achieve anything but can only destroy. May the Almighty annihilate him, and may Christianity prevail, so that governments may come into being similar to the above, to those in Europe, where every one has his own without fear of injustice, where justice reigns . . .[50]

Many other contemporary Greek sources stress the insecurity of life and property that characterised Ottoman rule during the period of Ottoman decline. Daniil Philippidis and Grigorios Konstantas in their *Geographia Neoteriki*, published in Vienna in 1791, a work which is a source of much highly interesting material on the nature of Greek society in the eighteenth century, attribute to this factor the emigration of Greeks, particularly the wealthy, that was a characteristic feature of this period.[51] Some perceptive Ottoman observers also noted the stark contrast between Ottoman practice and that of the nation states of Western Europe. Ebubekir Ratib Efendi, Selim III's ambassador in Vienna in 1792–3, observed that in European states:

. . . the laws, organizations, principles and taxes laid down by their Kings are observed properly by high and low persons. So long as their taxes are paid on time, no king or general or official can interfere with anyone because of it . . .[52]

Certainly, then, there is evidence that Greek merchants in the decades before 1821 increasingly chafed against conditions which militated against the full exploitation of the commercial opportunities available within the Empire. But what is the evidence that this generalised discontent on the part of the merchants was transformed into political action? Historians have often pointed to the predominance of merchants (rather over 50 per cent) in the membership of the *Philiki Etairia*, the secret revolutionary society that helped lay the organisational framework of the Greek revolt, and to the fact that its three founders, Xanthos, Skouphas and Tsakalov, were merchants. But, as George Frangos convincingly demonstrates in Chapter 4, those merchants who did enrol in the *Etairia* were in their great majority those who had failed to make the grade in the competitive world of commerce. The established and wealthy merchants for the most part wanted nothing to do with the society.

Certainly the popular image of the merchants as a class was unflattering. They were seen as basically unsympathetic to Greece's plight, more interested in profit than in independence. In the *Rossanglogallos*, the merchant declares:

> I have given no thought to Greece
> For all that it bears a tyrannical yoke.
> But I continually await loaded ships,
> From the Barbary Coast and the country of the Franks.
> . . .
> I weep for my nation, because it is under the yoke,
> But for freedom I do not give a penny. [53]

The anonymous author of the *Elliniki Nomarkhia* (1806), the most significant example of pre-independence polemical literature, diagnosed as the reasons for the servitude of the Greeks the 'ignorant priesthood and the absence of the best fellow citizens'. By these latter he meant the merchant bourgeoisie, who, however valid the reasons that had originally obliged them to exile themselves from Greece and however worthy their previous benefactions to the nation, now owed it to Greece to return to their homeland and place their undoubted skills and knowledge at the service of the struggle for independence. But, he added, most merchants established abroad did not give a damn for their country; they had become denationalised and had been transformed into 'true enemies and worse than Greece's Ottoman tyrants'. Once they had made money 'they sink into the mire of debauchery and wallow about like pigs until they die', perverted by the immorality which characterises the foreigner. The same applied to Greek students studying abroad. Instead of studying politics, law, tactics and 'sciences useful for our nation' they read fanciful poems 'of which there are more volumes in France and Italy than pumpkins in the Peloponnese'. The conversation of these miserly merchants 'begins with cotton and ends with beans, that of the young begins with the theatre and ends with women'. It was now the overriding patriotic duty of the merchants to return home, when they would very quickly feel the improvement wrought by their presence. For who else would be able to counter the power and influence of the *hocabaşıs* and the higher clergy?[54]

The anonymous author of the *Elliniki Nomarkhia* was not alone in regarding the *hocabaşıs* (*proestoi*, *proychountes*, primates or notables; see also Chapter 7), the nearest equivalent to a Greek propertied élite, as a group who, like the Phanariots, the higher clergy and many of the merchants, were wedded to the Ottoman status quo. Photakos Khrysanthopoulos, for instance, a hero of the War of Independence, noted in his memoirs that the

> *hocabaşı* imitated the Turk in everything, including dress, manners and household. His notion of living in style was the same as the Turks', and the only difference between them was one of names: for instance instead of being called Hasan the *hocabaşı*, he would be called Yanni, and instead of going to the mosque he would go to the church. This was the only distinction between the two.[55]

Part of their unpopularity is explained by the fact that the *hocabaşıs* acted as intermediaries between the Turkish officials and the Greek populations, frequently combining the roles of landlord and tax collector.[56] In areas where the Greeks enjoyed a measure of autonomy their powers were correspondingly increased. Nowhere were the *hocabaşıs* more powerful than in the Peloponnese. Here the primates comprised a distinct economic group, owning as much as a third of the total land owned by the Greeks. To their profits from the land, they added the proceeds of tax farming and incurred much consequent hostility, as it fell

to them to allot the proportion of taxes levied in a particular
paşalık on the individual Christian families. They also began
increasingly to engage in trade, and, as they were also landowners, they were able to control the price of primary produce.
In the Peloponnese the primates elected representatives to a kind
of advisory council to the Ottoman governor which met once a
year. Two of their number were elected to act as permanent
advisers to the *paşa*, and two other primates, known as *vekils*,
acted as virtual ambassadors of this Peloponnesian Greek élite
in Constantinople.[57]

The *hocabaşıs* or 'christian Turks', however, probably incurred
less odium than the upper strata of the hierarchy of the Orthodox church. As the English traveller, Sir William Gell, noted,
there was 'a saying common among the Greeks, that the country
labours under three curses, the priests, the cogia bashis, and the
Turks; always placing the plagues in this order'.[58] The relationship of church and state is discussed by Philip Sherrard in
Chapter 8. Of particular significance to the nascent national
movement was the growth of anti-clerical attitudes among
many of the most active protagonists of Greek independence.
As the national revival gathered momentum, the hierarchy of
the church became increasingly identified with educational
obscurantism and political reaction. Heresy trials, the burning
of offending books, and the hierarchy's opposition to an increasing emphasis in the schools and colleges on the natural sciences
and on Greece's classical heritage, were all manifestations of this
tendency. In an encyclical of 1819, the Ecumenical Patriarch
Grigorios V and the Holy Synod asked:

> What benefit does our youth derive from learning numbers
> and algebra, cubes and cube roots, triangles and tetragons,
> logarithms, calculus, ellipses, atoms, vacuums, vortices,
> power and attraction, gravity, the northern lights, optical
> and acoustic matters and a myriad such things . . . if in speech
> they are barbaric, if their writings are full of solecisms, if they
> have no idea of religion, if their morals are degenerate, if their
> forms of government are injurious . . . ?[59]

Even more offensive to the active proponents of Greek
independence was what they considered to be the craven attitude of 'ethelodouleia', or voluntary submission to the Ottoman

authorities, on the part of church hierarchy. A well-known, but by no means atypical, expression of such attitudes is contained in the *Didaskalia Patriki*, written by Anthimos, the Patriarch of Jerusalem, and printed at the press of the Ecumenical Patriarchate in Constantinople in 1798. Anthimos declared that God had deliberately raised up the Ottoman Empire to protect the Orthodox faith from contamination by the heresies of the West. The Orthodox flock as a consequence owed the Ottoman Porte a duty of absolute, unquestioning, and, indeed, grateful obedience.[60] With the increasing threat posed to the Ottoman Empire by France in the late 1790s numerous patriarchical encyclicals were issued warning against 'the wily snares of unrest and rebellion' being propagated in those parts by the French and issuing stern injunctions that any copies of Rigas Velestinlis' *Nea politiki doiikisis*, found circulating among the Orthodox flock, should be handed over for destruction.[61] When the Greeks did revolt in 1821, the Ecumenical Patriarch Grigorios V and the Holy Synod issued several encyclicals denouncing the insurgents and anathematising Alexandros Ypsilantis and his followers 'as traitors, haters of religion and atheists'.[62] Not surprisingly, such attitudes stimulated anti-clerical sentiments, both at a popular level as expressed in the *Rossanglogallos*, and among the nascent Greek intelligentsia, in the writings of illuminati such as Adamantios Korais, Daniil Philippidis, Grigorios Konstantas and the anonymous authors of the *Elliniki Nomarkhia* and the *Stokhasmoi tou Kritonos* (1819).[63]

The influence of this small and largely Western-oriented intelligentsia is discussed by Catherine Koumarianou in Chapter 3, while Alexis Dimaras and Robin Fletcher discuss related aspects of this question, the role of the non-military philhellenes and their influence on Greek intellectual and literary developments during the period of the War of Independence in Chapters 9 and 10. The very considerable increase in book publishing, the increasingly secular nature of Greek culture, the introduction of the learning of the Western Enlightenment into the Greek world by means of translations, the development of schools and academies with more advanced curricula, the growth of an awareness of Greece's past glories, amounting latterly to an obsession,[64] were all characteristic of this intellectual revival. Great stress was laid on education as the essential precondition for the liberation of the Greeks, but the proponents of these views were never very clear as to how, once the Greeks had reached a sufficient level of education, the transition from subjection to the Ottomans to independent nationhood was to be achieved.[65]

The intelligentsia, however, remained small and it is not clear to what extent the nationalist ideas propagated by Korais and his followers enjoyed any broad circulation among the great mass of the Greek population. But Greek culture and education did exercise a considerable influence over the other Christian populations of the Balkans, although later, of course, a violent reaction against this process of cultural hellenisation was to set in. This 'civilizing' mission of Greek culture and language is well expressed in the poem with which the priest Daniil of Moskhopolis prefaced his tetraglott (Greek–Rumanian– Bulgarian–Albanian) lexicon published in 1802, probably in Constantinople, in order to accustom the children of the Rumano-Vlachs to the Greek language. The poem begins:

> Albanians, Bulgars, Vlachs and all who now do speak
> An alien tongue rejoice, prepare to make you Greek,
> Change your barbaric tongue, your customs rude forgo,
> So that as byegone myths your children may them know.[66]

Daniil goes on to urge young Bulgarians, Albanians and Vlachs to wake from out of the 'deep slumber of ignorance' and learn Greek, which is 'the mother of wisdom'. Greek, moreover, he adds on a more practical note, would be highly useful 'in all your commercial undertakings'. What is particularly significant about this poem is that its author, Daniil, appears not to have been a Greek but a Vlach.

To some extent Greek also acted as a filter through which the learning and literature of the West percolated to the other Christian peoples of the Balkans. And not only in the Balkans, for the Arab Mīkhā'īl Mishāqa (1800–88), talking about his early education, recalled examining some of his uncle's books which included an Arabic translation by Basili Fakhr of 'The commentary of the Archimandrite Anthimus Ghazi on the book of the Englishman Benjamin about natural science'.[67] This must have been a translation of Anthimos Gazis' translation of Benjamin Martin's popularisation of Newtonian science, *The*

Philosophical Grammar, which was first published in London in 1735.

Attitudes such as those of Daniil of Moskhopolis, of course, did not go unchallenged by the other Christian populations of the Balkans even during the eighteenth century. Paisii Khilandarski, the progenitor of modern Bulgarian nationalism, in his Slavo-Bulgarian history (*Istoriia Slavenobolgarskaia*) compiled in 1762, specifically attacked the Graecophilia of the emergent Bulgarian bourgeoisie, and urged them to employ the Bulgarian language and interest themselves in Bulgarian history. 'There are those', Paisii wrote, 'who do not care to know about their own Bulgarian nation and turn to foreign ways and foreign tongues; they do not care for their own Bulgarian language but try to read and speak Greek and are ashamed to call themselves Bulgarians.'[68]

More truly representative of the collective mentality of the Greeks during the decades before independence than the effusions of the intelligentsia were the messianic and neo-Byzantine elements in Greek thought, as Cyril Mango has stressed in Chapter 2.[69] Prophecies and messianic beliefs circulated very widely in the Greek world and profoundly influenced the thinking of the great majority of the Greeks, both literate and otherwise. These prophecies, which for the most part foretold, either explicitly or implicitly, the liberation of the Greeks from the Hagarene yoke, circulated widely throughout the period of the *Tourkokratia*. Those that appear to have circulated most widely were the prophecies attributed to Agathangelos. These were purportedly written in Sicily in 1279 and printed in Milan in 1555. In fact, they were forgeries compiled by the archimandrite Theoklitos Polyeidis, a native of Edirne, towards the middle of the eighteenth century. For a time he was priest of the Greek church in Tokay in Hungary, and later (*c.* 1744) founded the Orthodox church established for the community of Greek merchants in Leipzig.[70] This sojourn no doubt partly explains the garbled references to the Kingdoms of Europe and in particular to Germany and its heretical religion with which the text is littered. In fact, there was very little in his prophecies to give comfort to the Greeks, save vague references to the discomfiture of the Hagarenes and exhortations to Russia to awaken from her slumbers and similar ambiguities. This did not prevent, and indeed perhaps contributed to, their very wide manuscript circulation.

It was by no means only illiterate peasants, half-educated didacts and monkish obscurantists who placed their faith in these prophecies. Ioannis Pringos, the very epitome of the 'progressive' bourgeois merchant, was one of those who attached credence to the sayings of the prophecies. For, during the course of the Russo-Turkish war of 1768–74, he noted in his diary for 22 July 1771, that now was the time for the prophecy of Leo the Wise to be fulfilled according to which 'two eagles shall devour the snake'. The two eagles he took to be the double-headed eagle of the Russian Empire, which was also the emblem of the Byzantine Empire, while the snake was none other than the Turk who had entwined himself around the moribund corpse of the Byzantine Empire. For, according to Leo, the Turk was to remain in the City (i.e., Constantinople) for 320 years, of which 317 had already passed since its capture in 1454 (sic). God, Pringos concluded, during the next three years would throw the Turk out of Greece and out of Europe.[71] Moreover Rigas Velestinlis (see below), an enthusiastic advocate of French revolutionary principles and of the violent overthrow of the Ottomans, also hedged his bets by being the first to print the highly popular prophecies of Agathangelos. This he appears to have done at the press of the brothers Markidis-Poulios during his first sojourn in Vienna in 1790–1, when he also undertook the printing of the *Skholeion ton delikaton eraston* and the *Physikis Apanthisma*.[72]

The manifest failure of the prophecies of Leo the Wise to be fulfilled after the crushing Russian victory over the Ottomans in the war of 1768–74, led some Greeks, such as Konstantinos Kaisarios Dapontes and Athanasios Komninos Ypsilantis, to conclude that such were the sins of the Greek race it could never hope for emancipation, for no other oracle to that effect survived (see Chapter 2). But others continued to place their hopes for Greece's emancipation in prophecies.

As always when trying to determine the 'unspoken assumptions' of a society, these are often difficult to document and quantify. Yet there are a number of indications that belief in the efficacy of the prophecies remained widespread right up to, and during, the War of Independence. Theodoros Kolokotronis,

a hero of the War of Independence, recorded in his memoirs
that his childhood reading had consisted of the prophecies,
together with the *psaltirion*, the *okhtoikhos* and the *minaion*. [73] An
interesting and rare example of the Greeks actually acting on the
basis of these messianic beliefs is contained in a report of Francis
Werry, the Levant Company's consul in Smyrna, dated 2 June
1821, shortly after the outbreak of hostilities:

> This day, the festival of the Greek St. Constantine, the
> founder of Constantinople, has cost the lives of 16 Greeks
> shot in the Bazar, so very fanatic are these deluded people.
> They yesterday openly congratulated each other (the lower
> orders) on the approach of the morrow, as the day appointed
> by heaven to liberate them from the Ottoman yoke and to
> restore their Race of Princes to the throne and possession
> of Constantinople. The Turks who entered on their fast of
> Ramazan yesterday heard this, and began their fast in the
> evening with human sacrifices and I fear much it will be
> followed up. [74]

While according to the historian, Ioannis Philimon, an edition
of the prophecies of Agathangelos was printed at Mesolonghi in
1824, while the war was in progress, in a conscious effort to
improve morale. [75] It is significant that while eulogising the
'golden letters' of Korais, the most 'energetic champion' of the
Enlightenment in Greece, Philimon emphasised the hold of
Agathangelismos on the great mass of the population.

It is somewhat paradoxical, but by no means surprising, that
it is about this great mass of the Greek population at this time,
the peasants and urban working and artisan classes of the towns
and cities of the Empire, that we know least. Observers of rural
conditions in Greece during the pre-independence period are
unanimous in stressing the wretched condition of the peasantry,
who had been the principal victims of growth of the *çiftlik*
system described above. Felix Beaujour, for instance, noted in
the late 1790s that 'the peasants die with hunger, while their
lords abound with gold'. He also commented on the tendency
for the peasants to flee the countryside, as in Western Europe,
'but with this difference, that our countrymen go to the cities in
search of profits and easy pleasures, whereas the Greek peasants

flee to a distance from their villages in order to avoid the insatiable desires and depredations of their beys'.[76]

Greek observers of Ottoman society also stressed their wretched condition. The author of the *Elliniki Nomarkhia* wrote that 'the peasants toil non-stop and suffer tribulations beyond description, they never have anything to spare of the fruits of their sweat, so that they may rest for as much as one day . . . the peasants, the most respected class of a state, the most stable support of civil happiness, live worse than their own animals'. If their total product is taken as ten, then after the landlord and the *hocabaşı* have taken their share, the peasant is left with only two.[77]

Nor was the condition of the urban working class, about whom we know even less than the peasantry, any better. Indeed, the author of the *Elliniki Nomarkhia* maintained that their plight was even more wretched:

> City dwellers are obliged to toil no less than the peasants, while their troubles are even more fearsome. Craftsmen work for almost 18 hours a day, and even then they cannot fulfill their obligations. The *proestoi* with their unjust impositions, with which they burden them, on the one hand, snatch from them the few fruits of their sweat, while on the other the multitude of festivals and obligations, prevent any greater gain that they might try to make.[78]

There is, moreover, considerable evidence of unrest on the part of this urban working and artisan class directed against the *proestoi* or *proychontes*, the ruling élite within the community. One of the best documented of these intra-community[79] factional disputes occurred in Smyrna in 1788 and is described in a poem entitled 'The Tragedy of Smyrna, written about the revolt of the mob against the *proychontes* in the year 1788' and cast in the form of a dialogue between Smyrna, Homer, Aristeides, the Mob, and the *proychontes* of the city.

According to the poem, the mob demanded a general gathering at which the leaders of the community would give a reckoning to the guilds as to why they continually burdened the poor with taxes. The outbreak of war between the Porte and Russia and Austria in 1787 had led to a tripling of tax burdens, which were not equitably shared throughout the community, and for this reason the mob demanded that the *proychontes* be replaced. The *proychontes* or *archontes* were duly deposed but, according to the poem, the mob then realised that they had been led astray ('Mas gelasan oi diavoloi') and the old *arkhontes* were invited to return. It seems likely that this was not, in fact, a spontaneous demonstration on the part of the mob, but rather that it had been manipulated by the masters (*protomastoroi*) of the guilds (*syntekhniai* or *esnafs*), possibly in league with Grigorios, then Metropolitan of Smyrna, and later Ecumenical Patriarch. The guilds were resentful because their own tax burdens were greater than those of the *arkhontes*.[80] Some years later equally violent squabbles broke out over the *Philologikon Gymnasion* in Smyrna, which had been established as a rival to the more conservative *Evangeliki Skholi*.[81] Again the Rev. William Jowett, a perceptive observer of Greek affairs, noted the stormy internal history of the virtually autonomous Greek community of Ayvalık (Kydonies) in Asia Minor,[82] while it has been suggested that factional disputes within the community contributed to the emigration of Greeks from Kozani to the Hapsburg Monarchy in the eighteenth century.[83]

A highly significant development in the eighteenth century was, as has been seen, the emergence of serious external threats to the integrity of the Ottoman Empire, above all from Russia. Moreover, Russian territorial ambitions against the Ottoman Empire were matched by an increasing Russian interest in the Greek populations of the Empire. Already these had begun to manifest themselves during the reign of Peter the Great, who sent propaganda pamphlets into Greece. This Russian interest assumed a concrete form during the Russo-Turkish war of 1768–74. Concurrently with Russian military and naval operations against the Empire, attempts were made to provoke a Greek uprising against the Turks in the Peloponnese. A key figure in this attempt was Georgios Papazolis of Siatista (see above), who wildly overestimated the potential strength of Greek support for such an undertaking, and the attempted insurrection in 1770 at the instigation of the Orloff brothers proved a total fiasco, the province being subject to devastating reprisals by Albanian irregulars.[84]

Many Greeks were bitterly disappointed that the Treaty of Küçük Kaynarca brought no improvement in their lot.[85] But if Russia never gained by the treaty a right of protection over the Orthodox populations of the Empire as is often claimed, nonetheless she made effective use of the right she did gain to station consuls in various cities of the Empire, while Korais noted that the Russian victory gave a great boost to Greek morale by showing that the Ottomans could be defeated.[86]

Moreover, Catherine the Great's interest in the Greeks, to some extent prompted by her correspondence with Voltaire, continued, and she began to toy with the idea of a Greek Empire including the Slav, as well as Greek, Orthodox populations of European Turkey, to be centred on Constantinople, with her own grandson Constantine as emperor.[87] And Greek hopes in Russia as the liberator persisted. When war broke out between Russia and Turkey between 1787 and 1792, the Greek merchants of Trieste financed a flotilla under Lambros Katsonis which fought alongside the Russians. But the manifest failure of the Russians to deliver the Greeks from their yoke, prompted some Greeks, at least, to look elsewhere for salvation, particularly after the outbreak of the French Revolution. As Theodoros Kolokotronis put it, the French Revolution had opened his eyes by showing him that kings could be toppled from their thrones.[88]

Some Greeks, such as Konstantinos Stamatis, were enthusiastic advocates of French revolutionary principles from the beginning, while Korais himself lived in Paris throughout the years of the Revolution, after attempts to secure a job for him at Oxford University had failed. But broadly speaking, interest among the Greeks in what was going on in France was limited until the French annexation of the Ionian Islands by the Treaty of Campo Formio in 1797, an acquisition which Bonaparte, already considering himself a second Alexander, considered as 'more important than the whole of Italy'.[89] The French occupation of the Ionian Islands was accompanied by all the trappings of 'revolutionary liberation', with the planting of trees of liberty and the burning of the *Libro d'Oro* of the Ionian nobility. Maniot women were reported to be burning candles before icons of Bonaparte, while the Stephanopoli brothers secretly visited the Mani at this time with instructions to report on the likelihood of a Greek uprising.[90] The Porte, which had hitherto largely been indifferent to revolutionary events in the infidel West, now took the French threat very seriously. In the spring of 1798 the Reis ül-Kuttab, Ahmed Atif Efendi, in a memorandum on the current political situation, denounced

> the conflagration of sedition and wickedness that broke out a few years ago in France, scattering sparks and shooting flames of mischief and tumult in all directions . . . [The French] had printed and published various works, consisting, God preserve us, of insults and vilification against the pure prophets and great Kings, of the removal and abolition of all religion, and of allusions to the sweetness of equality and republicanism.[91]

Particularly ominous in Ottoman eyes were the activities of French agents within Ottoman territory, and more particularly French contacts with Tepedelenli Ali Paşa. Ali's court poet, Hacı Sekhretis, for instance, recorded that an emissary of Bonaparte, Roze, 'came from Corfu, intending to cause the Christian *raya* to rise up against their sovereign'. To Ali himself, according to Sekhretis, Roze brought the offer of being created King of Rumeli, with jurisdiction over Venice and Corfu.[92]

It was the French Revolution which was the direct inspiration of the most interesting of the proto-martyrs of Greek independence, Rigas Velestinlis (see also Chapters 2 and 3). The son of a merchant, Rigas was born in Velestino in Thessaly in 1757. He was soon forced to emigrate and moved to Constantinople where he became the secretary of Alexandros Ypsilantis, then *megas dierminefs* of the Porte. From Constantinople he moved to the Principalities where he became secretary to a number of *hospodars*, among them Nikolaos Mavroyenis and Mikhail Soutsos, and acquired an impressive linguistic equipment.

On his second visit to Vienna in 1796 it is possible that Rigas founded a secret revolutionary society, but much uncertainty surrounds this. It is beyond question, however, that he engaged in an extensive programme for the publication of subversive literature. This included a map of Greece, whose frontiers were drawn very wide, together with an engraving of Alexander the Great, the symbolism of which was obvious.[93] But by far the most important of these publications was his 'revolutionary pamphlet'. This contained a revolutionary proclamation, a declaration of the Rights of Man, the *thourios* or war song, and most important of all, the project of a constitution, which reflected the very considerable influence of the French constitutions of 1793 and 1795. Rigas also sent a *Stratiotikon Engkolpion*, or military manual, to press but this was never printed.

According to this constitution, or to give it its full title, *The New Political Constitution of the Inhabitants of Rumeli, Asia Minor, the Archipelago and the Danubian Principalities*, the new state that was to arise from the ashes of the Ottoman Empire was to be known as the *Elliniki Dimokratia* or *Hellenic Republic*. Sovereignty was to reside in the people, who were to comprise all the inhabitants of this state, without distinction of religion or language: Greeks, Albanians, Vlachs, Armenians, Turks and any other race residing within the boundaries of the Empire. Geographically the new state was to embrace the whole of the Balkans and Asia Minor. Yet, despite Rigas's insistence on the principle of equality of all nationalities, the essentially Greek character of the new state is everywhere in evidence. The official language was to be Greek, while it was to be organised on a unitary rather than federal basis. A highly significant omission in the constitution was any reference to the role of the church, a striking departure from the Ottoman concept of the *millet*. Essentially what Rigas seems to have envisaged was a kind of restored Byzantine Empire with republican in the place of monarchical institutions, ruled, as in Byzantium, by an élite that was Greek by culture if not necessarily by race. But it is not altogether surprising that Rigas's schemes met with little rapport among the non-Greek Orthodox christians of the Balkans, who tended to look on him as a Greek chauvinist.[94]

In practical terms Rigas achieved very little. He set off to spread the gospel of revolution in the Balkan lands, but the moment he landed in Trieste in December 1797, on the first stage of his journey, he was arrested by the Austrian police, following betrayal by a merchant called Oikonomos. Following an Austrian police investigation, Count Pergen reported to the Emperor Francis II himself that Rigas and his fellow conspirators were engaged in an attempt 'die . . . griechische Nation gegen ihren rechtmässigen Herrscher aufzuwiegeln'.[95] On the Emperor Francis's orders, Rigas, and those of his accomplices who were Ottoman citizens, were handed over to the Ottoman authorities who had them strangled in June 1798. But although the immediate effects of Rigas's activities were negligible he did act as an inspiration to the more determined of the protagonists of Greek independence.

During the 1800s faith in the French as the future liberators of Greece began to decline. Korais, during Napoleon's early years, continued to place great faith in him,[96] but eventually became disillusioned, considering that Napoleon, instead of seeking to free the oppressed peoples of Europe of their despotic rulers, had sought himself to become despot of despots.[97] Korais, however, as did many Greeks, continued to draw comfort from the example of the Ionian Islands, which had passed from Venetian to French rule by the Treaty of Campo Formio (1797). After a brief period of French occupation, the islands were ruled by a Russo-Turkish condominium, which gave way to direct Russian rule until 1807, when the islands once more reverted to France. However, by 1814, all the islands were under British rule, and, in 1815, the 'United States of the Ionian Islands' came into being, under British protection. If the existence of the Ionian Islands as a separate state proved to be a fiction, nonetheless the example of Greeks enjoying even a highly restricted degree of self-government was a powerful one to the mainland Greeks.

In the years immediately before 1821 there was, despite the earlier disappointments experienced by the Greeks as a result of Russian policy, a swing back to the Russians as Greece's potential saviours. Certainly a major recruiting plank of the *Philiki Etairia* was the erroneous claim that the Society enjoyed the patronage of Alexander I and Kapodistrias and that the Greeks could count on whole-hearted Russian assistance in the event of a general uprising against the Ottomans (see Chapter 5).

This faith in Russia as liberator, however, was by no means universal, and, in an interesting prefiguration of political align-ments in Greece during the independence and post-independ-ence periods, the poet Ioannis Vilaras characterised to Dr. Henry Holland:

> . . . the present political sentiment of the Greeks, as dividing them into three classes; all seeking a change of condition, but seeking it in different ways. The insular and commercial Greeks, and those of the Morea, attached themselves to the idea of liberation through England; a second party, in which

he included many of their literary men and continental merchants, looked to the then existing power of France, as a more probable means of deliverance; while the lower classes, and those most attached to their national religion, were anxious to receive the Russians as their liberators.[98]

Yet at the same time, in the decades immediately before 1821, there was an increasing awareness on the part of the more politically aware Greeks and of the more active champions of Greek independence that such a faith in liberation from abroad was totally misplaced and that the Greeks must look to their own resources if they were every to gain liberation. For instance, according to the *Rossanglogallos*, Russia had declared three wars against Turkey, gathering together Greeks from many homes and promising in writing to free them, but her purpose was rather to enslave them ruthlessly. Then France began to preach freedom, but her arrival at the borders of Greece simply increased the sufferings of the Greeks. While denouncing tyranny she thirsted after money. Russia and England, meanwhile, seeing the French in Turkey, ran to throw them out but not to liberate Greece. The poem rails against the Western powers who, without the benefit of the wisdom of the Ancient Greeks, would have remained 'the slaves of ignorance', for their failure to exert themselves on Greece's behalf.[99] The anonymous author of the *Elliniki Nomarkhia* similarly urged his readers not to place false hopes in liberation from abroad, for the principal objective of the foreign powers was to further their own interests at the expense of others.

Did you not know, O Greeks, that today virtue is not to be found upon thrones? To rely on foreign assistance in securing her liberation, Greece would only be substituting one form of alien domination for another. A thousand times more blood will flow if foreigners meddle in the liberation of Greece. Rather than placing trust in foreigners, the Greeks should imitate the example of the Serbs.[100]

Although some Greeks were realistic enough to discount the possibility of foreign intervention on behalf of their struggles, many others preferred to pin their hopes on foreign intervention, although the evidence which might justify such hopes was slight indeed. All in all, given that the chances of outside intervention were remote, and the fact that there were powerful forces within Greek society which were wedded to, and had an active interest in, maintaining the Ottoman status quo, the prospects for a successful uprising against the Turks must to the realistic observer in the decades before 1821, both within Greece and without, have appeared remote. Indeed, John Cam Hobhouse in 1810, concluded that the likelihood of any 'general revolution' of the Greeks without foreign support was 'quite impracticable':

> ... for although the great mass of the people, as is the case in all insurrections, has feeling and spirit enough to make the attempt, yet most of the higher classes, and all the clergy ... are apparently willing to acquiesce in their present condition.[101]

Yet there were elements present in Greek society which were to prove capable of providing the basis of a revolutionary nucleus. And within ten years Hobhouse's gloomy prognostication was to be proved false, with the outbreak of a 'general revolution'. The immediate origins of this insurrectionary outbreak are discussed by George Frangos, C. M. Woodhouse, E. D. Tappe and Douglas Dakin in Chapters 4, 5, 6 and 7. It is hoped that this introductory survey will have indicated something of the nature of Greek society during the crucial fifty years or so before 1821 and, more particularly, have indicated something of the tensions that existed in Greek society itself, tensions that were to contribute powerfully to the factionalism and internecine warfare that broke out among the Greeks during the course of their bitter but eventually successful armed struggle against the Ottomans.

NOTES TO CHAPTER 1

1. Professor E. Kedourie has described the Greek as 'the first nationalism to appear outside Western Christendom, among a community ruled by non-Christians and itself hitherto violently hostile to all Western notions'. *Nationalism in Asia and Africa* (London, 1971) p. 42.

2. The tendency for all high offices within the Orthodox church to be monopolised by Greeks gained impetus with the suppression of the Serbian

patriarchate of Peć in 1766 and the Bulgarian archbishopric of Ohrid in the following year.

3. Quoted in N. J. Pantazopoulos, *Church and Law in the Balkan Peninsula During the Ottoman Rule* (Thessaloniki, 1967) pp. 44–5.

4. I. Vasdravellis, *Istorika Arkheia Makedonias* II: *Arkheion Veroias-Naousis (1598–1886)* (Thessaloniki, 1954) pp. 112–13.

5. Arnold Toynbee has described Ayvalık as the 'first piece of free Greek soil in modern times'. *The Western Question in Greece and Turkey* (London, 1922) p. 332. A contemporary observer, the Rev. R. Walsh, described Ayvalık as 'a free republic of active and intelligent Greeks, equal to any that formerly existed among their Ionian ancestors, in opulence, spirit and a feeling of independence'. *A Residence at Constantinople During a Period Including . . . the Greek and Turkish Revolutions* (London, 1836) II, p. 397. For Ayvalık, see also my 'Two accounts of the Academy of Ayvalık (Kydonies) in 1818–1819', *Revue des Études sud-est européennes*, X (1972) 633–67. On the elaborate system of self-government that existed in the Peloponnese during the decades before independence, see M. Sakellariou, *I Peloponnisos kata tin defteran Tourkokratian (1715–1821)* (Athens, 1939) pp. 87–98.

6. B. Lewis, 'Ottoman Observers of Ottoman Decline', *Islamic Studies*, I (1962) 74 ff. 'Some Ottoman Reflections on the Decline of the Ottoman Empire', *Studia Islamica*, IX (1958) 111 ff.

7. P. M. Holt, *Egypt and the Fertile Crescent 1516–1922* (London, 1966) p. 64. Chapter IV contains a useful account of the process of Ottoman decline, particularly in the Arab provinces.

8. T. Stoianovich, 'Land Tenure and Related Sectors of the Balkan Economy, 1600–1800', *Journal of Economic History*, XIII (1953) 402.

9. B. Lewis, *The Emergence of Modern Turkey* (London, 1961) pp. 441–2. Cf. A. Sućeska, 'Bedeutung und Entwicklung des Begriffes A'yân im Osmanischen Reich', *Südost-Forschungen*, XXV (1966) 3–26.

10. The *ayans* and *derebeys* maintained an ambiguous relationship with the central government which in times of war was often forced to rely on their assistance in raising troops. The Porte, for instance, relied on Hacı Hüseyin Karaosmanoğlu to restore order in Smyrna following the disastrous anti-Christian riots of March 1797. Cf. the report of the British consul, Francis Werry, 17 June 1797, to the British Minister to the Porte, Spencer Smith, Public Record Office FO 78/18. Cf. also the memorial addressed to Hüseyin Karaosmanoğlu by the foreign consuls in Smyrna, dated 10 April 1797.

11. The same decline in the authority of the central government also occurred in the Arab provinces of the Empire. Holt, *Egypt and the Fertile Crescent . . .*, pp. 69–70.

12. J. H. Mordtmann in *Königliche Museen zu Berlin. Altertümer von Pergamon*, I, i (Berlin, 1912) 88.

13. On Ali Paşa see the important article by Dennis Skiotis, 'From Bandit to Pasha: First Steps in the Rise to Power of Ali of Tepelen, 1750–1784', *International Journal of Middle East Studies*, II (1971) 219–44. See also S. P. Aravantinos, *Istoria tou Ali Pasa* (Athens, 1895) and J. W. Baggally, *Ali Pasha and Great Britain* (Oxford, 1938).

14. L. Vranousis (ed.), *Rigas* (Athens, 1953) p. 393. On Rigas, see below and Chapters 2 and 3.

15. See D. Skiotis, 'Mountain Warriors and the Greek Revolution' (a paper read at the Conference on War, Technology and Society in the Middle East at the School of Oriental and African Studies, University of London, 1970).

16. Cf. K. G. Koutzikos, *Viographia tou Pasvanzoglou . . . plirexousiou arkhigou (komantatou) eis Vidini, kai olon to Paradounavi . . .* (Pest, 1800) pp. 15–16; H. Holland, *Travels in the Ionian Isles, Albania, Thessaly, Macedonia, during the years 1812 and 1813* (London, 1815) p. 175 ff.; and D. Zotos, *I dikaiosyni eis to kratos tou Ali Pasa* (Athens, 1938).

17. Cf. G. E. Marindin (ed.), *The Letters of John B. S. Morritt of Rokeby Descriptive of Journeys in Europe and Asia Minor in the Years 1794–1796* (London, 1914) p. 133; and S. P. Cockerell (ed.), *Travels in Southern Europe and the Levant, 1810–1817: The Journal of C. R. Cockerell* (London, 1903) p. 141. For a useful account of the Karaosmanoğlu dynasty see Mordtmann in *Königliche Museen zu Berlin . . .*, pp. 84–91.

18. G. G. Papadopoulos and G. P. Angelopoulos, *To kata ton . . . Patriarkhin . . . Grigorion ton E . . .* (Athens, 1866) II, p. 520. Cf. P. M. Kontogiannis, *Oi Ellines kata ton proton epi Aikaterinis tis B rosso-tourkikon polemon (1768–1774)* (Athens, 1903) pp. 386–7. F. C. H. L. Pouqueville specifically notes that Greek refugees fled from the region of Dimitsana to the Karaosmanoğlu domains. *Voyage en Morée, à Constantinople, en Albanie . . .* (Paris, 1805) I, p. 121. M. G. A. F. Choiseul-Gouffier estimated that as many as 40,000 Greeks from Attica and the Peloponnese had settled within the Karaosmanoğlu lands, where, he stressed, 'l'ordre le plus étonnant' reigned. *Voyage pittoresque de la Grèce* (Paris, 1809) II, 37.

19. H. L. Bodman, *Political Factions in Aleppo, 1760–1826* (Chapel Hill, North Carolina, 1963) p. 55. See particularly Chapter III.

20. Approximately £220,000 and £80,000. The best overall picture of the Smyrna 'rebellion' is contained in the despatches of Francis Werry, the Levant Company's consul. These are contained in P.R.O. F.O. 78/18 and SP 105/126. See also Kh. Solomonidis, *Ymnos kai thrinos tis Smyrnis* (Athens, 1956) pp. 182–99; N. K. Kh. Kostis, 'Smyrnaika Analekta. To en Smyrni rebellion tou 1797 kata neas anekdotous pigas', *Deltion tis Istorikis kai Ethnologikis Etaireias*, VI (1901–5) 358–72; and N. A. Veis, 'To "Megalo Rebelio" tis Smyrnis (Martios tou 1797) kata neotatas erevnas', *Mikrasiatika Khronika*, IV (1948) 411–22. For further evidence of the way in which the janissaries acted as a law unto themselves see my article 'Smyrna in 1821: Documents from the Levant Company Archives in the Public Record Office', *Mikrasiatika Khronika*, XV (1972) 313–71.

21. The Venezuelan revolutionary leader, Miranda, recorded meeting Campbell during his visit to Istanbul in 1786. *Archivo del General Miranda* (Viajes por Grecia, Turquía y Russia) (Caracas, 1929) II, p. 155. He also listed the French military experts whom he encountered in the city (p. 156).

22. See F. Babinger, *Stambuler Buchwesen im 18. Jahrhundert* (Leipzig, 1919) pp. 10–18. The press was closed down in 1742 but reactivated in 1784. Campbell, 'a worthy clever fellow and very well connected', was involved in

an earlier attempt to revive the press in 1779 by James Matra, a secretary to the British Embassy in Constantinople. Letter of Matra to Sir Joseph Banks, 17 September 1779, BM Add. MS 33977, fol. 107v.

23. On Selim and his reforms, see the valuable study of Stanford J. Shaw, *Between Old and New. The Ottoman Empire under Sultan Selim III, 1789–1807* (Cambridge, Mass., 1971).

24. *Ibid.*, pp. 33–4, 83–4, 341.

25. As the British ambassador to the Porte, Sir Robert Liston, put it to Lord Grenville, the British Foreign Secretary, in a despatch of 25 April 1795, trafficking in *berats* was the 'universal practice'. 'It was natural that a patent which raised a tributary subject from a state of degradation, and procured respect to his person, security to his property, and the patronage of an Ambassador at the seat of Government should soon become an object of ambition.' The going rate for a Russian *berat*, which carried with it the valuable privilege of trading to the Black Sea, was as high as 10,000 piastres. Liston himself was able to make between £2000 and £3000 a year through selling *berats*. P.R.O. FO 78/16.

26. Shaw, *Between Old and New*, p. 120.

27. I. K. Vasdravellis, *Armatoloi kai klephtes eis tin Makedonian* (2nd ed.; Thessaloniki, 1970) p. 99.

28. On the *kapoi* see B. P. Panagiotopoulos, 'Nea stoikheia peri tou thesmou ton Kapon en Peloponniso', *Deltion tis Istorikis kai Ethnologikis Etaireias*, XI (1956) 78–85.

29. G. Papazolis, *Didaskalia, igoun ermineia tis polemikis taxeos kai tekhnis* (Venice, 1765).

30. Quoted in Skiotis, *loc. cit.*, p. 9, which gives a useful account of the *klephts* and *armatoloi*. On the klephtic ballads see J. W. Baggally, *The Klephtic Ballads in Relation to Greek History (1715–1821)* (Oxford, 1936). The autobiography of one of the most significant of these *klephts*, Theodoros Kolokotronis, is available in English translation by Mrs Edmonds, *Kolokotrones. The Klepht and the Warrior. Sixty years of Peril and Daring* (London, 1892).

31. T. Stoianovich, 'Factors in the Decline of Ottoman Society in the Balkans', *Slavic Review*, XXI (1962) 632.

32. On the diplomacy of Alexandros Mavrokordatos, see N. Camariano, *Alexandre Mavrocordato. Le Grand Drogman. Son activité diplomatique (1673–1709)* (Thessaloniki, 1970).

33. For a collated text of the poem see K. Th. Dimaras, 'To keimeno tou "Rossanglogallou"', *Ellinika*, XVII (1962) 188–201. An incomplete text of the 'Russ-Anglo-Gaul', together with a translation, is given in W. M. Leake, *Researches in Greece* (London, 1814) pp. 140–54. Other contemporary references to the satire include John Cam Hobhouse, *A Journey through Albania and other Provinces of Turkey* ... (London, 1813) II, p. 597 and Lord Byron, *Childe Harold's Pilgrimage*, I, i–ii (London, 1819) pp. 194–5. The most useful commentary on the poem is K. Th. Dimaras, 'Me pente anglous stin Ellada (1811–1814). Gyro se mia satyra', *Angloelliniki Epitheorisi*, III (1948) 293–300.

34. D. Dakin, 'The Greek Unification and the Italian Risorgimento Compared', *Balkan Studies*, X (1969) 7.

35. T. Stoianovich, 'The Conquering Balkan Orthodox Merchant', *Journal of Economic History*, xx (1960) 309.

36. H. Holland, *Travels in the Ionian Isles* . . ., pp. 148–9. Cf. W. Jowett, *Christian Researches in the Mediterranean between 1815 and 1820* (London, 1822) p. 72. For the expansion of Greek commerce during this period see, in addition to Stoianovich, F. Beaujour, *A View of the Commerce of Greece, Formed After an Annual Average from 1787 to 1797* (London, 1800); N. Svoronos, *Le Commerce de Salonique au XVIIIe Siècle* (Paris, 1956); V. Kremmydas, *To emporio tis Peloponnisou sto 18 aiona (1715–1792)* (Thessaloniki, 1972); N. Camariano, 'L'organisation et l'activité culturelle de la compagnie des marchands grecs de Sibiu', *Balcania*, vi (1943) 201–41; S. Loukatos, 'O politikos vios ton Ellinon tis Viennis kata tin Tourkokratian kai ta aftokratorika pros aftous pronomia', *Deltion tis Istorikis kai Ethnologikis Etaireias*, xv (1961) 287–350; O. Füves, *Oi Ellines tis Oungarias* (Thessaloniki, 1965); and S. Lambros, 'Selides ek tis istorias tou en ti Oungaria kai Austria makedonikou Ellinismou', *Neos Ellinomnimon*, viii (1911) 257–300, xviii (1923) 376–86, xix (1925) 225–32.

37. A striking indication of the extent of this Greek *diaspora* is contained in the decision in 1795 of the Council of Lieutenancies in Buda (Budai Helytartótanács) to create the post of general inspector of the Greek schools that existed in 17 towns of Hungary: Békés, Belényes, Eger, Gyöngyös, Györ, Gyula, Hódmezóvásárhely, Kecskemét, Komárom, Miskolc, Nagyvárad, Oravica, Pest, Tokaj, Újvidék, Ungvár, Vác. A. Horvath, *I zoi kai ta erga tou Georgiou Zavira* (Budapest, 1937) pp. 5–6.

38. For the Greeks of Alexandria, see A. G. Politis, *L'Hellénisme et l'Égypte moderne* (Paris, 1928) i, i–ii.

39. For the statutes of the Greek community of Trieste towards the end of the eighteenth century see *Statuti, e regolamenti della nazione, e confraternità greca stabilita nella Città, e Porto Franco di Trieste* . . . (Venice, 1787).

40. On this community see S. Loukatos, *Ellines kai Philellines ton Indion kata tin Ellinikin Epanastasin* (Athens, 1965); I. Tantalidis, *Indiki Allilographia* . . . (Constantinople, 1852); and Anon., *Historical and Ecclesiastical Sketches of Bengal* . . . (Calcutta, 1827) pp. 221–4. According to this last source 'several native orphans and forlorn youth of both sexes (*perhaps fifty*) serving in Grecians families have been baptized and educated at the expence of their masters: there are now several of this description in Bengal, who understand the ancient Greek, and read and write the modern language with facility' (pp. 223–4). The community also produced in Dimitrios Galanos an indologist of outstanding ability; see S. A. Schulz, 'Demetrios Galanos (1760–1833): A Greek Indologist', *Journal of the American Oriental Society*, LXXXIX (1969) 339–56.

41. G. B. Leon, 'The Greek Merchant Marine (1453–1850)' in S. A. Papadopoulos (ed.), *The Greek Merchant Marine* (Athens, 1972) pp. 32–43.

42. J. L. S. Bartholdy, *Bruchstücke zur nähern Kenntniss des heutigen Griechenlands* . . . (Berlin, 1805) p. 169. A Greek translation of Kotzebue's play had been published as *Misanthropia kai metanoia* (Vienna, 1801).

43. Beaujour, *A View of the Commerce of Greece*, p. 187 ff.

44. Korais, *Mémoire*, p. 18. Originally published in French, Korais'

memoir has recently been translated into English by E. Kedourie in his *Nationalism in Asia and Africa*, pp. 153–88.

45. Cf. the remarks of von Schladen, the Prussian ambassador to the Porte in a report of 1819: 'Mehr als 50 junge Männer bereisen in diesem Augenblicke, Italien, Frankreich und Deutschland auf öffentliche Kosten, zu welchen noch nach ganz kürzlich Alexander Mauro, Handelsmann in Constantinople 15000, und N. Babazy aus Taganrock 50000 Piaster beytrugen'. 'Über Buch-und Druckwesen in der alten Türkei. Ein Bericht des Preussischen Gesandten zu Konstantinopel aus dem Jahre 1819', *Zeitschrift der Deutschen Morgenländischen Gesellschaft*, ns xxv (1950) 597. Nikolaos Papadopoulos' four-volume commercial encyclopaedia *Ermis o Kerdoos*, published in Venice in 1815, 'at the expense of the honourable and patriotic commercial corporation (*systima*) of the Greek wholesale merchants in Constantinople', specifically attributed Greece's intellectual renaissance to the growth of commerce (preface).

46. Cf. Stoianovich, 'The Conquering Balkan Orthodox Merchant', 313.

47. E. de Hurmuzaki, *Documente privitóre la Istoria Românilor*, suppl. i, vol. ii, 1781–1814, *Documente culese din Archivele Ministeriului Afacerilor Străine din Paris*, ed. A. I. Odobescu (Bucharest, 1885) p. 94, quoted in A. Elian, 'Conspiratori greci în Principate şi un favorit mavroghenesc: Turnavitu', *Revista Istorică*, xxi (1935) 362.

48. See Svoronos, *Le Commerce de Salonique*, pp. 347–67, for an interesting discussion of the consequences of this commercial revival.

49. See V. Skouvaras, *Ioannis Pringos (1725?–1789). I elliniki paroikia tou Amsterdam. I skholi kai i vivliothiki Zagoras* (Athens, 1964); S. Antoniadis, 'Het dagboek van een te Amsterdam gevestigde Griekse koopman', *Tijdschrift voor Geschiedenis*, LXIX (1956) 57–66. Interesting extracts from his diary are published by N. Andriotis, 'To khroniko tou Amsterdam', *Nea Estia*, x (1931) 846–53, 914–20.

50. Andriotis, 'To khroniko tou Amsterdam', 851–2. Cf. Skouvaras, *Pringos*, p. 51. See also G. K. Kordatos, *Rigas Pheraios kai i valkaniki omospondia* (Athens, 1945) p. 28 and L. S. Stavrianos, 'Antecedents to the Balkan Revolutions of the Nineteenth Century', *Journal of Modern History*, xxix (1957) 343, where the passage is also quoted.

51. Daniil Philippidis and Grigorios Konstantas, *Geographia Neoteriki* (Vienna, 1791) reprinted A. Koumarianou (Athens, 1970) p. 46. They estimated the number of Ottoman Greeks (*Tourkomeritai*) in the Hapsburg dominions alone at 80,000 families.

52. S. J. Shaw, *Between Old and New*, p. 96. Cf. also the remarks of Mahmud Raif Efendi (Ingiliz Mahmud) in his account of the first permanent Ottoman Embassy, of which he was secretary, to London in the 1790s. Ahmed III Library, Topkapı Sarayı, Ms. no. 3707, f. 56.

53. Dimaras, 'To keimeno tou "Rossanglogallou"', 194–5.

54. Anonymou tou Ellinos, *Elliniki Nomarkhia* (Italy, 1806) p. 150 ff., reprinted in N. Tomadakis (ed.), (Athens, 1948) and G. Valetas (Athens, 1949 and 1957). My references are to Valetas's edition of 1957.

55. Photakos Khrysanthopoulos, *Apomnimonevmata peri tis Ellinikis Epanastaseos* (Athens, 1899) i, pp. 33–4 quoted in A. Toynbee, *A Study of*

History, VIII (London, 1954) p. 683. Cf. also Dimaras 'To keimeno tou "Rossanglogallou"', 195–6 and K. N. Sathas, *Istorikai diatrivai . . . III. I Alipasias tou Tourkalvanou Khatzi Sekhreti* (Athens, 1870) p. 214.

56. The Greek communities of the towns were similarly governed by this class of primates. Miranda recorded that, at the time of his visit in 1786, Patras was governed by a Turkish governor, who ruled with the assistance of 'una junta de dos, ó tres personas griegas que llaman Primati *primados* – los quales distribuien entre las gentes de su nacion la quota respectiva al pagamento de las contribuciones que con frecuencia se imponen al Pueblo pr. la corte de Constantinopla'. *Viages por Grecia, Turquía y Russia,* pp. 113–14.

57. On the Peloponnesian *hocabaşıs* see, e.g., T. A. Stamatopoulos, *O esoterikos agonas prin kai kata tin epanastasi tou 1821* (Athens, 1971) I, pp. 94–123.

58. W. Gell, *Narrative of a Journey in the Morea* (London, 1823) pp. 65–6.

59. K. Th. Dimaras (ed.), *O Korais kai i epokhi tou* (Athens, 1953) p. 302 ff.

60. For a translation of the *Didaskalia Patriki,* see my 'The "Dhidhaskalia Patriki"' (1798): an Orthodox Reaction to French Revolutionary Propaganda', *Middle Eastern Studies,* V (1969) 87–115. Cf. also the remarks of Nikodimos Agioreitis on *oikonomia* in his massive *Pidalion . . . tis mias, agias, katholikis, kai apostolikis ekklisias . . .* (Leipzig, 1800) p. 36 quoted in T. Ware, *Eustratios Argenti. A Study of the Greek Church under Turkish Rule* (Oxford, 1964) p. 102. On this whole question A. Camariano, *Spiritul revoluţionar francez şi Voltaire in limba greacă şi română* (Bucharest, 1946) is indispensable.

61. See, for instance, G. G. Papadopoulos and G. P. Angelopoulos, *To kata ton . . . Grigorion ton E,* II, 498–9; P. G. Zerlentis, 'Patriarkhon grammata diataktika pros tous nisiotas peri doulikis ypotagis eis tous kratountas', *Deltion Istorikis kai Ethnologikis Etaireias,* IX (1926) 100; and E. Phanourakis, 'Anekdota ekklisiastika engrapha ton khronon tis Tourkokratias', *Kritika Khronika,* I (1947) 499–500.

62. See, for example, J. Mansi, *Sacrorum Conciliorum nova et amplissima collectio . . .* XL (Paris, 1909) pp. 151–5.

63. Some of the more percipient members of the Orthodox hierarchy, indeed, recognised the dangers inherent in this growth of anti-clerical, if not irreligious, attitudes and sought to counter them. See Ignatios Oungrovlakhias, in his anonymous *Apologia istoriki kai kritiki yper tou ierou klirou tis Anatolikis Ekklisias kata ton sykophantion tou Neophytou Douka . . .* published in [Pisa] in 1815.

64. One of the most curious manifestations of this growing sense of the past was the publication in Constantinople in 1819 of a *karamanlıca* version of Aristotle's Physiognomonika *Aristotelisin insan saraflaması.* This was printed in Turkish with Greek characters for the use of the substantial Turkish-speaking Orthodox populations of the Empire, who were princially concentrated in Asia Minor, although pockets were to be found in European Turkey. Indeed, according to M. Gedeon, during the last decades of the eighteenth century there were few Orthodox congregations even in Constantinople that could understand preaching in Greek. 'To kirygma tou Theiou Logou en ti Ekklisia ton kato khronon', *Ekklisiastiki Alitheia,* VIII (1888) 200.

65. Foremost among the champions of emancipation through education, of course, was Adamantios Korais. His sense of the realities of the contemporary international situation was not well developed. Shortly after the outbreak of hostilities, for instance, he wrote to the President of the Republic of Haiti, President Boyer, asking for an expeditionary force to be sent to Greece; see P. M. Kontogiannis, 'Epistolai anekdotai Korai kai pros Korain', *Khiaka Khronika*, v (1923) 140–4. Korais' views on the overriding importance of education were shared by Kapodistrias, Tsar Alexander I's Greek joint Foreign Minister (see Chapter 5).

66. Daniil of Moskhopolis, *Eisagogiki didaskalia periekhousa lexikon tetraglosson ton tessaron koinon Dialekton, itoi tis aplis Romaikis, tis en Moisia Vlakhikis, tis Voulgarikis, kai tis Alvanitikis* . . . ([Constantinople?], 1802). These four lines are in the translation of A. J. B. Wace and M. S. Thompson, *The Nomads of the Balkans* (London, 1914) p. 6. The Greek text of the poem, with a Rumanian translation, has been reprinted in I. Bianu and N. Hodoş, *Bibliografia românească veche* (Bucharest, 1910) II, pp. 440–2.

67. A. Hourani, *Arabic Thought in the Liberal Age 1789–1939* (London, 1962) pp. 58–9.

68. Quoted by M. V. Pundeff, 'Bulgarian Nationalism', in P. F. Sugar and I. J. Lederer (eds.), *Nationalism in Eastern Europe* (Seattle, 1969) p.101.

69. See also C. A. Mango 'The Legend of Leo the Wise', *Zbornik Radova Vizantoloshki Institut*, VI (1960) pp. 59–93 and 'Byzantinism and Romantic Hellenism', *Journal of the Warburg and Courtauld Institutes*, XVIII (1965) 29–43. Cf. also N. A. Veis, 'Peri tou istorimenou khrismologiou tis Kratikis Vivliothikis tou Verolinou (Codex Graecus fol. 62–297) kai tou thrylou tou "Marmaromenou Vasilia"', *Byzantinische-Neugriechische Jahrbücher*, XIII (1937) pp. 203–44 lst.

70. The young Goethe in the 1760s was particularly impressed by the colourful Greek contingent attending the Leipzig fair. *Aus meinem Leben Dichtung und Wahrheit, Goethes Werke*, IX (Hamburg, 1955) pp. 244–5.

71. Andriotis, 'To khroniko tou Amsterdam', 914.

72. See the interesting article by A. Politis, 'I prosgraphomeni ston Riga proti ekdosi tou Agathangelou. To mono gnosto antitypo', *O Eranistis*, VII (1969) pp. 173–92. The ambivalent co-existence of Western rationalist ideas with neo-Byzantine obscurantism is further illustrated by the case of Nikolaos Zertzoulis, a teacher at the Greek Academy of Jassy in Moldavia and a translator of Newton into Greek, who compiled in 1767 a 'Brief Interpretation of the Oracles of Leo the Wise Concerning the Resurrection of Constantinople', Mango, 'The Legend of Leo the Wise . . .', 89. Zertzoulis (Cercel), a native of Metsovo, had studied for seven years in Western universities and knew Latin, French and Italian. In addition to translating Newton, he had also translated from Wolff and Baumeister and Pieter van Muschenbroeck's *Cours de Physique expérimentale et mathématique*. A. Camariano-Cioran, *Academiile Domneşti din Bucureşti şi Iaşi* (Bucharest, 1971) pp. 103, 105, 157.

73. T. Kolokotronis, *Apomnimonevmata*, ed. T. Vournas (Athens, n.d.) p. 70.

74. P.R.O. SP 105/139.

75. Ioannis Philimon, *Dokimion Istorikon peri tis Philikis Etairias* (Nafplion,

1834) p. 68, quoted in Politis, 'I prosgraphomeni ston Riga proti ekdosi tou Agathangelou . . .', 175.

76. Beaujour, *A View of the Commerce of Greece*, pp. 88–6. For Selim III's measures to combat the flight to the towns see Shaw, *Between Old and New*, pp. 75–6.

77. *Elliniki Nomarkhia*, 137–8. Probably the most detailed and accurate picture that we have of the realities of rural life during this period, at least for a part of the Morea and of Western Continental Greece, is contained in a document of 1796, published with a useful introduction, by S. I. Asdrakhas 'Pragmatikotites apo ton elliniko 18 aiona', in K. Th. Dimaras (ed.), *Stathmoi pros tin nea elliniki koinonia* (Athens, 1965) pp. 1–47. Cf. also G. Konstantinidis, 'To Karlili kai i phorologia aftou, peri ta teli tou 18 kai tas arkhas tou 19 aionas kat'anekdoton patriarkhikon engraphon ek tou etous 1793', *Armonia*, I (1900) 465–74 and Sakellariou, *I Peloponnisos*, passim.

78. *Elliniki Nomarkhia*, 139–40.

79. At the same time there was often serious inter-communal tension between the non-muslim populations of the Empire. Ill feeling between Jews and Greeks in Constantinople was endemic, so much so a Jew entering one of the predominantly Greek villages on the Bosphorus, Arnautköy, was in danger of a beating. P. Rizos (ed.), *Mémoires du Prince Nicolas Soutzo, Grand-Logothète de Moldavie, 1798–1871* (Vienna, 1899) p. 10. It was regarded as particularly galling that the corpse of the Ecumenical Patriarch Grigorios V was handed over to a Jewish mob after his execution in 1821. In 1818 a major riot between Orthodox and Uniate Christians in Aleppo resulted in 11 deaths. Bodman, *Political Factions in Aleppo*, p. ix. In the same year there was serious friction between Catholics and Orthodox Greeks in Smyrna. Journal of William Jowett, 10 May 1818, *Church Missionary Society Archives* C. M/E 3 and Philpin de Rivière, *Vie de Mgr. de Forbin-Janson, missionnaire, évêque de Nancy et de Toul, primat de Lorraine, fondateur de la Sainte-Enfance* (Paris, 1891) pp. 104–10.

80. S. K. Karatzas. *Smyrnis tragodies. Dyo anekdota poiimata skhetika me tarakhes sti Smyrni (1788, 1810)* (Athens, 1958) pp. 11–29.

81. *Ibid.*, pp. 63–80; and Ph. K. Bouboulidis, 'Anekdoton stikhourgima peri ton skholikon pragmaton Smyrnis arkhomenou tou 19 aionos', *Mikrasiatika Khronika*, VIII (1959) 402–5.

82. R. Clogg, 'Two accounts of the Academy of Ayvalīk . . .', 643–4.

83. O. Füves, *Oi Ellines tis Oungarias*, p. 12. Some of the most bitter factional disputes took place in the predominantly Vlach town of Moskhopolis. Here tension between *hocabaşıs*, guilds and workers led, at Easter, 1735, to the massacre of the *hocabaşıs* in the monastery of the Prodromos. Ph. Mikhalopoulos, *Moskhopolis. Ai Athinai tis Tourkokratias 1500–1769* (Athens, 1941) p. 41.

84. See A. Camariano-Cioran, 'La guerre russo-turque de 1768–1774 et les Grecs', *Revue des Études sud-est européennes*, III (1965) 513–47 and T. A. Gritsopoulos, *Ta Orlophika. I en Peloponniso epanastasis tou 1770 kai ta epakoloutha aftis* (Athens, 1967).

85. In a pro-French propaganda tract, *Stokhasmoi enos philellinos*, published, purportedly, in Vienna, in 1798, the author charged that the Russians at

Küçük Kaynarca, had not thought to insist on 'the slightest article which might lighten the misery of our nation' (p. 2).

86. Korais, *Mémoire*, pp. 21–2.

87. Constantine, of course, was a deliberately emotive name, for the last Emperor of Byzantium had been Constantine Palaiologos. Catherine, it is said, hired Greek women to suckle the infant Constantine. W. Eton, *A Survey of the Turkish Empire* . . . (London, 1799) p. 432.

88. Kolokotronis, *Apomnimonevmata*, p. 70.

89. Quoted in E. Z. Karal, *Fransa-Misir ve Osmanlı Imparatorluğu (1797–1802)* (Istanbul, 1938) p. 38.

90. Cf. R. Clogg, *Dhidhaskalia Patriki*, p. 88 ff. See also A. Camariano-Cioran, 'Les Îles Ioniennes de 1797 à 1807 et l'essor du courant philo-français parmi les Grecs', *Praktika Tritou Panioniou Synedriou*, I (Athens, 1967) pp. 83–114.

91. Ahmed Cevdet Paşa, *Tarih-i Cevdet*, VI (Istanbul, 1877) quoted in B. Lewis, 'The Impact of the French Revolution in Turkey: Some Notes on the Transmission of Ideas', *Cahiers d'Histoire Mondiale*, I (1953) p. 121.

92. Sathas, *Istorikai diatrivai*, pp. 200, 213.

93. G. Laios, 'Oi khartes tou Riga', *Deltion tis Istorikis kai Ethnologikis Etaireias*, XIV (1960) pp. 231–312.

94. On Rigas see, e.g., L. I. Vranousis, *Rigas* (Athens, 1953) Vasiki Vivliothiki 10; A. J. Manessis, 'L'activité et les projets politiques d'un patriote grec dans les Balkans vers la fin du XVIIIe siècle, *Balkan Studies*, III (1962) pp. 75–118; and N. I. Pantazopoulos, *Rigas Velestinlis. I politiki ideologia tou Ellinismou. Proangelos tis epanastaseos* (Thessaloniki, 1964).

95. K. Amantos, *Anekdota engrapha peri Riga Velestinli* (Athens, 1930) p. 28.

96. Cf., for instance, *Ti prepei na kamosin oi Graikoi eis tas parousas peristaseis? Dialogos dyo Graikon katoikon tis Venetias, otan ikousan tas lampras nikas tou Aftokratoros Napoleontos* (Venice, 1805).

97. *Vios Adamantiou Korai syngrapheis para tou idiou* . . . (Paris, 1833) p.23.

98. Holland, *Travels in the Ionian Isles*, p. 274. Holland noted that 'this distinction as to the state of opinion in Greece is certainly well founded.'

99. Dimaras, 'To keimeno tou "Rossanglogallou"', 198–9. Leake observed that in these concluding lines of the poem 'the traveller will recognize the exact language, which he must often have heard in the country'. *Researches in Greece*, p. 140.

100. *Elliniki Nomarkhia*, pp. 198–9, 220–1.

101. J. C. Hobhouse, *A Journey through Albania and Other Provinces of Turkey in Europe and Asia to Constantinople During the years 1809 and 1810* (London, 1813) II, p. 597.

2 The Phanariots and the Byzantine Tradition

CYRIL MANGO

Two conflicting judgments have often been expressed concerning the Phanariots. The first is that they were a thoroughly iniquitous lot who lived by intrigue and base adulation, who were indifferent to the real interests of their compatriots and who cynically exploited the Rumanian principalities that they were appointed to govern; who, furthermore, constituted a sinister cabal that exerted a profound influence on the affairs of the Ottoman Empire and entirely controlled the Greek Church. This unfavourable judgment is stated most fully in a book entitled *Essai sur les Fanariotes*, published in 1824 by one Mark Philip Zallony, a Roman Catholic Greek who knew the Phanariots well and who was afraid that they might assume control of the independent Greek state that was then in the process of being born.[1] It is in a purely derogatory sense that the epithet 'Byzantine' has often been applied to the Phanariots.

The other judgment is that the Phanariots, in spite of certain unavoidable vices that were due to the corruption prevailing in the Ottoman Empire, were animated by the purest patriotism; that they made a great contribution towards civilising their Rumanian subjects; above all – and this is the point I should like to stress – that they worked in the fields of politics, education and literature for the regeneration of the Greek people and of *ellinismos*. Needless to say, this second judgment has been voiced by the majority of Greek historians.[2] Other, more balanced views have been expressed concerning the Phanariots,[3] but the two I have mentioned are those most frequently encountered.

We may begin with a brief historical sketch. In speaking of the Phanariots we do not mean all the Greek inhabitants of a particular quarter of Istanbul; we mean more specifically a Greek oligarchy that resided largely in the Phanar (whither the Ecumenical Patriarchate moved in 1600) and that owed their privileged position, in one way or another, to service in the Ottoman administration. The first Phanariot in this restricted sense is considered to have been Panayotis Nikousios (1613–73), son of a petty tradesman, who rose to the position of Grand Interpreter to the Porte and who contributed to the conquest of Candia by the Turks in 1669.[4] Panayotis did not, however, establish a dynasty since his only son wasted all his money on alchemy.[5] The privilege of founding a dynasty was reserved for Panayotis's successor, Alexandros Mavrokordatos, who, in spite of many vicissitudes, served as Grand Interpreter for nearly forty years (1673–1709) and who is chiefly remembered for his leading role in the conclusion of the treaty of Karlowitz in 1699.[6] Until 1821 the highly influential post of Grand Interpreter remained a prerogative of the Phanariot Greeks who also succeeded in securing for themselves another, not inconsiderable position, that of Interpreter to the Navy. The latter's chief function was to serve as intermediary between the Turkish Grand Admiral and the islanders of the Aegean.

A much greater prize was, however, awaiting the Phanariots. The two Rumanian principalities of Wallachia and Moldavia had long been tributary to the Turks, but enjoyed a considerable measure of independence under the rule of local princes. The latter, we may note in passing, allowed their country to become deeply infiltrated by Greek interests, ecclesiastic, cultural and economic. This situation continued until the beginning of the eighteenth century when, in the context of the war between Peter the Great of Russia and Charles XII of Sweden, the two *hospodars*, Brîncoveanu and Cantemir, aligned themselves with forces hostile to Turkey. The Porte now decided to have these provinces governed by men it could more effectively control, and began choosing the incumbents among the Phanariots. The first Greek prince of Moldavia was Nikolaos Mavrokordatos, Alexandros' son, appointed in 1709 and, once again, in 1711; the same man was transferred in 1715 to the governorship of the richer province of Wallachia. The Phanariot administration of the two principalities continued until the outbreak of the Greek Revolution in 1821 and, during this period, Moldavia experienced 36 changes of princes and Wallachia 38. Allowing for periods of foreign occupation, the average length of rule was 2.5 years. All the *hospodars* of the two principalities were recruited from among eleven families.[7]

The results of the Phanariot administration of Rumania were, by most accounts, disastrous.[8] 'It is impossible,' writes R. W. Seton-Watson, 'to conceive a more disheartening task than that of recording in detail the history of these hundred years in Wallachia and Moldavia, and the western reader would only read it with impatience and under protest.'[9] The Greeks themselves freely admitted the wickedness of their own régime. The Phanariot historian, Athanasios Komninos Ypsilantis, exclaims:

> What harmful innovations have occurred in these unhappy lands . . . on account of the Greeks! I pass over in silence all the things I know . . . and in particular the innovations introduced by the *hospodar* Nikolaos [Mavrokordatos] and his son, the *hospodar* Konstantinos: they form a shameful story. This only I say that the Greeks have destroyed the old privileges of these two principalities that were beneficial to their inhabitants, and they will surely see at God's tribunal Who it is that they have sinned against.[10]

Another contemporary Greek, Konstantinos (Kaisarios) Dapontes, looks back to the days of Brîncoveanu, the last native prince of Wallachia, as to a golden age. 'Wallachia,' he says, 'was like a rose-garden and most populous; there were then 700,000 families living there, and now there are scarcely 70,000.'[11]

There is no need for our purpose to give a more detailed historical account of the Phanariots, nor would I be competent to do so. I should like, however, to touch on some factual matters that are relevant to our discussion.

In the first place, it has to be made clear that the Phanariots were in no way descended from a medieval Byzantine aristocracy. Broadly speaking, the noble Byzantine families (or, at any rate, families that bore the illustrious old names) disappeared at Constantinople towards the end of the sixteenth century.[12] In the course of the seventeenth there arose a new élite of provincial origin, and it is from among its ranks that the

Phanariots eventually emerged.[13] The claim to aristocratic Byzantine ancestry is a myth that the Phanariots themselves strove to propagate and that later became enshrined in a book called *Le livre d'or de la noblesse phanariote* by E. R. Rangavis.[14] Fortunately, this myth was bolstered not by any deliberate falsification, such as was perpetrated in the late seventeenth century by the 'iatrosophist' Ioannis Molyvdos 'Comnenus',[15] but only by vague references to unspecified 'Byzantine authors' and to documents preserved in family archives which, needless to say, have never been produced. It is not necessary to demonstrate that, e.g., the Aristarkhis family had no good claim to be descended from the Emperor John I Tzimiskes, that the Mourouzis family had no demonstrable kinship with the Comnenes of Trebizond, that the Rangavis family had nothing to do with the Emperor Michael I Rhangabes or the Ypsilantis family with the eleventh-century patriarch John Xiphilinus, that the Neroulos family could not reasonably claim the fifth-century Egyptian poet Nonnus among its ancestors. The truth is rather more prosaic. It will be enough to consider here the eleven families that attained so-called princely status. The Mavrokordatos' came from Chios, first appearing at Constantinople in the early seventeenth century: their lineage can only be traced back to the sixteenth.[16] The Ghika family was Albanian and also emigrated to Constantinople in the early part of the seventeenth century, soon rising to high honours thanks to the protection of a fellow-Albanian, the Grand Vizier Mehmet Köprülü.[17] The Ypsilantis and Mourouzis families, which were intermarried and may have been partly of Laz extraction, came from Trebizond, where they seem to have been engaged in petty shipping and farming; they migrated to Constantinople about 1665 and attained a measure of prominence only in the first half of the eighteenth century.[18] The Racovitza (Racoviţă) and Callimachi families were both Rumanian, the first of noble ancestry, while the second was descended from a Moldavian peasant called Calmăşul who climbed the hierarchical ladder at Constantinople, hellenised his name to Kallimakhis, and was made *hospodar* of Moldavia in 1758.[19] The Soutsos family was certainly established at Constantinople in the second half of the sixteenth century; according to another tradition (perhaps malicious), its ancestor was a certain

Diamantakis Drakos of Epirus, the son of a milkman (*sütcü* in Turkish) who lived in the seventeenth century.[20] The Rosetti or Rossetti family was clearly of Italian origin, but was already settled at Constantinople in the seventeenth century.[21] The Karatzas (Karadja) family bore a common Turkish name meaning 'black' or 'swarthy': it seems to have come from Caramania in Asia Minor and was resident at Constantinople in the second half of the sixteenth century. There exist, however, other accounts of its origin.[22] The Mavroyenis family, which fancifully claimed kinship with the Morosinis of Venice, came from Paros and Mykonos and reached Constantinople only after 1750.[23] The Khantzeris (Handjeris or Handjerlis) were also latecomers: the oldest member of the family to have attained a position of prominence was, rather exceptionally, a cleric – Samuil, who became Patriarch of Constantinople in 1763.[24]

In short, the leading Phanariot families were a hodgepodge of enterprising Greeks, Rumanians, Albanians and Levantine Italians. Most, if not all of them originated outside Constantinople, and they attained high position in the course of the seventeenth and eighteenth centuries. They cannot, therefore, be regarded as having a more direct pipeline to the Byzantine tradition than other contemporary Greeks living within the Ottoman Empire.

The second question I should like to raise concerns the financial resources of the Phanariots. Naturally, it is not easy to obtain any precise information on this matter since they took good care to cover their tracks. Broadly speaking, however, it may be said that their resources, which were considerable, were due, in the first instance, not to trade in the normal sense of the word, but to various lucrative positions that they managed to obtain within the Turkish system.[25] Thus, the Mavrokordatos fortune was founded by Alexandros' father-in-law, a certain Scarlato or Scarlati who, from being a poor man, made himself a millionaire by holding the government office of *beylikçi* which enabled him to fix customs duties.[26] When, after the Turkish failure at Vienna, Mavrokordatos was imprisoned and fined 300 purses, he was able, though with some difficulty, to produce the greater part of this enormous sum within a year.[27] By way of comparison, the annual tribute of Wallachia to the Porte was at that time 280 purses.[28] He could hardly have made himself so rich on his salary as dragoman which he found insufficient even for his expenses while he was accompanying the Grand Vizier on campaign, and had to supplement by claiming the revenues of the metropolis of Adrianople.[29] Of course, as dragoman he had access to some fringe benefits like the yearly retainer of 4000 *livres* he drew from the French Embassy and the very substantial bribe he is said to have received from Austria as a reward for the Treaty of Karlowitz.[30]

Manuil Ypsilantis, the first member of that family to have attained prominence, was in the early years of the eighteenth century chief purveyor of furs to the Grand Vizier, an office he inherited from his brother-in-law. He accompanied his Turkish master on the Morean expedition of 1715 and came back a very rich man.[31] After a long and devious career which brought him into politics, he was impaled by order of the government (1737) and his fortune confiscated: it amounted to the staggering sum of 1800 purses, including the estate of his brother and that of his nephew which were seized at the same time.[32]

These two examples may show how Phanariot families rose to the surface. Once, however, the Danubian principalities were opened to their ambition, opportunities for enrichment were vastly increased. That, of course, depended on personal initiative. A few of the Greek *hospodars* proved to be honest, such as Konstantinos Mavrokordatos (1711–69) who, although he had ruled Wallachia six times and Moldavia four times, was obliged to sell his ancestral house at Constantinople and to pawn his grandfather's library to an English merchant.[33] The majority of *hospodars*, however, did very well for themselves. Zallony, who is admittedly a biased observer, says that after a reign of only two years a *hospodar* might have amassed 10,000,000 francs.[34] Ioannis Karatzas, who ruled Wallachia from 1812 to 1818, did even better: he got away with 90,000,000 piastres which he deposited in foreign banks.[35] The intense rivalry for the *hospodar's* office shows all too clearly what benefits were involved. Furthermore, these were not confined to the *hospodar's* person, but also extended to a large circle of relatives and clients on whom he conferred offices and patents of nobility in Rumania.[36] According to the same Zallony, a Greek *boyar* could count on anything between 100,000 and 1,000,000 francs as the illicit reward of his service. Among the most coveted posts were those of *Grand Postelnik* or Chief Minister who was able to sell various dignities to the local nobility, of *Spathar*, i.e., chief of militia, of *Ağa*, i.e., chief of the municipal police of Bucharest, of *Comisso*, i.e., the prince's equerry, of *Caminar* which involved no duties but was rewarded with a cut from the tax on wine, of *Armash* who inspected the Gypsies and the collection of gold from the rivers.[37] Furthermore, if he was an enterprising man, the Phanariot could combine his Rumanian profits with some lucrative concession obtained from his Turkish protectors, as did, e.g., in the mid-eighteenth century, the notorious Stavrakoğlu who, while holding the title of *Spathar* and acting as agent (*kapıkâhyası*) for the *hospodar* Constantine Racovitza, also won for himself the monopoly of selling tobacco at Constantinople.[38]

After serving his term in Rumania, the successful Phanariot could afford to build for himself a town house in the Phanar and a country villa on the Bosphorus, if he did not have them already.[39] Apart from this, he seldom purchased any landed property. He spent a great deal on imported furniture, rich clothing, crockery and jewellery for his wife.[40] The rest of his capital he loaned at interest as unobtrusively as possible so as not to excite the suspicion of the authorities.[41] The Church, as we shall see presently, was a frequent recipient of such loans.

It should be apparent from the above that the Phanariots, as a class, had carved out for themselves a very comfortable niche in the existing Ottoman system. The game they played was not without its dangers – witness the number of *hospodars* and dragomans who served prison sentences or were beheaded – but it was obviously worth the candle. Furthermore, the Phanariots had nothing to gain by changing a system that they had learnt so well to manipulate. If anything, they might have wished to extend the same form of exploitation to other provinces of the Ottoman Empire, and they are said to have had designs of this kind on Serbia, the Peloponnese and Cyprus.[42] There was a profound contrast between the Phanariot class and that of the Greek merchants that rose to prominence and riches in the eighteenth century. In the perspective of history we may realise that the Greek merchant, too, did well out of the Ottoman Empire, but this is not a view he held at the time. What he knew all too well was that his efforts were constantly thwarted by Ottoman officialdom the arbitrary impositions of which he could escape only by flying the Russian or the British flag. The Phanariot, therefore, was a man who fed on the existing system, while the merchant fed himself by circumventing it. The former tended to be a reactionary, the latter a liberal.

The third question I should like to raise concerns the intimate relationship between the Phanariots and the Church. In this respect the Phanariots merely continued an existing tradition: already in the sixteenth century influential Greek _arkhons_, like Mikhail Kantakouzinos, were able to appoint and depose patriarchs, and, before the advent of the Phanariots proper, Rumanian princes often had a controlling voice in the affairs of the Greek Church. The influence exercised by the Phanariots on the Church of Constantinople cannot be exactly defined. In terms of recognised institutions, it was limited to the existence of certain appointments called _offikia_ that were open to laymen and entitled their holders to a seat on the Synod. These posts, like that of Grand Logothete, Grand Skevophylax, Grand Chartophylax, etc., were usually occupied since the end of the seventeenth century either by Phanariots or their protégés.[43] It may be worth noticing that the Phanariots themselves very seldom took holy orders: I can mention only two patriarchs of the eighteenth century, Ioannikios Karatzas and Samuil Khantzeris, who belonged to prominent Phanariot families.[44] What appears on paper is, however, only the tip of the iceberg: the real hold of the Phanariots on the Church was political and financial. Political, because the Phanariots enjoyed the confidence of the Turkish authorities; financial, because the Church was chronically in debt[45] and was obliged to use the Phanariots as its bankers. We should remember that all important ecclesiastical offices were sold for ready cash: that of Patriarch cost at the beginning of the eighteenth century 3,000 florins, i.e., $16\frac{1}{2}$ purses, but this soon went up to 80 purses or even more.[46] Since the nominees seldom had so much money at their disposal, they had to borrow it at about 10 per cent interest. It is said that the Phanariots regularly invested their assets in subsidising the appointment of patriarchs and metropolitans, which enabled them, of course, to pick their own candidates and keep them in a state of lasting subservience.[47]

While it is true that the Phanariots constantly interfered in the affairs of the Church, often in a most unceremonious manner, it is equally true that they remained steadfastly faithful to the Church and identified themselves with its interests as they interpreted them. Their benefactions, which were not perhaps commensurate with their wealth, were directed almost entirely to the Church: gifts of money, of real estate, of plate, of vestments, even of wax for candles. When they subsidised education, it was education under ecclesiastical auspices.[48] Many Greek *hospodars* founded monasteries in Rumania which they usually assigned to the Holy Sepulchre, Mount Sinai or Mount Athos: there can be no doubt that this represented a form of investment.[49] The involvement of the Phanariots was not limited to the Church of Constantinople. The Church of Rumania was, of course, entirely in their pocket since all senior ecclesiastical appointments were at the *hospodar*'s pleasure; furthermore, they showed an active interest in the affairs of the other Eastern Patriarchates, especially that of Jerusalem which was, incidentally, a major landholder in Rumania. Panayotis Nikousios, Alexandros and Nikolaos Mavrokordatos laboured ceaselessly to defend the Holy Sepulchre and other places of pilgrimage in Palestine against the encroachments of Roman Catholics. The great volume of correspondence between leading Phanariots and the Patriarchs of Jerusalem[50] offers sufficient evidence of this concern, which also had obvious financial implications.[51]

I have attempted by way of introduction to discuss certain characteristics of the Phanariots that must have conditioned their behaviour as a class. I should now like to turn to their literary culture in order to find out whether they represented a definite way of thinking, a tradition, and whether this could be called a Byzantine tradition. In speaking of Phanariot literature, I am including under this heading not only the writings of bona fide Phanariots, which are not very numerous, but also those produced in their milieu, whether in Constantinople or Rumania. I shall begin with a few general remarks.

At the risk of making a sweeping generalisation, I would venture to say that Greek literature after the fall of Constantinople splits up into two main streams. The first, which may be labelled Franco-Greek (in the demotic acceptation of *Frangos*), is largely the literature of the Greek islands: it includes the so-called Rhodian and Cypriot love songs, the chronicle of Makhairas, the Cretan plays of the seventeenth century and the *Erotokritos*. Most of these works have some literary merit; with the possible exception of Makhairas, they are all dependent, however loosely, on western prototypes and are not explainable in terms of Byzantine antecedents. In so far as post-conquest Greek literature has attracted the attention of western scholars, this attention has been confined almost entirely to the Franco-Greek stream.

The other main stream, which is quite copious but entirely devoid of literary merit, represents the writings of Greeks living under Ottoman domination. Their content is largely theological, but there are also chronicles, collections of letters, laudations, epigrams, poems commemorating memorable events and school textbooks. This stream perpetuates the literary genres of medieval Byzantium, exhibits the same range of interests, the same stock of assumed knowledge, the same rhetoric, the same linguistic dichotomy, the same lack of any poetic feeling as does Byzantine literature. The writings of the Phanariots belong to this second tradition, of which they form the historical termination.

Furthermore, it seems to me that the literary culture of the Phanariots has been greatly exaggerated. It is difficult to understand today the admiration that has been lavished on a work so essentially mediocre as the *Peri kathikonton* (*Concerning Obligations*), acknowledged to be the masterpiece of Nikolaos Mavrokordatos.[52] Yet Nikolaos was unquestionably one of the most cultivated Phanariots. As for Konstantinos Dapontes, the distinguished alumnus of the academies of Bucharest and Jassy and 'the most productive Greek author of the eighteenth century',[53] his tedious verbiage will defeat the patience of the most determined reader. The literary world of the Phanar, the 'world of tchelebi Yorgakis', as George Seferis has aptly called it,[54] will remain forever enshrined in the *New Erotokritos* of Dionysios Photeinos, purged, as the author informs us, of its barbarous and nearly incomprehensible Cretan dialect, and rendered into the 'mellifluous speech of educated Greeks'.[55]

We may now examine a few specimens of Phanariot writing

so as to show both their mentality and something of their content. The first document that claims our attention is the collected letters of Alexandros Mavrokordatos. These are mostly in high rhetorical style and were actually used in the Greek schools as models of epistolography along with the letters of Libanius and Synesius and the *Peri epistolikon typon* of Theophilos Korydalefs.[56] I shall single out from them a few topics of interest.

First, there is Alexandros' attitude towards his Turkish masters. He states repeatedly that he has served them faithfully:

> We conform to the prescription of the Gospel, 'Render unto Caesar the things which are Caesar's'; it is not the custom of us Christians to confuse what is temporary and corruptible with what is divine and eternal.[57]

The trouble stems from the fact that the Turks are extremely contemptuous towards Christians. To make matters worse, the Sultan is constantly changing his ministers. 'I have succeeded by dint of great exertion,' he says, 'to win one vizier's favour; but now he has fallen and another has taken his place, and then another. Each time I have to start afresh.'

In matters of ethics Alexandros counsels prudence or, as we would say, dissimulation. One of his correspondents had been ordered to audit government expenditure over the previous ten years and was afraid of exposing influential embezzlers. 'You should have excused yourself,' says Alexandros, 'on the pretext of being incapable of the task. Now, however, that you are under orders, you ought to engage as many collaborators as possible so as to spread the responsibility.'[58] Another correspondent had been cruelly treated by the authorities and was seeking Alexandros' advice. 'Be patient,' he says, 'and prudent. Whatever punishment is inflicted on you, be it the confiscation of your property or even imprisonment, call it a great blessing so all can hear you.'[59]

With regard to contact with the West, Alexandros has this to say:

> It often leads to the corruption of the ancestral customs that adorn our nation. I have often deplored the fact that Greeks who have gone abroad have not only acquired disgusting and spurious manners, but have also polluted their minds with

alien doctrines and have drawn thousands of simple souls into the same abominations. Would that they had suffered ship-wreck upon their departure.[60]

Finally, with regard to language, Alexandros distinguishes between two idioms, the Hellenic, i.e., ancient Greek which is used for display, and the vulgar used for serious communications. In writing from Belgrade to Dositheos, Patriarch of Jerusalem, he says, 'Forgive me if I have erred in describing these matters in Hellenic as if I was playing a game, whereas I should have been serious and used the vulgar dialect.'[61] On the other hand, he is greatly incensed when his sons, whom he had left at home in the care of a schoolmaster, wrote him in the vulgar tongue.

When will you cease, O beloved ones, chattering in the dialect of the marketplace? Two or even three months have gone by, and you have not sent me a single letter wrought in Attic, such as would be an exemplar of your diligence and would serve to console me on this dreadful expedition. Has your course of rhetoric come to no good end? Is this the result of your studies that you do not hesitate to speak barbarously to your father whom you know to prize the charms of rhetoric and artful elegance more than nectar and ambrosia?[62]

Alexander was not in the end disappointed: his dutiful son Nikolaos reduced him to tears of joy by sending him a letter conceived in such convoluted Hellenic, that he even had to be gently reprimanded for using expressions that were too contrived.[63] Here is the father's delighted reaction:

Let those who disparage the present time for its unproductive-ness and poverty keep silent. Nature has not been reduced to such sterility. Nay, God has given an Athens to Hellas, and to Athens He has given a Libanius.[64]

Anyone who is acquainted with Byzantine epistolography will immediately recognise a familiar strain in these letters. For the educated, Libanius still rules the Muses. But what do we find when we step down one rung on the ladder of sophistication? It is, even more emphatically, Byzantium. Here is the list of recommended reading compiled by Konstantinos Dapontes for the benefit of the Princess Eleni Mavrokordatou:

Let me tell you those books that I find to be full of sweetness. Here they are: The *Oktoikhos* of John Damascene, the *oikoi* in honour of the Virgin [i.e., the Acathist Hymn] – and add to them those in honour of St. John the Baptist as being of equal grace; the seven prayers to the Virgin contained in the missal (*synopsis*); the Exposition of the Liturgy by Nicholas Cabasilas; the Chapters of the deacon Agapetus addressed to Justinian, the ornament of the ages; the book by Stephen on the Making of Gold; not to mention your Constantine [i.e., Dapontes himself] who is like honey unto the heart.[65]

An instructive list considering it was drawn up in the middle of the eighteenth century.

What little there is of Phanariot historiography is also revealing. Alexandros Mavrokordatos wrote a vast historical work divided into three parts, called *Iudaica*, *Romaica* and *Mysica*, of which only the first has been published.[66] In the Preface the author tells us that Greeks were ignorant of history because so many of their books had been destroyed; furthermore, being enslaved, very few of them went abroad, and those who did so sought commercial gain rather than instruction. The author, who had had the opportunity of travelling in the West and knew many languages, proposed, therefore, to offer to his compatriots the fruits of his wide reading. If, on the strength of this promise, we expect to find in the *Iudaica* any reflection of Renaissance scholarship, we are quickly disappointed. On the first page the author informs us that history is divided into six periods: 1 and 2 from Creation to Abraham, 3 and 4 from Abraham to the Incarnation, 5 and 6 from the Incarnation to the Second Coming. This is to be followed by a seventh period, which is that of 'endless repose in the eternal mansions.' The *Iudaica* covers periods 1 to 4 and is based on the authority of the Old Testament. When we lay down the heavy tome, we do so with the realisation that things had not changed much since the days of Zonaras and Manasses: Moses, the greatest of historians, the seven aeons of universal history corresponding to the seven days of the week are still with us.

The book that tells us most about the activities of the Phanariots (not without bias and considerable inaccuracy) is undoubtedly the historical work of the physician Athanasios

Komninos Ypsilantis, commonly known as *Ta meta tin Alosin*, i.e., *Events after the Conquest*. The published part, consisting of Books VIII, IX, X and extracts of Book XII, is only a small section of a vast ecclesiastical history in twelve books that starts with Julius Caesar and goes down to 1789.[67] The skeleton of the work is provided by the succession of the Patriarchs of Constantinople starting with the apostle Andrew: it is they who occupy the centre of the stage, while the affairs of the four other apostolic sees, of Byzantine emperors and Turkish sultans are dealt with marginally. In other words, we have before us a work that stands in direct succession to Socrates and Sozomen, Theodoret and Nicephorus Callistus; and its avowed purpose was to propagate Orthodoxy and confound the heretics.[68]

In reading works of Phanariot literature, such as those of Konstantinos Dapontes, who served as secretary to the *hospodars* Konstantinos and Ioannis Mavrokordatos, and the History of Athanasios Ypsilantis, one cannot help noticing again and again the extent of their geographical horizon. To be sure, Western Europe was not entirely ignored, but the part of the world that especially interested the Phanariots extended from Moscow in the north to Alexandria in the south. It was the world not of *ellinismos*, but of Orthodoxy, and its centre was naturally Constantinople which, to quote the expression of Iakovos Argeios, the tutor of Nikolaos Mavrokordatos, 'presides today not only over Europe, but also over Asia and Africa'[69] – as, in fact, it did thanks to the existence of the Ottoman Empire. When the notorious Stravrakoğlu, whom I have already mentioned, built his palatial residence on the Bosphorus, he decorated his own room with views of Wallachia and Moldavia, and his wife's room with views of Constantinople and Moscow[70] – not, I might add, with a view of the Parthenon. Dapontes' *Catalogue of Distinguished Men* (1700–84) deals with the following categories of people in this order: patriarchs of Constantinople, Alexandria, Antioch and Jerusalem; Orthodox bishops, priests and monks; Czars of Russia; Phanariot *hospodars* and interpreters; other *arkhons* of Constantinople, tradesmen and finally teachers.[71]

That the dream of recreating the Byzantine Empire was very much alive in Phanariot circles may be taken for granted. The same Konstantinos Dapontes saw in 1738, when he was at

Bucharest, a vision of the double-headed eagle wearing the imperial crown, as well as of Constantine and Helena.[72] The Oracles of Leo the Wise had spoken of a mysterious ox that would bellow when the awaited emperor John appeared to liberate Constantinople: now the emblem of Moldavia was an ox-head and all the *hospodars*, on their accession, assumed the ceremonial name of John.[73] The most influential Greek oracular work of the eighteenth century, the so-called Book of Agathangelos, was dedicated to Grigorios Ghika, *hospodar* of Wallachia.[74] As envisaged at the time, the restoration of the Byzantine Empire was to come about not by internal revolution, but by a providential intervention either of the Russian Czar or the German Emperor (or both combined), and it was widely believed that this was to happen 320 years after the Fall, i.e., in 1773. This very nearly came to pass. The Russo-Turkish war that broke out in 1768 resulted, however, not in the liberation of Constantinople, but in the Treaty of Küçük Kaynarca which, favourable as it was to Greek interests, aroused profound disappointment. I quote the reaction of Konstantinos Dapontes:

The time appointed by the oracles for the restoration was 320 years after the Conquest, and it so happened that this time coincided with the six years' war when [the Russians] approached the City, surrounded it and were on the point of taking it, but did not take it. For this reason the Russians will no longer be able to capture it no matter what means they use or what forces they bring down to the Crimea . . . For if God, constrained by our sins – may He forgive me for daring to say so – prevented that which was affirmed by the oracles from happening at the appointed time; if, I say, He saw fit that the utterances of so many astronomers, scholars and saints should prove vain in preference to giving the Empire to men unworthy not only of this Empire but of life itself, how is it possible henceforth that the resurrection of the Romaic Empire should happen when no assurance or oracle concerning this has remained? This being so, neither the Greeks nor the Russians will reign in the City unto the end of the world. May merciful God take pity on us and grant us the Heavenly Kingdom, and never mind about the earthly one.[75]

The disappointment of these deeply felt messianic hopes came about at a time when French rationalism was beginning to exert some impact upon the better educated Greeks – first upon the mercantile Greek diaspora and, a little later, upon the rising Greek bourgeoisie resident in the Ottoman Empire. In spite of ecclesiastical opposition, several attempts were made to introduce the 'new learning' into the curriculum of Greek schools in the place of the Aristotelianism of Theophilos Korydalefs that had held sway since the beginning of the seventeenth century.[76] French novels, often of the worst kind, were avidly read at Constantinople, and even a few Phanariots took up the cause of Enlightenment by translating more serious French works into Greek. Rallou, daughter of the *hospodar* Alexandros Soutsos, is said to have translated the Marquise de Lambert's *Avis d'une mère à sa fille*, Aikaterini Soutsos rendered into Greek Mably's *Entretiens de Phocion*, Konstantinos Manos is credited with a translation of Barthélemy's *Voyage du jeune Anacharsis*, etc.[77] All of this was harmless enough. When, however, the French Revolution broke out, when French agents began disseminating subversive proclamations in Ottoman territory, when, in particular, Napoleon landed in Egypt (1798) and so attacked directly the world of Islam, some stand had to be taken. The Church of Constantinople reacted violently by hurling its anathemas at French godlessness and affirming that the Sultan's Empire had been set up by God's decree. These and similar views were expressed in a number of pamphlets of which the most notorious is the *Patriki didaskalia* (*Paternal Doctrine*) published at the Patriarchal Press of Constantinople in that same year 1798 under the name of Anthimos, Patriarch of Jerusalem.[78] The circumstances surrounding the publication of this and other reactionary tracts are, unfortunately, very obscure. It is likely enough that the Phanariots had a hand in them, although I have no conclusive proof of this. I should like, however, to draw attention to a statement made by Zallony, namely, that in the course of a conversation he had in 1818 with the metropolitans of Nicomedia, Derkoi, Sophia and Thessaloniki he was informed by them that the Phanariots imposed the following conditions on the clergy: to keep alive an undying hatred of the Roman Catholic Church; to forbid all marriages between Orthodox and Roman Catholics; to insist on the observance of 195 fast days per year; to promote the pilgrimage to Jerusalem; finally – and this is the important point – to declare that the concept of political liberty had been inspired by the devil, whereas the Sultan's Empire existed by God's grace.[79]

Western godlessness, egalitarianism and antiquarianism triumphed in the end, but not without having produced a strange Phanariot hybrid in the proclamations of Rigas Velestinlis. This famous revolutionary who, we may remember, made his career entirely within the Phanariot framework, traced in 1796 his blueprint for regenerated Greece. The well-known map he printed in that year includes, in fact, the entire Balkan peninsula as well as western Asia Minor, while its lower left-hand corner is occupied by an inset plan of Constantinople which was evidently meant to be the capital.[80] Rigas elaborated his rather fuzzy ideas in the Revolutionary Manifesto of 1797 which is addressed to

> The People descended from the ancient Hellenes who inhabit Rumeli, Asia Minor, the Mediterranean islands, Vlakhobogdania, and all those who groan under the unbearable tyranny of the most foul Ottoman despotism or who have been forced to depart to foreign kingdoms so as to escape this heavy yoke, all, I say, Christian and Turk alike without any distinction of religion.[81]

The ornamental detail and phraseology of this manifesto are admittedly of Western inspiration: Rigas speaks of Hellenes, not of Romaioi, although he has no clear conception of who these Hellenes may be; he lays down the design of the revolutionary flag which, by way of compromise, was to represent the club of Hercules surmounted by three crosses; he wants the soldiers to wear classical helmets and heroic costume, i.e., black jerkins, white shirts and red hose. If we make allowance for all this romantic claptrap, what emerges is not a Hellenic democracy, but, in fact, a somewhat dechristianised Byzantine democracy.[82]

The people of Vlakhobogdania were not, of course, greatly stirred by the appeal to join the new Hellenic Commonwealth, as Alexandros Ypsilantis was to discover in 1821. The story of his failure does not need retelling. One might be tempted to call it a farce had it not ended in tragedy, when the Turks, justifiably alarmed by the turn of events, carried out an indiscriminate massacre of the leading Phanariots in Constantinople and even hanged for good measure the unfortunate Patriarch Grigorios V who was a fanatical opponent of the Revolution. This marks the end of the Phanariots as a significant element in history. Many of them settled in Greece. Some remained in Turkey and even succeeded in regaining influential posts in the Ottoman administration, like Spyridon Mavroyenis (1816–1902) who was chief physician to Abdul Hamid, like his son Alexandros (d. 1929) who served as Turkish ambassador to Washington. Some Phanariots stayed in Rumania. A few emigrated to Western Europe.

R. W. Seton Watson writes:

> The Greek Revolution of 1821 is inaugurated in Moldavia and Wallachia by the son of a former hospodar, but ends like one of those dissolving views that are thrown upon the screen. For a moment it is Greek, then the outlines fade and waver and vanish, and suddenly in the twinkling of an eye the Greek is gone and has been replaced at every point by the Roumanian . . . There is no other example of the leaders of a national revolt so completely misconceiving the nature of their own problem as to address themselves in the first instance to a people which was not only alien in blood, but indifferent and even hostile to all their aims and outlooks.[83]

In this 'misconception' lies the paradox of the Phanariots. It would be injudicious to pass a general judgment on an aristocracy that was constantly divided and whose members, especially at the end of the eighteenth century, championed the conflicting interests of Russia, Austria and France while remaining Ottoman civil servants. I do not believe that there ever existed a Phanariot master-plan for a settlement of the Eastern question. I am aware that some Phanariots became infected with liberal ideas, and that a few of them even won the crowns of 'ethnomartyrdom'. But if we are to draw a conclusion, it is that the Phanariots, not by virtue of their descent, but by virtue of their position in the Ottoman Empire, the sources of their wealth, and their close identification with the Church, represented a

Byzantine tradition that was basically anti-national.[84] Those of them that espoused the 'new ideas' simply superimposed them, as did Rigas Velestinlis, upon their innate Byzantinism without realizing that the two were mutually exclusive. For all of their political finesse, they did not perceive that their world had ceased to exist. Those Phanariots and Patriarchs who implacably opposed French philosophy and revolution had perhaps a clearer understanding of what was about to happen.

NOTES TO CHAPTER 2

This paper was read at a symposium entitled 'After the Fall of Constantinople', held at Dumbarton Oaks, Washington, D.C., in May 1968. It is presented here without any substantial alterations, i.e., as a sketch and nothing more. 'La question phanariote', wrote Émile Legrand in 1888, 'est beaucoup plus compliquée qu'elle ne le paraît de prime abord; elle n'est pas de celles que l'on tranche au pied levé; elle demande au contraire à être mûrie par une longue étude, et nous abandonnons volontiers à d'autres le soin de la résoudre.' *Bibliothèque grecque vulgaire*, IV, p. v. Legrand's wish has not, unfortunately, been realised. Much has been written about the Phanariots, mostly in a polemical or sentimental vein, but we still lack a comprehensive study based on the enormous mass of available source-material, Greek, Rumanian and Turkish. Hence the danger of passing general judgments as I have had to do.

Among books that are readily accessible, N. Iorga's *Byzance après Byzance* (Bucharest, 1935, 1971) remains very useful in spite of the opacity of its style. J.-C. Filitti, *Rôle diplomatique des Phanariotes de 1700 à 1821* (Paris,1901) deserves mention, although it is hardly relevant to the subject of our discussion. Manuel Gedeon and Émile Legrand have both in their voluminous works made notable contributions. By contrast, A. A. Pallis, *The Phanariots: A Greek Aristocracy under Turkish Rule* (London, 1951) is decidedly superficial. Nor does Sir Steven Runciman, *The Great Church in Captivity* (Cambridge, 1968) Chapter 10, offer any new insights. I particularly regret not having been able to attend the symposium 'L'époque phanariote' held at Thessaloniki in October 1970, the programme of which is given in *Balkan Studies*, XI (1970) 318–23. Its proceedings have not yet been published.

1. I quote from the first French edition (Marseille, 1824). There is a second French edition under the title *Traité sur les princes de la Valachie et de la Moldavie* (Paris, 1830); an English translation in Charles Swan, *Journal of a Voyage up the Mediterranean* (London, 1826) II, p. 271 ff.; and a Greek translation, *Pragmateia peri ton igemonon tis Moldovlakhias* (Athens, 1855).

2. Among the earliest apologies we may quote Jacovaky Rizo Neroulos (himself a Phanariot), *Cours de littérature grecque* (2nd ed.; Geneva–Paris, 1828) p. 33 ff. See also Skarlatos Byzantios (a protégé of the Kallimakhis family), *I Kônstantinoupolis*, I (Athens, 1851) p. 574, indignantly refuting the

'slanderer Tzalonis'; E. I. Stamatiadis, *viographiai ton ellinon megalon diermineon tou Othomanikou kratous* (Athens, 1865) pp. 14 f., 24. K. Paparrigopoulos, *Istoria tou ellinikou ethnous* (4th ed.; Athens, 1903) v, p. 570 ff., considers the chief achievement of the Phanariots to have been the hellenisation of Roumania which would have been complete had their government been allowed to last another fifty years! Among more recent apologies see K. Amantos, 'Oi Ellines eis tin Roumanian pro tou 1821', *Praktika Akadimias Athinon*, xix (1944) 416, 429 ff.; Archimandrite H. Konstantinidis, *To ekpolitistikon ergon ton Phanarioton* (Istanbul, 1949) p. 11.

3. Already by Ch. Pertusier, *La Valachie, la Moldavie et de l'influence politique des Grecs du Fanal* (Paris, 1822). The re-appraisal of the Phanariots in this century owes much to N. Iorga. See, for example, his *Roumains et Grecs au cours des siècles* (Bucharest, 1921) p. 48 ff. Th. H. Papadopoullos, *Studies and Documents relating to the History of the Greek Church and People under Turkish Domination* (Brussels, 1952) p. 49 ff., is critical of the Phanariots for the unexpected reason that they undermined the jurisdiction of the Church.

4. On Panayotis see K. Dapontes, *Istorikos katalogos* in Sathas, *Mesaioniki Vivliothiki*, III (Venice, 1872) pp. 165–6, who says that he was the son of a furrier of obscure family; Athanasios Komninos Ypsilantis, *Ta meta tin Alosin* (Constantinople, 1870) p. 161 ff.; I. Sakkelion, 'Panayotaki tou Mamona . . . dialexis meta tinos Vanli [sic] efendi', *Deltion Istorikis kai Ethnologikis Etaireias*, III (1890) 240 ff.; Stamatiadis, *Viographiai . . .*, 29 ff.

5. Ypsilantis, *Ta meta tin Alosin*, p. 165; Stamatiadis, *Viographai . . .*, p. 29 ff.

6. On his career see especially A. Stourdza, *L'Europe orientale et le rôle historique des Maurocordato (1660–1830)* (Paris, 1913) p. 30 ff.; K. Amantos, 'Alexandros Mavrokordatos o ex aporriton', *Ellinika*, v (1932) 335 ff.; and N. Camariano, *Alexandre Mavrocordato, le Grand Drogman. Son activité diplomatique 1673–1709* (Thessaloniki, 1970).

7. For a chronological list of the hospodars see, for example, C. C. Giurescu (ed.), *Istoria României în date* (Bucharest, 1971) p. 455 ff.

8. This judgment is already expressed in the *History of Moldavia* by Nicholas Costin issued in 1729 under the *hospodar* Grigorios Ghika and immediately translated into Greek (Paris, Bibl. Nat., Suppl. gr. 6). See C. B. Hase, 'Notice d'un manuscrit . . . contenant une Histoire inédite de la Moldavie', *Notices et extraits des manuscrits de la Bibliothèque du Roi*, xi/2 (1827) 282. Cf. E. Habesci, *The Present State of the Ottoman Empire* (London, 1784) p. 198 f.; W. Wilkinson, *An Account of the Principalities of Wallachia and Moldavia* (London, 1820) pp. 44 f., 95; M. Kogalnitchan, *Histoire de la Valachie, de la Moldavie et des Valaques transdanubiens* (Berlin, 1837) I, p. 371 ff., etc. For an indictment of the Phanariot regime backed by economic statistics see N. A. Mokhov, *Moldavija epokhi feodalizma* (Kishinev, 1964) p. 359 ff.

9. R. W. Seton-Watson, *A History of the Roumanians* (Cambridge, 1934) p. 127.

10. Ypsilantis, *Ta meta tin Alosin*, p. 263. Ypsilantis was admittedly very hostile to the entire Mavrokordatos family. Legrand goes so far as to suggest

that he was paid by the Turks to write his History, but this I find most unlikely: Legrand, *Ephémérides daces*, II (Paris, 1881) p. xii f.

11. K. Dapontes *Istorikos katalogos*, *loc. cit.*, p. 160. He adds: 'The Turks, too, did not gobble up then as much as they do now, or rather, to tell the truth, they [the native princes] did not give them as much to eat as we are giving them.'

12. Cf. A. Vakalopoulos, *Istoria tou neou Ellinismou*, II/I (Thessaloniki, 1964), p. 354 ff. It is interesting to observe that a board of trustees set up by the Patriarch Ioasaph in 1564 comprised the following laymen: Antonios Kantakouzinos of Galata, the *arkhon* Mozalos [i.e., Mouzalon] son of Gabras, Konstantinos Palaiologos, and Karatzas of Caramania: M. Gedeon, *Khronika tou patriarkhikou oikou kai naou* (Constantinople, 1884) p. 137 f.

13. La Croix, *La Turquie chrétienne* (Paris, 1695) p. 6 f., who served at Constantinople in the 1670s, gives the following list of 19 noble Greek families: Juliani, Rosetti, Diplomatachi [Diplovatatzi?], Mauro Cordati, Chrisosculi, Vlasti, Cariofili, Ramniti, Mamenadi, Cupraghioti, Musselimi, Succii, Veneli, Cinchidi, Contaradii, Mauradii, Ramateni, Francidi, Frangopoli. Cf. J. Aymon, *Monumens authentiques de la religion des Grecs* (The Hague, 1708) p. 479. Note that of the above families only three (the Rosetti, Mavrokordatos and Soutsos) emerged in the top rank of Phanariot aristocracy. La Croix (p. 4 f.), makes the further observation that the true Byzantine aristocracy was extinct save for the families of 'Cantacuzene, Paleologue, Assanii et Rali', which, however, 'auroient même beaucoup de peine à prouver leur Généalogie'; and that their representatives had sunk to the level of menial artisans.

14. E. R. Rangavis, *Le livre d'or de la noblesse phanariote* (1st ed.; Athens, 1892). I am quoting from the 2nd edition (Athens, 1904).

15. See O. Cicanci and P. Cernovodeanu, 'Contribution à la connaissance de la biographie et de l'oeuvre de Jean (Hierothée) Comnène', *Balkan Studies*, XII (1971), 146 f.

16. See E. Legrand, *Généalogie des Maurocordato de Constantinople* (Paris, 1900).

17. The 'founder' of the family was George Ghika, prince of Moldavia (1658–9) and thereafter of Wallachia (1659–60). Cf. E. Kourilas, 'Grigorios o Argyrokastritis', *Theologia*, XI (1933) 219 ff.; Rangavis, *Livre d'or*, p. 85 ff.; C[arra], *Histoire de la Moldavie et de la Valachie* (Jassy[?], 1777) p. 87 ff.

18. See the exhaustive study by S. Skopeteas, 'Oi Ypsilantai', *Arkheion Pontou*, XX (1955) 150 ff. S. Ioannidis, *Istoria kai statistiki Trapezountos* (Constantinople, 1870) p. 136 ff., claims that these two families reached Constantinople after 1697.

19. For a contemporary account of the rise of the first Kallimakhis see Dapontes, *Istorikos katalogos*, p. 174 ff. Cf. Ypsilantis, *Ta meta tin Alosin*, p. 350.

20. There exists a list of manuscripts belonging to the *arkhon* Ioannis Soutsos (ca. 1570): R. Foerster, *De antiquitatibus et libris manuscriptis Constantinopolitanis commentatio* (Rostock, 1877) p. 19. See also note 13 *supra*. For the Drakos tradition see Ypsilantis in Hurmuzaki, *Documente privitoare la*

istoria Românilor, xiii, ed. A. Papadopoulos-Kerameus (1909), p. 189; S. Byzantios, *I Konstantinoupolis*, p. 114, n. 1. The Soutsos and Drakos families appear to have been intermarried: an Alexandros Drakos Soutsos is recorded as Grand Khartophylax (1741–60).

21. See note 13 *supra*. Antonios Rosetti, prince of Moldavia (1675–8), is said to have been the son of the Constantinopolitan nobleman Laskaris Rossetos, Great Logothete of the Patriarchate, and of Bella, grand-daughter of Mikhail Kantakouzinos. Dapontes, *Khronographos* in Sathas, *Mesaion. Vivl.*, iii, 17. Rangavis, *Livre d'or*, p. 183 ff., derives the family from Genoa. I do not know whether they were related to the Rossettis of Coron: Moustoxydis, *Ellinomnimon*, 1 (1843) pp. 157, 295.

22. See note 12 *supra*. Rangavis, *Livre d'or*, p. 75 ff., says that the family came from Epirus, while Skopeteas, 'Oi Ypsilantai', 150, claims it for Trebizond. Given the commonness of the name, more than one family may be involved.

23. The notorious Nikolaos Mavroyenis (b. 1738), Dragoman of the Fleet, then *hospodar* of Wallachia (1786–90), was the son of Petros Mavroyenis, Austrian vice-consul at Mykonos. An exorbitant laudation of Nikolaos by Manolaki Persianos is reprinted by Legrand, *Bibl. grecque vulgaire*, vii (1895) p. 365 ff. The same personage figures prominently in Thomas Hope's *Anastasius, or Memoirs of a Greek*, where this 'individual of the Tergiumanic genus' is described as belonging to the 'most distinguished family in the island of Paros' (2nd ed.; London, 1820) 1, p. 38 ff. See also Th. Blancard, *Les Mavroyéni: histoire d'Orient de 1700 à nos jours*, 2 vols. (Paris, 1909).

24. On Samuil see Germanos, metropolitan of Sardis, in *Orthodoxia*, xi (1936) 300 ff.; Papadopoullos, *Studies and Documents*, p. 387 ff. He was a rich man and, presumably, a native of Constantinople. I have not been able to ascertain the origin of the family whose name is probably derived from Turkish *hançer* = dagger.

25. The notion that the Phanariots were 'merchants on a grand scale' (A. J. Toynbee, *A Study of History*, ii (London, 1934) p. 224) is, I believe, incorrect. There may have been a few exceptions like Adamakis Mourouzis who is described as a rich merchant from Trebizond. He married the granddaughter of Panayotis Nikousios. Having been accused of embezzlement, he barely saved his life by paying 50,000 scudi. Stamatiadis, *Viographiai*, p. 56 (who erroneously calls him Asimakis).

26. Legrand, *Généalogie des Maurocordato*, p. 48. See also the Venetian document of 1631 quoted by A. Stourdza, *L'Europe orientale*, p. 354: '. . . un greco nominato Scarlato, il quale da modesta fortuna sali a grande richesse nell'amministrazione dei dazii, in modo da lasciare, morendo, un milion d'oro in contanti oltre molti beni stabili'. Cantemir is, as often, quite wrong in stating that Skarlatos made himself rich by holding the office of '*Sorguj*, or purveyor to the court for sheep and oxen'. *History of the Ottoman Empire*, trans. Tindal (London, 1734) p. 356 n. 12. This is repeated by Zallony, *Essai*, p. 22, and by others.

27. P. G. Zerlentis, 'Ioannou tou Karyophyllou ephimerides', *Deltion Istorikis kai Ethnologikis Etaireias*, iii (1889) 305 ff.; Dapontes, *Khronographos*, p. 31; id., *Istorikos katalogos*, p. 167 f. 1 purse = 500 piastres.

28. Ypsilantis, *Ta meta tin Alosin*, p. 233; thereafter increased to 400 purses (*ibid.*, p. 234).

29. Dapontes, *Khronographos*, p. 33; id., *Istorikos katalogos*, p. 168. Cf. Th. Livadas, *Alex. Mavrokordatou . . . epistolai 100* (Trieste, 1879) p. xciv f., and letter 73, p. 125 ff. addressed to Neophytos, metropolitan of Philippopolis, who wished to borrow money from Mavrokordatos. The letter may be summarised as follows: 'I have no landed property, no ships, no workshops. I live by lending capital at interest. My salary does not cover half of my expenses. Many of my creditors have failed me. You may have my friendship, but not my money.'

30. Stourdza, *L'Europe orientale*, p. 63 n. 1; Seton-Watson, *History of the Roumanians*, p. 93. A sidelight on Alexandros' parsimony and, incidentally, on the degree of influence he enjoyed is provided by the following incident. Having married his daughter Roxandra to the prince Matthaios, son of Grigorios Ghika, he subsequently felt obliged to have his son-in-law banished to Cyprus because the latter was a drunkard and 'was dissipating his [Alexandros'] daughter's fortune' (Dapontes, *Khronographos*, p. 61).

31. Skopeteas, 'Oi Ypsilantai', 221.

32. Ypsilantis, *Ta meta tin Alosin*, p. 342, who puts the blame for this on Konstantinos Mavrokordatos.

33. *Ibid.*, p. 375. It is amusing to note that the historian, instead of commending Konstantinos for his honesty, accuses him of bad management.

34. Zallony, *Essai*, p. 64. Wilkinson, who was British Consul at Bucharest and, therefore, reliably informed, puts the private income of the Prince of Wallachia at about 2,000,000 piastres (*An Account of the Principalities*, p. 68). At that time (1818) 30 piastres equalled £1. He makes it clear, however, that the Prince had almost unlimited opportunity of manipulating the system to his advantage.

35. Seton-Watson, *History of the Roumanians*, p. 193. Cf. Wilkinson, *An Account*, pp. 122, 206 ff.

36. Nikolaos Mavrokordatos, who did not trust his compatriots, forms an exception in this respect. In the instructions to his son Konstantinos which he composed in 1727, he says: 'You should have a small retinue and few Phanariots' (Legrand, *Ephémérides daces*, 1, p. 341). He himself gave an important post to only one Greek. Konstantinos, contrary to his father's advice, appointed many Greeks (Ypsilantis, *Ta meta tin Alosin*, p. 340).

37. These offices are described by Wilkinson, *An Account*, p. 51 ff.; Pertusier, *La Valachie*, p. 55 ff.

38. Legrand, *Recueil de poèmes historiques en grec vulgaire* (Paris, 1877) p. 191 ff.

39. Thus Alexandros Ypsilantis owned a house at Kuruçeşme (on the Bosphorus) worth 500 purses or more, 'since he lifted (*esikose*) much wealth from Wallachia, more than anyone does these days' (Dapontes, *Istorikos katalogos*, p. 172). Many interesting details on the residences of the Phanariots at Arnautköy may be found in Gennadios, metropolitan of Heliopolis, *Istoria tou Megalou Revmatos* (Istanbul, 1949), p. 157 ff.

40. Carra, *Histoire de la Moldavie*, p. 206, remarks: 'Ce qu'il y a de singulier chez ces despotes de Moldavie et de Valachie, c'est que toutes leurs

richesses, argent, bijoux, hardes & ameublemens sont toujours dans des malles ou coffres de voyage, comme s'ils devoient partir à chaque instant; & dans le fait, ils n'ont pas tort, car ils ont sans cesse à craindre d'être déposés par force ou enlevés ou assassinés . . . .'

41. Cf. *supra*, note 29. We may also quote the case of the Grand Dragoman Alexandros Ghika who was put to death in 1741. His sequestered property, worth more than 700 purses, consisted of a house at the Phanar and another at Kuruçeşme, bonds to the amount of 380 purses, and 20 purses in cash (Dapontes, *Istorikos katalogos*, p. 172 f.). On financial loans there is much interesting material in N. M. Vaporis, *Some Aspects of the History of the Ecumenical Patriarchate of Constantinople in the Seventeenth and Eighteenth Centuries* (New York, 1969).

42. Zallony, *Essai*, p. 207.

43. See La Croix, *La Turquie chrétienne*, p. 191 ff.; Gedeon, *Khronika tou patriarkhikou oikou*, p. 191 ff.; Papadopoullos, *Studies and Documents*, p. 60 ff.

44. Both of these Patriarchs represented the extreme right wing, and were responsible for suspending the teaching activity of Evgenios Voulgaris whom they considered to be too 'modern'. See Patriarch Konstantios I, *Viographia kai syngraphai ai elassones* (Constantinople, 1866) p. 358 f.; Gedeon, *Khronika tis Patriarkhikis Akadimias* (Constantinople, 1883) p. 163.

45. The amount of the debt naturally varied greatly. In 1641, when it was paid off by Basil Lupu, prince of Moldavia, it amounted to 300 purses: Ypsilantis, *Ta meta tin Alosin*, p. 145. La Croix, *La Turquie chrétienne*, p. 144 ff. (referring to ca. 1670) estimates the annual income of the Patriarchate at less than 40,000 écus, whereas the debt stood above 400,000 écus. On the eve of the Greek Revolutionary War it was more than 3000 purses: Papadopoullos, *Studies and Documents*, 132.

46. Ypsilantis, *Ta meta tin Alosin*, p. 296. This lamentable practice was started by Symeon of Trebizond who, in 1465, bought the patriarchal office for 500 florins, a sum that was gradually increased by his successors. See V. Laurent, 'Les premiers patriarches de Constantinople sous domination turque', *Revue des études byzantines*, XXVI (1968) 233 ff. On the institution of the *peşkeş* (fee paid to the Ottoman Treasury for the appointment of an Orthodox bishop) see, for example, J. Kabrda, *Le Système fiscal de l'Église orthodoxe dans l'Empire ottoman* (Brno, 1969) p. 59 ff.

47. Zallony, *Essai*, p. 157 f.

48. On Phanariot piety and benefactions to the Church see M. Gedeon, 'Phanariotika ypomnimata', *Ekklisiastiki alitheia*, III (1883) 325 ff., 372 ff.; id., *Khronika tis Patriarkhikis akadimias* (Constantinople, 1883) pp. 107, 150, 230 ff., 234 f.

49. In Moldavia in 1803 about 20 per cent of the land was in the possession of monasteries (Mokhov, *Moldavija*, p. 377). Wilkinson, *An Account*, p. 70, remarks: 'Some of the monasteries are now the richest establishments in the country. The greater number are in the gift of the reigning princes, who let them out for a space of time to the highest bidders.'

50. Collected by Legrand, *Bibl. grecque vulgaire*, IV (1888), and VII (1895); Hurmuzaki, *Documente*, XIV/2 (1917).

51. In addition to foreign pilgrims, the Greeks, too, perhaps in imitation

of the Moslems, took up the custom of going to Jerusalem in pilgrimage. They could then style themselves *hacı*, after 'pouring 4,000 or 5,000 piastres down the throats of the *Agiotaphitai*', to quote the expression of Korais, *Bekkariou peri adikimaton kai poinon* (2nd ed.; Paris, 1823), p. lviii, n. 1.

52. Published at Bucharest in 1719. This work owes more to the Bible and the Church Fathers than to the Greek and Latin classics. The only 'modern' reference it contains (p. 109) is to Christopher Columbus who is commended for having caused the Gospel to be preached in the New World.

53. B. Knös, *L'histoire de la littérature néo-grecque* (Uppsala, 1962) p. 489.

54. Seferis, *Erotokritos* (Athens, 1946).

55. First published at Vienna in 1818. I have used a two-volume edition (Smyrna, 1863).

56. On this textbook, first published in 1625, see H. Rabe, 'Aus Rhetoren-Handschriften', *Rheinisches Museum*, LXIV (1909) 288 f.; C. Tsourkas, *Les débuts de l'enseignement philosophique et de la libre pensée dans les Balkans. La vie et l'oeuvre de Théophile Corydalée* (Thessaloniki, 1967) p. 98 f.

57. Ed. Livadas, No. 85, p. 145 f. Alexandros expresses similar views in his *Phrontismata* (Vienna, 1805), quoted by Amantos in *Ellinika*, V (1932) 339. Nikolaos Mavrokordatos is also critical of those who challenge the authority of the Sultan (*Peri Kathikonton*, p. 110). Cf. likewise his letter to Khrysanthos, Patriarch of Jerusalem, in Hurmuzaki, *Documente*, XIV/2, No. DCCLXIV.

58. Ed. Livadas, No. 59, p. 95 f.

59. *Ibid.*, No. 60, p. 96 f.

60. *Ibid.*, No. 77, p. 130 f.

61. *Ibid.*, No. 87, p. 146 ff.

62. *Ibid.*, No. 14, p. 20.

63. *Ibid.*, No. 15, p. 22; No. 18, p. 23 ff.

64. *Ibid.*, No. 20, p. 27 f.

65. Dapontes, *Kathreptis gynaikon* (Leipzig, 1766) II, p. 396. Agapetus was used as a textbook at the Academy of Bucharest (Legrand, *Bibl. grecque vulgaire*, VII, 80). The *peri khrysopoiias* is a work on alchemy attributed to Stephen of Alexandria (seventh century). The Preface to the *Mirror* constitutes an interesting cultural document. It may be summarised as follows: It would have been an admirable thing if we strove to understand the text of the Old Testament as did Sts. John Chrysostom, Gregory and Basil. But, alas, we have completely forgotten our noble ancestral language, that of the Hellenes (meaning the language of the Bible!), and so must depend on translations into vulgar Greek. Which is why I have retold in simple language various stories from the Old Testament and have added to them, for the sake of amusement, a few more recent stories.

66. A. Mavrokordatos, *Istoria iera itoi ta Ioudaika* (Bucharest, 1716).

67. Books VIII–X are those published by G. Aphthonidis (Constantinople, 1870). Extracts translated into French by Ph.A. Dethier, *Monum. Hung. hist.*, XXI/2 (1875?) 435–512. Parts of Book XII ed. A. Papadopoulos-Kerameus in Hurmuzaki, *Documente*, XIII (1909) 159–92; addenda to the Aphthonidis ed., *ibid.*, 513–31.

68. Aphthonidis ed., p. xvi.

69. Alexandros Mavrokordatos, *Ta Ioudaika*, Preface.

70. Legrand, *Recueil de poèmes historiques*, p. 202.

71. Sathas, *Mesaioniki vivliothiki*, III p. 71 ff.

72. Dapontes, *Kathreptis gynaikon*, II p. 400 f.

73. See E. Kourilas, 'Ta khrysovoulla ton igemonon tis Moldovlakhias kai to symvolon Io i Ioannis', *Eis mnimin S. Lamprou* (Athens, 1935) 245 ff.

74. E. Kourilas, 'Theoklitos o Polyeidis', *Thrakika*, v (1934) 142.

75. Dapontes, *Istorikos Katalogos*, p. 119 f. Similar passage in verse in his *Geographiki istoria* (Legrand, *Ephémérides daces*, III, p. lxv ff.). Cf. also the sentiments of Ypsilantis, *Ta meta tin Alosin*, p. 534.

76. In Rumania the reorganisation of the curriculum dates from the rule of Alexandros Ypsilantis (1776). See D. V. Economidès, 'Les écoles grecques en Roumanie jusqu'à 1821', *L'hellénisme contemporain*, Ser. 2, IV (1950) 248 ff. At the Patriarchal school of Istanbul the 'new learning' was excluded until the early nineteenth century (Gedeon, *Khronika tis Patriarkhikis Akadimias*, p. 245 ff.). It is interesting to observe in this connection that the poet Georgios Soutsos in his play called *The Catechumen or the Cosmogonical Theatre* (Venice, 1805) could still maintain that, although Newton's system had some merit, that of Moses remained 'the most perfect and the most divine of all others, old and new'. So much for the spread of Enlightenment.

77. See M. Gedeon, 'Peri tis Phanariotikis Koinonias', *O en Konstantin-oupolei Ellinikos Philologikos Syllogos*, XXI (1892) 65 ff. The same works were being translated into Greek and published by others. Mably, rendered into Greek by I. Kaskambas, appeared at St. Petersburg in 1813; *Anacharsis* was published in Vienna (1819) in the version of G. Sakellarios and Rigas.

78. See the thorough investigation by R. Clogg, 'The "Dhidhaskalia Patriki" (1798): An Orthodox Reaction to French Revolutionary Propaganda', *Middle Eastern Studies*, v (1969) 87 ff.

79. Zallony, *Essai*, p. 133 ff.

80. Cf. G. Laïos, 'Oi khartes tou Riga', *Deltion Istorikis kai Ethnologikis Etaireias*, XIV (1960) 231 ff. Rigas was not alone in imagining a Greece that would stretch to the Danube. The same solution was advocated for practical reasons by D. Dufour de Pradt, *De la Grèce dans ses rapports avec l'Europe* (Paris, 1822) p. 75, who, however, did not believe that the population of the Balkan peninsula was descended from the ancient Hellenes. Rumelia and Bulgaria, he thought, were inhabited almost entirely by Turks.

81. Rigas, *Vasiki Vivliothiki*, x, ed. L. I. Vranousis (Athens, 1953), p. 371.

82. I refrain from reproducing here the immense bibliography on Rigas. The Byzantine component of his thought is well brought out by D. Zakythinos, 'O Rigas kai to orama tou oikoumenikou kratous tis Anatolis' in *I Alosis tis Konstantinoupoleos kai i Tourkokratia* (Athens, 1954) pp. 127–35.

83. Seton-Watson, *A History of the Roumanians*, p. 192.

84. G. Finlay, *History of Greece*, ed. Tozer, v, p. 245, is, I believe, essentially right in saying: 'This Greek official aristocracy [the Phanariots] ... was quite as anti-national in its policy as the ecclesiastical hierarchy established by Mohammed II.'

3 The Contribution of the Intelligentsia towards the Greek Independence Movement, 1798–1821[*]

CATHERINE KOUMARIANOU

The years 1798 and 1821 have a dual significance in the history of modern Greece: they are turning points in the development of modern Greek life, marking the natural end of certain historical processes while, at the same time, constituting the beginning of further struggles and endeavours. Their precise nature may, in each particular case, have been different, but they all had a common aim: national liberation and the creation of an independent Greek state with its own distinct national character.

In 1798 the arrest of Rigas, the failure of his movement and the more general failure of a number of his associates to continue and complete his unfinished work, marked the end of one crucial phase of the Greek question. However, this year also marked the beginnings of a new cultural upsurge in the Greek world, which, owing to a more varied, complex and politically mature activity, led, in the year 1821, to the outbreak of the War of Independence. Naturally, the pursuit of a common aim and the final outcome did not depend solely on the subjective conditions which prevailed at a given moment in the Greek world; there were always objective factors to be taken into account, and these factors themselves had a dual significance. Their role was largely positive in the fields of ideology and culture, but gave rise to ambiguity in the question of ways and means, a field which was determined by political expediency and the demands of a given moment.[1]

* Translated by E. J. W. King.

The liberation, which was the result of the uprising of 1821 and of a military conflict lasting nearly ten years, did not merely bring an end to foreign domination, nor indeed was that its sole objective: its main aim was to bring about, after a successful end of the armed struggle, the beginning of a new phase, propitious for the development of a modern Greek consciousness. This may explain the sharp internal contradictions which emerged in the course of the War of Independence among the different sections of the nation. While the Greeks all had one common aim – liberation – they were often in opposition and divided into different ideological camps. Although these contradictions often assumed a violent form, ultimately they expressed the will of a people to emerge from the confusions of the past, to discover its own personality and national character, and to forge its future in accordance with its own criteria.

The extent to which this struggle, almost uninterrupted for 150 years of independent life, has been successful, is not the subject of this study. The question is still open and awaits further discussion. The aim of the present study is to put forward some propositions which will enable us, as far as possible, to evaluate the role and the significance of the Greek intelligentsia in the development of the movement for independence, which in turn determined the course modern Greek society was to take. The chronological framework of this study is limited to the last decades of the eighteenth century and the first two of the nineteenth.

It is indisputable that Rigas' movement was the result and expression of a long, slow process on the intellectual and ideological plane which took place in the Greek world during the eighteenth century. This process reflected changes which occurred in the economic life of the Greeks during the course of the century. A natural result of the development of the Greek economy, in Greece itself and in the Greek diaspora, was the participation, in a more vigorous and determined manner, of new sections in the life of the nation. These new groups of people now claimed a position of equality, if not dominance, in modern Greek society. They put forward new demands, they questioned and often disputed the role of other social groups and the effectiveness of certain institutions. The appearance of these new social forces, which constituted the basis for the creation of the Greek bourgeoisie, acted as an important stimulus in various sectors of Greek life, leading to a substantial diversification of Greek society, and in particular to an astonishing flourishing of culture at the end of the eighteenth and the beginning of the nineteenth centuries.

The great concern of these new social forces with education was demonstrated in a number of ways. Schools were founded, curricula were modernised with the introduction into schools of the natural sciences, new textbooks were written, Greek printing presses were founded, libraries were created, and scholarships were provided for young Greeks to study in Western universities. The nascent bourgeoisie was becoming increasingly aware of its rights and sought to train its leadership. Contacts with the West, which in earlier times had been encouraged by a section of the enlightened higher clergy and by the Phanariots, now took on a new significance. Wider social strata had come of age and so they had the power to satisfy their thirst for learning and their need for a meaningful and effective education. What in previous decades had been the privilege of certain limited groups was now opened up to a broader cross-section of society. Education took on a new, more substantial importance. It began to develop at an altogether faster pace.

As a result of the intervention and influence of these new social forces, developments which had been following a slow, evolutionary course increased their momentum. In the specific case of education this can be illustrated by reference to two educational books published at an interval of sixty years. The first was written by the Patriarch of Jerusalem, Khrysanthos Notaras, an enlightened cleric and scholar. On the title page he declares that his work is intended for 'young noblemen', in other words for the offspring of the Greek 'princely' families who ruled in the Danubian Principalities. In the second case Iosipos Moisiodax, a scholar and teacher, again in the Principalities, who had played a major role in disseminating the ideas of the Enlightenment in the Greek world, announced in the preface of his Geography the forthcoming publication of two books, '... the first of which comprises two complete textbooks in Mathematics, one for the use of the nobility and the other for

use in schools; and the second, two textbooks in Physics, one for
the nobility and the other for use in schools.' A new concept had
now been formulated in the field of education, a concept which
unquestionably reflected and expressed the diversification
which had taken place in people's attitudes and consciousness.[2]

Throughout the course of the century the output of books
printed in Greek for Greeks increased markedly, and this output
shows the wealth and variety of subjects which concerned the
Greek intelligentsia. A comparative analysis, at intervals of
twenty-five years, reveals proportions of the following order.[3]

	1700–25	*1726–50*	*1751–75*	*1776–1800*
Religion	80	163	318	395
Grammar	10	13	46	104
Miscellaneous	17	34	91	250
Total	107	210	455	749

It is quite clear that these figures show that, in comparison
with the sum of publishing activity, the predominance of the
religious book remained constant throughout the century.
However, as the decades pass the proportions change and they
tend to equalise in the last quarter of the century. Also noteworthy is the growth in numbers of books with a miscellaneous
content. During the first 25 years the 'miscellaneous' category
contains only 17 publications while in the last it rises to 250, a
relative increase of 14.7 to 1 compared with 4.9 to 1 for religious
books. This truly impressive increase is not without explanation.
On the contrary, it reflects the wider cultural awareness of a new
public, with a clear interest in new and varied reading matter,
quite apart from the purely functional. Almanacs, books on
morality, books on health, commercial guides, methods for
teaching foreign languages, literature, both scholarly and popular, all show a substantial broadening in the interests of the
people as a whole. This trend had a direct relation to the social
changes we have already noted.

In connection with this publishing activity special mention
must be made of translations. As the century passed, many
Greeks were able to travel, either to the urban and trading
centres of the Ottoman Empire, or to those of the West, to
regions where flourishing Greek trading communities had been

established. Consequently, these social groups had more opportunities to become familiar with Western culture, to study, use and translate foreign books. Furthermore, translations were regarded by many enlightened Greeks as the quickest and most suitable way to equip the schools with textbooks of immediate use, and more generally to present to the Greek public works which Greek scholars themselves were not yet capable of producing. In previous years there had been sporadic attempts at translations, and these had been by no means negligible; they included Locke's *Essay on Human Understanding*, Voltaire's *Memnon* (both translated by Evgenios Voulgaris) and Rollin's *Histoire Ancienne*, published by Alexandros Kangkellarios, to name but a few. Now, however, the work of translation took on new dimensions and almost constituted a planned programme inspired largely by Iosipos Moisiodax and particularly by Dimitrakis Katartzis.[4]

It is to Katartzis that we are also indebted for the first serious attempts at a theoretical analysis of the language question. A supporter of the 'natural' language, he used it in his writings and teaching – at least at one stage of his career – in the belief that only through the popular tongue would it be possible for learning to reach the broader strata of society. The Greek intelligentsia were thus given an impulse in their efforts towards the effective dissemination of knowledge. Thanks to the introduction of a new element – the demotic tongue – education was to become the possession of all men. In this respect it is obvious that the Greek intellectuals were greatly influenced by the French *Encyclopédistes*, and in particular by their ideas concerning a wider participation in education and culture.

Around Katartzis a group of outstanding young scholars, among them Rigas, attempted – with partial success – to put into operation a programme to renew Greek cultural life. They aimed to restructure the teaching in schools, and also to cater for the more general intellectual interests of the public.[5] Many of their literary and scholarly achievements owe their source and inspiration to the influence of Katartzis' personality, and to his advice and teaching. However, these young Greeks – most of whom belonged to the rising merchant class – were destined, because of their youth and their social origin, to give a new import to the aspirations of the Greeks. The ideological content of Katartzis' teaching could not completely satisfy them. It should also be remembered that in the last decade of the eighteenth century the French Revolution not only acted as an inspiration to the peoples of Europe, and in particular to the subject peoples, but it also provided the political and ideological content for movements which, until then, had been unable to express in concrete terms even their immediate aims, or to organise their activities coherently. For the Greeks, the presence of French republican forces in the Ionian Islands in the years 1797–8, quite apart from the moral force it exercised, constituted a very real stimulus to concrete political activity aimed at national liberation. And so towards the end of the century, partly as a result of the activities of the intellectuals, a section of Greek society was ideologically prepared and ready alongside, or even led by, these intellectuals to take up the struggle to overthrow national oppression.

The principal representative of this movement was Rigas. His association with Katartzis had greatly strengthened his respect for education and opened for him new intellectual horizons; his contact with Greeks of similar aspirations in the Danubian Principalities and in Vienna had sharpened his political awareness. In the last decades of his life, he was able successfully to combine his intellectual interests with political activity.[6] He was thus politically and intellectually mature at the time of the French Revolution. He was fully prepared to receive its new ideology and it was this which formed the basis of his movement. Encouraged by the revolutionary fervour of the time, he stepped up his own conspiratorial activity and put into practice his revolutionary plans. While the main aim of his programme was an end to tyranny and the expulsion of the Ottomans from the Balkans, it was not devoid of ideological and social content, as his political writings of the period show. Rigas' failure and his tragic death perhaps mark the end, for a time at least, of political activity among the Greeks.[7] However, the ideological conflict between the representatives of the old institutions and the followers of new ideological movements was intensified in this period with the appearance of a series of 'polemical pamphlets', of unimaginable violence, and it continued to dominate the Greek world during the following decades. In the years immediately preceding the War of

Independence this conflict shifted to other spheres, for example to the language question, which on the surface could be regarded as simply a dispute over methods of education. But disputes of this kind were, in fact, essentially symptoms of deep ideological and social cleavages. It was these contradictions which dominated the War of Independence, when they manifested themselves in the form of the 'Civil War' and of the 'Dissension'.

The natural consequence of Rigas' failure was a respite in the political activities of the Greeks at the beginning of the nineteenth century. This respite was essential for the reorganisation of the revolutionary forces, and was, in any case, temporary. Besides, in the early years of the century there were several movements of a revolutionary nature, such as the rising of the Souliots and the movement of Efthymios Vlakhavas. Although they did not take on the form of a general uprising, they were important revolutionary gestures which conserved in full vigour the fighting spirit of the people and kept alive hopes for national liberation. Furthermore, in the same period various political initiatives were taken by individuals and groups of people, with the aim of ensuring the participation of European powers in support of Greek liberation. However naive we may consider these attempts, they do show the general climate of anticipation which was diffused throughout the Greek world.[8] In themselves they were not destined to lead to anything decisive, but viewed as a part of the Greek question as a whole, alongside other similar developments, they take on a new weight and significance. It was only in the following decade, as a result of the groundwork undertaken by various different forces, that a suitable organisational form was developed. Societies, some secret, were formed which undertook concrete activities on an intensified scale, now with the immediate aim of throwing off foreign domination.

The establishment in 1800 of the Free Ionian Republic acted as another strong stimulus for the Greeks, who now, for the first time, saw some correspondence between their hopes and political reality. What had for a long time been the object of secret aspirations now took on some kind of concrete form. In particular the existence of the semi-autonomous Ionian state meant that the possibilities existed to create, develop and put into practice the political and social machinery necessary if the aims of the Greeks were to be fulfilled.

I have already referred to the question of the external factors which affected Greek affairs during this period, whether by slowing down and hindering developments, or by accelerating them and encouraging their realisation. To be more precise, we should speak of the Western presence and the Western influence which operated at various levels in the Greek society.

There is no doubt that Western thought and Western culture were decisive factors in the development of Greek consciousness during this period. As a result of these Western influences the Greeks were enabled to emerge from the confusions of the past and to define their ideological and intellectual orientation, and so to formulate and give concrete expression to their national aspirations. The development of a Greek national consciousness, and the formation of new attitudes were very much indebted to the intensive intellectual, ideological and political contacts established in the last decades of the eighteenth century with the Western world. The force of this contact was felt in two directions. On the one hand there was a movement of Greeks from Greece who gained experience of the Western world actually in Europe, while on the other there was a wave – in this case of travellers and visitors of various kinds – who came to Greece – and facilitated such contacts within Greece itself. In this period travel took on new dimensions. The earlier Philhellenism of foreign classical scholars and antiquarians had for the most part been confined to an interest in ancient Greece. To it was now added a Philhellenism of a different kind in which modern Greece began to have a significant place. The results of this new attitude can be seen in books such as those of Felix de Beaujour and Pouqueville – consular officials played a substantial part in creating this new climate with their interest in the social, economic and intellectual achievements of modern Greece – or of Byron and Leake. These works had the effect of attracting the interest of a wider European public, which until then had not had the opportunity to learn of the accomplishments of the contemporary inhabitants of the classical world. In addition they allowed the Greeks themselves to make interesting comparisons, and to weigh and evaluate what foreign writers had to say, whether they wrote from a sympathetic point of view, or were largely antagonistic towards the modern Greeks.

The fact that young Greeks were, in ever increasing numbers, going to the West for the purpose of study or trade, meant that they were in a position to become involved in the intellectual, ideological and political currents of the West, to experience new ways of life and new conditions and methods of work. The natural result of this was that they should compare and correlate and be inspired to similar activities in Greece. Many of the vague aspirations and spontaneous movements of the Greeks were given concrete form by the French Revolution. The effects of the revolutionary events in France, combined with the revolutionary enthusiasm vibrating throughout the West, are seen in the first serious Greek news publication – the *Ephimeris*. From December 1790 until, probably, January 1798 this newspaper fed the Greek public, both inside and outside Greece, with abundant material concerning revolutionary developments in France. It was published by the brothers Markidis-Poulios, who, as is apparent from the archives, were closely connected with French politics at that time and who were also friends and collaborators of Rigas. Their political stand was determined by their belief in the blessings of liberty and by their decision to use their paper to develop the conditions necessary to bring about a lasting solution to the national question in Greece.

The appearance of the *Ephimeris* marks the beginning of the Greek press, since previous similar attempts had led to nothing. In the second decade of the nineteenth century there was an extraordinary growth in this field with the publication of a number of literary journals and newspapers, and this is a sufficient indication of the vigorous participation of the Greek intelligentsia in the life of the nation on the eve of the War of Independence. The most important of the literary periodicals to be published were *Logios Ermis*, 1811–21, *Melissa*, 1819–21, and *Kalliope*, 1819–21. These and newspapers such as the *Ellinikos Tilegraphos*, 1812–36, enable us to follow – in all its intensity – the development of Greek intellectual and social life, and to evaluate the part played by groups and individuals in the process of developing a modern awareness in the Greek

world. In addition, by describing the attitudes and behaviour in
these pre-revolutionary years, they provide us with a key to
understanding the source of phenomena which in the course of
the war gave rise to disharmony, controversies and serious
conflicts.

When considering the vigorous intellectual activity which
characterised the first two decades of the nineteenth century,
we must examine the significance of the economic conditions
then prevailing in the Greek world. Greek trading houses,
scattered as they were around the Ottoman Empire and the
countries of Europe, had formed links with foreign traders; this
fact and the existence of European consuls and merchants in the
urban centres of the Greek world led to fruitful contacts, which
although initially economic, soon began to influence social and
intellectual life and to stimulate social change. Similar developments were to be seen in culture and ideology. In 1802, Athanasios Parios, a representative of the most bigoted ecclesiastical
conservatism, produced a pamphlet entitled *Antiphonisis* (*Reply*).
It was published under a pseudonym, and in it he stigmatised
those who '. . . run at all speed to Europe, for lessons in
philosophy', and attempted to dissuade 'Christians' from sending '. . . their sons to Europe on business . . .'[9] It is clear from
this and other similar texts of the time that the representatives
of conservatism were disturbed by the economic progress of the
Greek world and by the effect that it might have in developing
a progressive consciousness. Already at that time demands were
being formulated which openly questioned the validity of
traditional institutions.

This economic well-being was the result of the riches amassed
by Greek merchants and shipowners, in particular after the
signing of the treaty of Küçük Kaynarca (1774), and the
advantages which this gave them. It was precisely this which
gave the new social strata the power to make their presence felt
and the desire to undertake initiatives in social and intellectual
fields. Finance was provided by Greek merchant houses to
subsidise new schools, to give scholarships for study in Western
universities and to pay for the publication of books. These
developments opened new perspectives in education, while at
the same time giving significant encouragement to the aspirations of the Greek intelligentsia and enabling them to undertake

publishing programmes of wide scope, such as Korais' *Elliniki Vivliothiki*, which was financed in its initial years by the trading house of the Zosimas brothers.

It is indisputable that these contacts between the Greek and the Western worlds, which were felt particularly in the intellectual sphere, and to an ever increasing degree in the early nineteenth century, accelerated the process which began with the modernisation of Greek education and led finally to the road of regeneration and liberation. Furthermore, for a section at least of the Greek intelligentsia, who saw in education one of the most effective means to ensure liberation and independence, educational reform and more generally the enrichment of cultural life was in itself a political act.

The fact that these developments took place to a large degree outside Greece, in the Danubian Principalities, or in the Greek communities abroad, does not detract from their significance. In the first place there was an intellectual and political movement of similar intensity inside Greece – in Thessaly, Ioannina, Constantinople, Smyrna, Kydonies (Ayvalık) and the islands. Moreover, the movement that developed in the diaspora was always orientated towards Greece itself. Any doubts on this score are soon removed by a reading of the ten volumes of *Logios Ermis*, which cover the vital decade 1811–21; from this it is clear that all the efforts of the Greek intelligentsia, including those who were active outside Greece, were directed towards developing cultural and national life inside Greece.[10] It also shows that the Greeks, obliged through historical and economic necessity to live outside their own land, were helped by their contact with other ways of life to formulate their national demands, based on their own historical tradition and enriched by elements taken from Western civilisation. Consequently, I do not believe that the Greek intelligentsia had no answer to the question 'To what goal would education carry them'.[11] Indeed the main question facing them was whether and to what degree their demands could be met and their aims fulfilled, given that this did not depend exclusively on their own wishes and endeavours, but rather on political expediency and the demands of a given moment. Of this the Greeks had bitter experience; the near future was to confirm that this was a factor far from favourable to Greek aspirations.

The question of the policies adopted at various times by the European countries with regard to Greek affairs, in particular from the end of the eighteenth century onwards, is very complex and it is not my intention to discuss it here. As a general observation, however, I do not think it would be far from the truth to say that the policy of the Powers was negative, often antagonistic, and never generous towards a situation which implied new responsibilities and was controlled by forces which were working towards solutions that European politicians preferred to ignore. On this point, C. M. Woodhouse describes, in epigrammatic form, the general attitude that prevailed towards Greek affairs, when he writes: 'The last thing anybody contemplated was an independent nation-state.'[12]

Nevertheless, particularly during the years after Küçük Kaynarca (1774), the Greeks persisted in their long struggle, in the fields of culture and politics, and they finally attained their goal, after the War of Independence that began in 1821, with the creation of a free Greek state. This did not help to alter the negative attitudes of the European powers towards the Greek question. Until the very last moment, and even later, the European powers were reluctant to accept an autonomous Greece, a fact which was instrumental in creating an abortive state, confined to a very small part of Greek soil. From its very foundation this state was confronted with a mass of complex and formidable problems.

The *Elliniki Nomarkhia* is one of the most remarkable works of the Greek revival, because of the way in which the anonymous author analyses the problems confronting the nation, and also because of his bold proposals for their solution:

> Come, brothers, the time of deliverance is upon us. Do not weep for a little blood shed for your freedom and your happiness . . . Take up the sword of righteousness and let us storm against the cowardly Ottomans, and grind our chains to dust . . .

As for his advanced social views, I cite the following extract:

> Let us now examine the reasons why it will be easy to bring about the regeneration of the Greeks. The first is the progress

of our nation in learning. O what a difference can be seen
between the Greece of ten years ago and the Greeks of today!
A great difference, my brothers, a very great difference, and
every day things get better. Now the Muses have begun to
return and to rise up again on the gold-tinted mountains of
Greece. Apollo has appeared in his ancient palace; today the
city does not exist which does not have two or three schools
. . . The schools are no longer deserted as before but each one
contains fifty or a hundred pupils, and when they have read
sweet Xenophon, wise Plutarch and the other historians and
philosophers of our ancestors, then they see the mire of
tyranny and weep for the misfortunes of our homeland. They
no longer mumble, as they used to do, the name of Freedom
with fear, in case the elders or the prelates hear and denounce
them as atheists; instead they pronounce it with the boldness
that slaves cannot possess. They never cease from admonish-
ing their ignorant friends and by their example they induce
everyone to think for once as they ought to, a thing which
they have never done before. In one word, in order for everything to be as they would wish, the only thing they lack is
Freedom.[13]

The *Elliniki Nomarkhia* is a bold, unrelenting, courageous
book, it is not, however, the work of an optimist and this gives
its author's analyses greater value and seriousness. More
specifically, we should pay close attention to the opinions of the
writer on the subject with which we are now concerned, and
particularly his views concerning the progress made in education – the 'flight of ignorance', to use his own expression – and
the beneficial influence exercised by culture in the formulation
of national consciousness, an influence which was felt increasingly in the years when the *Nomarkhia* was being written. 'They
no longer mumble the name of Freedom with fear . . . instead
they pronounce it with the boldness that slaves cannot possess.'
It is clear from this that, for the author of the *Nomarkhia*, the
principal function of education was not simply the pursuit of
knowledge, but the creation of the conditions which would
allow the individual to develop a personal ethic. For the Greeks
it was to be an effective means leading ultimately to the gaining
of freedom.

The opinions of the author of the *Nomarkhia* are given support by other contemporary evidence. One of the most persuasive is the one offered by Korais: 'La fermentation actuelle des esprits en Grèce', as formulated in the *Mémoire sur l'état actuel de la civilisation dans la Grèce*, which also commands respect because of the authority of its writer's personality. Written three years before the *Nomarkhia* (i.e. 1803) and intended for delivery in Paris at a meeting of the *Société des Observateurs de l'Homme*, that is for a wider, European public, it constitutes a survey and at the same time a balance sheet of the latest Greek achievements. In it Korais describes the progress which had been made in the economic sphere, '... plusieurs maisons [of commerce] grecques se virent en possession de richesses extraordinaires...'; in shipping, 'les insulaires... maîtres d'un grand nombre d'excellents voiliers, fabriqués par leurs propres mains d'une manière aussi solide qu'élégante...'; in social life, 'le luxe commence à s'y introduire; et tant qu'il sera alimenté par le commerce sans l'épuiser, il augmentera de plus en plus leur civilisation et leurs lumières. On y voit déjà des maisons bâties avec toutes les commodités possibles...' He underlines the continuing struggle against the Ottomans, singling out the Souliots, '... ils défendent depuis plusieurs années leur liberté...' He stresses above all the great progress which had been made in the field of education, underlying in particular the importance of the 'révolution morale' which was taking place in Greece at that time.[14]

The term 'révolution morale' is not merely accidental. Since it is used more than once in the *Mémoire*, by such a sensitive and perceptive observer of Greek affairs as Korais, it must surely be considered – when taken together with the 'fermentation actuelle des esprits en Grèce' – as an epigrammatic, but authoritative, expression of the real changes which had taken place in the dominant consciousness of the Greek world. Quite apart from the wealth of useful information on the state of the Greek world to be found in this work, its prime importance lies in the fact that it gives an impression of the moral climate which governed the lives, work and aspirations of the Greeks at the turn of the eighteenth century. It is clear that the *Mémoire* was not intended to be an informative, factual account. Written from a deeply moral standpoint, with dramatic force and 'dialectical expertise', as Korais's biographer observes,[15] it performed a valid political act, aiming at clear and well-defined objectives: the refutation of all the unjust statements which had been made against the Greeks in the past, the presentation of irrefutable evidence as to their present-day achievements, and the justification of their position in their natural world, Europe.

In the same period Korais began work on the *Elliniki Vivliothiki*, a publishing programme initiated in 1805 and lasting many years, which aimed to familiarise the Greek public with the ancient writers. In the *Prolegomena* with which he introduced the various texts, he examined contemporary Greek problems, giving special emphasis to educational matters. He set out his own attitude towards them, and proposed ways and means of overcoming the problems. He worked ceaselessly in this endeavour, along with his other intellectual pursuits, for the fifteen years preceding the outbreak of the War. Even during the war he continued, with special classical texts chosen to serve the needs of a time of crisis, to strengthen the morale of a nation at war, or to help in the political education of the Greeks. Now, however, quite apart from this work, he also published texts which were purely political in nature, in which, despite his advanced age, he re-discovered the fighting passion of earlier times, when, inspired by the French revolution, he had written and published polemical pamphlets, some advocating new ideas, others seeking to counter conservative attitudes but all with the common aim of preparing individuals to take a conscious part in the struggle to gain their freedom.

Korais has often been criticised for his opinion that the revolution of 1821 broke out somewhat prematurely. Similar observations were also expressed by other responsible Greeks, among them the metropolitan Ignatios of Oungrovlakhia and Alexandros Mavrokordatos. Their reasons were the same: they considered that if such a harsh and unequal struggle was to be undertaken successfully, if, in other words, the Greeks were to be ensured not only freedom, but, equally important, independence and good government, then a period of moral and material preparation was indispensable. They did not believe that this process of preparation had yet been fully carried out. Right or wrong, this point of view is understandable although I do not intend to discuss it further here. What I would like to underline, however, is that regardless of the various theoretical doubts which they expressed about the timing of the Revolution, each of those three men, far from hindering the war, on the contrary furthered its development in whatever way and with whatever means possible. More specifically, since it is Korais who concerns us here, I would say that his position on the Greek question as it stood in 1821 – a position which was adopted by a large section of the Greek intelligentsia – is expressed precisely in the following excerpt from a letter of his to his friend Neophytos Vamvas. This is perhaps the first letter which he wrote after hearing of the outbreak of the revolutionary movement in Greece.

> It is no longer the time for us to consider whether the revolution has broken out at the right time, or whether its leaders have done the right thing; the stupidity of the authorities . . . in brazenly declaring the total destruction of our race has given national form to the revolution. We are faced with the necessity either of victory, or of death. [16]

It is indisputable that in the twenty years preceding the War of Independence the Greek intelligentsia threw all its weight and concentrated a large part of its energies towards carrying out its immediate aims of education and regeneration; according to all the evidence these aims constituted the indispensable basis for the fulfilment of the long-term objectives of the Greek people: liberation and independence.

The publishing output of the years 1800–20 is very helpful on this point, since it shows the numerical proportions of books published, and indicates the intellectual preoccupations of the Greeks. The index of Greek publications for the preceding 25 years (1776–1800) gives a total of 749 publications, while the total for the 20 years 1800–20 easily surpasses 1300. There was then, in quantitative terms, a 100 per cent increase in publishing activity within this period. As for the subjects which interested the publishers, they are characterised by a new breadth and variety, and increasingly they tend to encompass many different areas of learning. To give one example of the vigour of this publishing activity, I return to the question of the literary periodicals and newspapers which were produced in the years before the war, by Greek publishers for a Greek public. After the demise of the Markidis-Poulios' *Ephimeris*, the movement rediscovered its momentum in the years after 1811 when Greek journalism made outstanding progress. Thus, in 1819 there were seven literary periodicals being published, and one news journal published three times a week – the *Ellinikos Tilegraphos* – in comparison with the one that was being published in 1811. When, immediately after the outbreak of war in 1821, attempts were made to create a press inside Greece, their success was directly due to the fact that the ground had been prepared by these earlier developments.[17]

Also characteristic of this period was a noticeable growth of interest in Greek antiquity. This was not characterised solely and exclusively by the study and publication of the classical texts. Ancient monuments became the object of particular concern: practical means for their safety and preservation were devised and published in the statutes of the Athenian *Philomousos Etairia*,[18] together with other political aims possibly concealed in its programme. This attitude on the part, at least of a section, of the Greek public shows an increasing awareness of the responsibility demanded by their ancestral heritage; it also demonstrates changing attitudes towards a subject of such importance, on which the Greeks have often been criticised for their ignorance and indifference. Their stand on this question showed that now they were not only proud of their ancestral heritage, but above all they were responsible heirs. Later, even during the Revolution, the Greeks took more drastic measures to prevent the destruction and transportation of antiquities. A typical case is that of Fauvel, the French consul at Athens. He was for many years the main dealer involved in the sale of Greek antiquities to foreigners. To his intense annoyance in 1832 he was refused permission to export a whole cargo of antiquities.[19] Times had changed and, if nothing else, at least the Greeks attempted to throw off the unscrupulous morals which they had inherited from centuries of subjection.

There are other developments worth mentioning in this period. The modern Greek theatre was created, with works written, for the most part, by Greek writers, and with subjects – often taken from ancient Greek history – intended to boost morale. In the schools, the Lancasterian method was introduced a few years before 1821. Attempts were made to employ young teachers who had studied at Western universities, and to equip the schools with worthwhile libraries. Printing presses were set up inside Greece – at Chios, Constantinople and Kydonies (Ayvalık). All of this shows that the Greek intelligentsia, assisted by the enlightened section of the merchants and shipowners, had in this period embarked on a well-thought out, deliberate struggle, on the intellectual and social plane, and were preparing the final stage before their freedom could be won.

I will do no more here than mention the controversial language question which dominated Greek intellectual life, particularly between 1815 and 1820 when the dispute increased in intensity. The fact that the question of language was paramount in Greece throughout the nineteenth century, and that it has still not been satisfactorily resolved, shows that the Greek intellectuals of the pre-revolutionary years made a correct analysis of its importance, in terms of intellectual and social developments. Persistently and resolutely they attempted to work towards a solution.

The War of Independence came to cut short all the endeavours and initiatives of the Greek intelligentsia. Battle now had to be joined on another level. It is no exaggeration to say that the great majority of Greek intellectuals continued to struggle throughout the War, in the armed forces, in the National Congresses, or through the press and the printed word. They struggled to ensure that what they had fought for so persistently in the pre-revolutionary years should not languish and die. In the face of the unimaginable difficulties of the War, and a mass of contradictions which often ended in disastrous conflicts, modern Greece attempted to win not only its freedom, but its national character. In this toil of Sisyphus, which has left its mark to this day on the Greek nation, the intellectuals did not remain neutral or indifferent – quite the contrary.

NOTES TO CHAPTER 3

1. For the influence of Western culture on the Greek world see the essays of K. Th. Dimaras, *La Grèce au Temps des Lumières* (Geneva, 1969).
2. Khrysanthos Notaras, *Eisagogi eis ta Geographika* (Paris, 1716), 2nd ed. (Venice, 1718); Iosipos Moisiodax, *Theoria tis Geographias* (Vienna, 1781).
3. I am indebted for the table to K.Th. Dimaras' study, 'L'apport de

l'Aufklärung au développement de la conscience néohellénique', published in *La Grèce au Temps des Lumières, op. cit.*, pp. 103–32, particularly pp. 104–5. It is likely that the calculations and comparisons may have to be somewhat modified when P. Iliou has completed his work on the Greek book and its development, particularly during the eighteenth century. See his preliminary findings in 'Pour une étude quantitative du public des lecteurs grecs à l'époque des Lumières et de la Révolution (1749–1832)', *Association Internationale d'Études du Sud-Est Européen* (Sofia,1969).

4. On translations and their importance, Korais wrote at length in his *Mémoire sur l'état actuel de la civilisation dans la Grèce* (Paris, 1803), pp. 456–8. The 'Mémoire' is published in the volume *Lettres inédites de Coray à Chardon de la Rochette (1791–1796)* (Paris, 1877) pp. 451–90. It has been translated by E. Kedourie in *Nationalism in Asia and Africa* (London, 1971) pp. 153–88.

5. Particularly relevant are the writings of Daniil Philippidis and Grigorios Konstantas; see especially their *Neoteriki Geographia* (Vienna, 1791), a work which they wrote jointly under the joint name of 'Dimitrieis' (reprinted in Athens, ed. A. Koumarianou, 1970). See also the translations by Philippidis of books intended for use in schools, such as Condillac's *La Logique*, Lalande's *L'Astronomie*, etc.

6. During this period Rigas produced books for use in schools such as the *Apanthisma Physikis* (Vienna, 1970), translated and adapted the short stories of Réstif de la Bretonne, under the title *Skholeion ton delikaton eraston* (Vienna, 1790, reprinted in Athens, ed. P. E. Pistas, 1971), wrote heroic poetry, translated Abbé Barthélemy's *Le Voyage du Jeune Anacharsis en Grèce* (1797), published maps of Greece and compiled political texts (1796–7). See Chapter 1.

7. Recent studies have shown that a group of Greeks, friends and supporters of Rigas, attempted to continue his work for the liberation of Greece in the period immediately after Rigas' death. See A. Koumarianou, 'Nees prospathies tou Konstantinou Stamati gia tin apeleftherosi tis Ellados', *Praktika tou Tritou Panioniou Synedriou*, 1 (Athens, 1967) 154–74. In the same volume see also the articles by Leandros Vranousis, 'Ena perizitito kerkyraiko kheirographo: o kodikas tis allilographias tou Perraivou', 47–57 and Vasilis P. Panagiotopoulos 'Protaseis tou P. Markidis-Poulios gia tin engkatastasi ellinikou typographeiou stin Ionio Politeia', 292–7. The material in the archives of the Quai d'Orsay, which I have had the opportunity to study, is very revealing on the endeavours of the Greeks and, particularly, on official French policy towards Greek affairs at the turn of the eighteenth century.

8. Particularly relevant is a text which was written in Thessaly in 1809, and which was sent to France to be given to Napoleon. The document is mentioned in the correspondence between the French hellenist Barbié du Bocage and Anthimos Gazis, the sender of the letter. See *Daniil Philippidis, Barbié du Bocage, Anthimos Gazis, Allilographia 1794–1819*, edited with notes by A. Koumarianou, in the series *Nea Ellinika Keimena* (Athens, 1966) letter 82, p. 154. Further studies in the archives enabled me to trace the letter – entitled 'Supplication' (Deisis) – among the papers of Konstantinos Nikolopoulos, who was for years the librarian of the Institut de France,

where he also kept a personal archive. It is written in ancient Greek by an anonymous teacher from Ambelakia in Thessaly, and it consists of an invocation to the Emperor of France to support the national aims of the Greeks.

9. Nathanail Neokaisareos, *Antiphonisis pros ton paralogon zilon ton apo tis Evropis erkhomenon philosophon . . .* (Trieste, 1802) p. 59, which contains the 'Advice, dissuading those who send their sons to Europe, for the sake of business'.

10. In his recent work *Oi Logioi kai o Agonas* (Athens, 1971), Alkis Angelou shows the full extent to which the Greek intelligentsia participated in the War of Independence. This participation was simply the continuation of earlier activity by the progressive section of Greek society, particularly during the twenty years preceding the War.

11. C. M. Woodhouse, *The Story of Modern Greece* (London, 1968) p. 127.

12. *Ibid.*, p. 124. For European policy see also ch. IV, pp. 99–124. See also N. Svoronos, *Histoire de la Grèce moderne* (Paris, 1964) pp. 25–40, the chapter entitled 'L'Éveil National', where he discusses the economic, social, political and educational activity of the Greeks and, briefly, the attitude of the Powers.

13. *Elliniki Nomarkhia itoi Logos peri Eleftherias . . . syntetheis te kai typois ekdotheis idiois analomasi pros opheleian ton Ellinon, para Anonymou tou Ellinos* (Italy, 1806). Reprinted by N. B. Tomadakis (Athens, 1948) pp. 175–8.

14. See Korais, *Mémoire, op. cit.*, pp. 458, 459, 460, 465, 469, 478.

15. D. Thereianos, *Adamantios Korais* (Trieste, 1889) I, p. 344.

16. A. Korais, *Epistolai*, ed. N. Damalas (Athens, 1885) III, pp. 663–6.

17. On this point I should like to stress the fact that although Greek historiography has not produced the kind of general works of synthesis whose authority would prevent certain hasty and inopportune – not to say incorrect – judgments on the development of modern Greek society, nevertheless there are recent works which facilitate more accurate interpretations. K.Th. Dimaras's *Istoria tis neas ellinikis logotekhnias*, because of its scope, its exhaustive documentation and its extensive bibliography, is the essential basis of any study of modern Greek culture. A greater knowledge of the Greek background is indispensable, even when dealing with relatively minor topics, if we are to avoid statements like the following: 'But the newspapers throughout their life were regarded by the majority of the Greeks as the playthings of the Philhellenes and they never put down roots or lost their connection with foreigners. Once the subsidies ran out they all ceased publication.' This is not only a misinterpretation, it is also inaccurate. See William St. Clair, *That Greece Might Still Be Free; The Philhellenes in the War of Independence* (London, 1972) p. 187. On the specific subject of the modern Greek press, see A. Koumarianou, *O Typos ston Agona, 1821–1827*, 3 vols. (Athens, 1971).

18. *Logios Ermis* (1814) no. 6, 98–100 and 100–3, the 'Catalogue of subscribers to the Athenian Philomousos Etaireia', among which are many English names.

19. A. Koumarianou, 'To taxidi tou Choiseul-Gouffier stin Ellada', in *Periigiseis ston elliniko khoro* (Athens, 1968) p. 48.

4 The *Philiki Etairia*: A Premature National Coalition

GEORGE D. FRANGOS

The *Philiki Etairia*, or Friendly Society, was a secret organisation established in 1814 by three impoverished Greek immigrants in Odessa, the newly-founded Russian city on the north shore of the Black Sea. By 1821, on the eve of the Greek revolt, the *Etairia* had managed to attract representatives from nearly every major social and regional group of the Greek world. According to a collated list of the organisation's membership,[1] over half or 53.7 per cent (N=479) described themselves as merchants.[2] The second largest occupational category, the 'professionals' (those whose occupation required more than an average education: teachers, physicians, students, non-merchant secretaries, etc.), accounted for 13.1 per cent (N=117) of the society's membership. The third largest group, which constituted 11.7 per cent (N=111) of the known membership, were provincial notables, mostly from the Peloponnese. Clergymen of all ranks joined the *Etairia*, accounting for 9.5 per cent (N=85) of its members. Military men or mercenaries, that is to say former *armatoloi-klephts* who had been or still were in the service of foreign armies were the fifth largest occupational group or 8.7 per cent (N=78) of the society's recruits. The one group that was poorly represented in the society was the peasants, by far the largest social and occupational group in the Greek-speaking areas of the Ottoman Empire; they accounted for 0.6 per cent (N=6) of the *Etairia*'s known membership.

CATEGORIES OF OCCUPATION

Occupation		Number	Per Cent
Merchant		479	53.7
merchant	445		
merchant secretary or clerk	10		
ship owner or captain	24		
Professional		117	13.1
lawyer	13		
physician	26		
teacher	51		
student	6		
non-military foreign government service	11		
non-merchant secretary	10		
Local Notables (*Proestoi*)		111	11.7
local notables	111		
Clergy		85	9.5
metropolitan	9		
bishop	8		
archimandrite	10		
archdeacon	9		
monk	12		
abbot	7		
priest	30		
Military		78	8.7
military (not specified)	54		
in Russian service	15		
in British service	8		
Peasant		6	0.6
peasant	6		
Artisan		7	0.7
artisan	7		
Sailor		28	3.1
sailor	28		

Despite this crucial omission, the wide social and occupational distribution in the organisation's membership has prompted some writers to claim that the *Etairia* was a genuine 'national' coalition in which class and regional interests were submerged for the sake of the Greek fatherland.[3]

A close examination of the *Etairia*'s membership reveals that the members of the major social groups that joined the society were not representative of their group as a whole. Social classes, even when dominant, are rarely homogeneous. Social analyses of the Greek world before the revolt of 1821, undertaken by Marxist historians, have also failed to recognise fine but significant distinctions that existed within larger social categories. The observation that the society was dominated by merchants is not sufficient evidence to claim that the *Philiki Etairia* represented the conscious vanguard of a progressive bourgeoisie.[4]

It was no accident that the society was established in Russia. Like the other nationalist movements of the Balkans, the so-called Greek awakening occurred outside the native fatherland in the cities of western and central Europe: Adamantios Korais did his work in Paris; Rigas Velestinlis, or 'Pheraios', worked in Vienna, the city that saw the publication of the first Greek language newspaper.[5] However, this is not to say that all the Greek-speaking Orthodox Christians in the Ottoman Empire were unaware that they constituted a distinct ethnic group. Thanks in part to the special features of Ottoman rule (the *millet* system, local autonomy, weakening central authority), at the start of the nineteenth century many Greeks of the Ottoman Empire were not without their own institutions, a situation which permitted in some areas, like the Peloponnese, a virtually independent or at least autonomous cultural, social and even political life. The Greek élites had viewed themselves for some time as a superior class of Christians forming a counterpart to the Osmanlı. The hierarchy of the Orthodox Church, the Phanariots and the provincial notables were leaders as well as representatives of a distinct ethnic community, defined by language and culture as well as religious tradition. They were, of course, aware of their special position, but in most cases they were even more conscious of their roles as Ottoman administrators. The Patriarch, as leader of the Orthodox *millet* was a defender of his faith; but in the years before the Greek revolt he functioned also as a defender of the Empire.[6] It would be a mistake to assume that this ethnic identity was felt by all Greeks or that it was synonymous with what is understood as modern national consciousness. An awareness of ethnic distinction does not constitute in itself – nor is it sufficient to produce – that vision of a human community in which individuals place loyalty to their nation as a whole above the traditional allegiances of family, region and caste. Modern nationalism is associated with the appearance of the nation-state which emerged out of western European traditional and feudal society during and after the French Revolution of 1789. It was intimately linked with that transformation of culture and society that social scientists have identified as the process of 'modernisation' – that is to say, the passing of a traditional world into modernity.[7] Most Greeks lived in the rural and primitive regions of the Ottoman Empire. Though their communities were organised along ethnic and religious lines, their social structure was traditional and pre-modern. An individual's first allegiance was to his family. He referred to his village, or at most his region, as his *patrida* or fatherland.

Theodoros Kolokotronis, the *armatolos* who joined the *Philiki Etairia* in 1818 and later became a leader in the Greek revolt, described the men of his village before 1821:

> The society of men was small. It was not until our revolution that all the Hellenes became acquainted. There were men who knew no village one hour away from their own. They thought of Zante as we now think of the furthest place in the world. America appears to us as Zante appeared to them; they referred to it as *Frangia*.[8]

Neither was the Byzantine Hellenism perpetuated by the church and the Phanariots equivalent to a genuine national ideology. It looked foward to the re-establishment of a multi-national but medieval empire united, not by a principle of national union, but by the dominance of a Greek aristocracy. It was in the communities of the Greek diaspora, scattered throughout Europe and distant from the native Greek-speaking areas of the Ottoman Empire, that a genuine and modern nationalism developed among the Greeks. It was there that they came into direct contact with the Enlightenment and the French Revolu-

tion. But neither the exposure to the modern institutions of the
West nor the radical ideas of the Revolution alone could
produce nor solely account for the development of a modern
national consciousness. The central feature of the expatriate
Greek communities was their establishment and governance by
merchants – a new breed of men whose social as well as economic needs were modern. These needs seemed to be answered
by the political and ideological forms that characterised the
European revolutionary tradition that found its clearest expression in the upheavals after 1789. If Greek merchants and
intellectuals responded positively to the ideas of the French
Revolution they did so for the same reasons their western
counterparts did.

As early as 1514 Greek merchants had established a community in Ancona. But it was not until the eighteenth century
that a substantial Greek-speaking merchant class emerged
both in and out of the Ottoman Empire. It grew in response to
several favorable circumstances that stimulated commerce and
maritime activity in the Balkans and the eastern Mediterranean,
especially the conditions established by the treaties of Karlowitz
(1699), Küçük Kaynarca (1774), and Jassy (1792).

Thousands of Greeks left the Empire to establish trading
houses in the emporia of Europe. These became the nuclei of
Greek communities (*koinotites*), created to complement not only
the economic requirements of their members but to fulfil their
social and cultural needs as well. When the Greeks of Ancona
were granted special trading privileges, they were also permitted to establish their own Greek Orthodox church. The
koinotita of Trieste was called a 'legally constituted national-
civil and domiciliar-administrative economic brotherhood'.[9]

An example of the special nature of these communities can be
seen in the organisation and activity of the Greek merchant
community of Sibiu (Hermannstadt) in Transylvania.[10] Greek
trading houses had been established there as early as 1545 and
in 1636 the Greeks were granted the right to establish a merchant company. In addition to trading privileges, the company
was permitted to elect its own officials to govern the affairs of the
company *and* the affairs of the community. In effect, the company became the institutional basis of the *koinotita*. Its president
was called *proestos* (notable), a title used by Peloponnesian

oligarchs. In 1640 the company hired a priest to conduct
baptisms, weddings and funerals. By 1776 a teacher was added
to the company's payroll and a school house was built several
years later in 1797. A substantial entrance fee and annual dues
were required of its members. An important feature of this and
other communities of the diaspora is that the merchant houses
were family-based enterprises. Furthermore, in Sibiu, by the
end of the eighteenth century, the directorship of the company,
the main constituents of which were the heads of other family
houses, became the virtual property of one family, the Safranos,
which was among the oldest and wealthiest in the city.

A crucial point in understanding the nature of these Greek
communities as well as the membership of the *Philiki Etairia* is
that emigration of Greeks from the Ottoman Empire occurred
in several waves. The first modern exodus took place after 1699
with the increase in trade in Central Europe prompted by the
treaty of Karlowitz. Immigrants passed through several stages
or levels of economic activity: very often, before their emigration, they worked as artisans, pedlars and muleteers. Abroad
they began work as commission agents, forwarders and clerks
in the employ of more established merchants. If they were
successful they became independent merchants and eventually,
if their success continued, they became bankers who lent money
to other merchants and established large family-based enterprises (for example, the Zosimas, Vasileiou, Postolakas and
Hacı Iannuş families).[11] It was men who had reached these
higher levels and whose families had arrived from the Ottoman
Empire during earlier waves of emigration, who were in control
of the Greek communities of the diaspora in the years before
1821. In a very real sense, a successful revolution and transformation of Greek society had already occurred. Their communities were miniature national societies established and
fashioned to their own requirements. They understood the
significance of their achievement and desired to share it with
their compatriots in the Ottoman Empire. However, they were
not willing to pay the price of revolution to fulfil it. They
supported men like Korais who believed that national independence could be and should be achieved only after the
Greeks back home became 'enlightened' and educated enough
to understand the responsibilities of nationhood. Their act of

revolution took place peacefully after they had been 'educated' by their emigration. Furthermore, their ties to their native areas weakened through the years. This helped to break down among them the regionalism that characterised provincial Greek society, but it also removed the immediacy of their bond to it. An illustration of this, though extreme, was expressed by a Greek of Bucharest who wrote an anonymous letter to the Austrian consul in Wallachia in 1821, condemning the *Philiki Etairia*:

> Yes, it is true that my fatherland (*patrida*) is Greece, but I grew up in Wallachia. It is here that I lead my life; it is here that I have found success; it is from this place that I took a wife and it grieves me much to see the misery of this, my second fatherland.[12]

The founders and early members of the *Philiki Etairia* were not satisfied with merely exporting ideas. They wanted to bring their own concrete experience to the native areas from which they emigrated, for the bulk of the *Etairia*'s membership were recent arrivals. They had been part of the last great wave of immigration before 1821 that accompanied the surge of commercial activity in the Balkans during the wars of the French Revolution. They were drawn from the rural provinces of the European parts of the Empire where many had been, and still were, primarily artisans and pedlars. They came alone to seek their fortunes in the cities and towns of southwestern Russia and the Rumanian Principalities, the areas that benefited most from the trading opportunities afforded by the French wars. They were men who had not yet been successful enough to invite their families to the 'new' world, nor were they solvent enough to pay the entrance fees and membership dues required by the established merchant company communities. They were simple and obscure men, unfamiliar with the sophisticated trading methods that the older merchants had acquired. When peace finally settled over Europe after 1814, they were ruined by the economic depression that followed; they had neither the resources nor the backing of their more established and organised compatriots to help them withstand the crisis. The established merchants never joined the *Philiki Etairia*.

According to the collated list of the *Etairia*'s membership a total of 425 or 41 per cent, out of the 1027 who reported their area of initiation into the society, were recruited in the Rumanian Principalities and the cities of southwestern Russia: 55 in Wallachia; 189 in Moldavia and 181 in Russia; 122 joined the society in Odessa. The majority who joined in these areas listed themselves as merchants or 'engaged in trade'. Of those initiated in Wallachia 62 per cent were merchants, in Moldavia 68.7 per cent and in Russia 85.5 per cent. The second largest occupational group in these areas, as in the *Etairia* as a whole, were the 'professionals': 18 per cent in Wallachia, 14 per cent in Moldavia and 4.3 per cent in Russia. Of these, the largest single sub-group were teachers: 20 out of 36. Of the remainder, 7 were non-merchant secretaries, 5 were physicians and 3 listed themselves as students. Nearly every Greek-speaking region of the European part of the Ottoman Empire was represented in the membership in Russia and Rumania. Only 7 listed themselves as Rumanian or Russian born. In Moldavia, 25.9 per cent were natives of the Peloponnese, 13.6 per cent were from the Aegean Islands and 10.5 per cent were from Epirus.

The *Etairia* failed to recruit any members in the substantial and older Greek merchant communities of London, Paris, Marseilles and Amsterdam. Only 1 member was recruited in Vienna. In Italy 14 Greeks joined the society: 3 in Barletta, 3 in Leghorn, 5 in Naples, 2 in Trieste and 1 in Pisa.

Typical of the society's membership was L. Leontidis, a Constantinopolitan merchant who had been in the pay of Napoleon's *Grande Armée* and who described himself as a 'bankrupt merchant'.[13] Still another was E. Glykoudis who was listed as a 'ship owner' and a native of Ithaki. In his letter of initiation into the society he wrote:

I, my friend, find myself here (in Galatz) without work. As long as commerce is dead I am ruined. The reason I am not at sea is that I owe 10,000 *grosia* and can't find work to pay the debt ... I was a ship captain with my own capital ... It troubles me, now that we've met, that I am without work. For when a man has work he is respected and better listened to. If I had work and were at sea I could initiate many good friends of the Fatherland.[14]

In 1814, Skouphas, one of the three founders of the society, was greeted with 'rude and barbaric jeering and was looked upon as a rogue' by the well-to-do merchants of Moscow to whom he had appealed for support for the *Etairia*.[15]

The founders and early members of the society were caught in the gap between the traditional world of the rural communities of the Empire and the more modern merchant company communities of the diaspora. By emigrating, they had lost access to the former and by their low economic status they were denied the protection of the latter. They found a solution to their alienation in the promise of a nation-state that would recognise them as its redeeming sons. They created their own society whose ultimate motive was clear: 'the liberation of the fatherland from the terrible yoke of Turkish oppression'. However, they never developed a concrete criticism of Ottoman society nor produced a clear blue-print of what the fatherland would be after the 'liberation'. Nevertheless, they were possessed by a vision of a community of Greeks whose cohesion would go beyond the ties of social class, of region and village, and even family. They were simple and semi-literate men of rural origin who, through the process of immigration, underwent a profound social and psychological transformation that characterises the passing of a traditional world into modernity. Their understanding of this transformation was primitive and crude, yet they responded, in a half-conscious way, with what has since become a universal phenomenon: the creation and adoption of a new social, political and individual identity – the nation. These very features make the *Etairia* such an interesting subject for analysis, for its level of development fell midway between more advanced organisations like the Italian Carbonari and the Russian Decembrists and those that Eric Hobsbawm has called 'primitive rebels'.[16]

This failure to develop a concrete position enabled the *Etairia* to succeed in initially attracting individuals from nearly every social group. Yet the society's success was, by definition, the basis for its ultimate failure: the *Philiki Etairia* disintegrated when the Greek revolt began; the major groups that took part in the revolt acted not as Etairists but as members of a traditional pre-modern social order. The implications of the *Etairia*'s vision were a threat to the society it had resolved to liberate. The

notables of the Peloponnese joined the *Etairia* believing they had
found a foreign ally; at first they had accepted the *Etairia*'s
deliberate misrepresentation that it had Russia's official backing
– as an aid in their struggle to extend the authority they already
possessed. They were not about to relinquish their social and
political positions for the sake of others, even other Greeks. The
Etairia had recruited from almost all classes of Greeks, but it
failed fully to initiate, or to be more precise, fully to convert
them to the cause for which it stood.

One of the striking features of the several letters of initiation
that have survived is the frequent use of the word *patrida*
(fatherland) to describe the new recruit's native village, island
or region. In these letters *patrida* was used to connote the English
word 'hometown' rather than 'fatherland' which is its literal
meaning, or 'nation' in its present-day usage. It was only in the
Etairia's oaths of initiation that *patrida* was consistently used in
its modern usage.[17] For example, Dimitrios Mamounis, a
merchant ship captain and a native of the Aegean island of
Psara, was initiated into the society in Constantinople. He
wrote to the *Arkhi*: 'Because I have wandered for such a long
time from my *patrida* Psara . . . I have not had the opportunity
to do a decent thing in my life.' Ioannis Kaphareus, a native of
Psara, who could not contribute any money to the *Etairia*, wrote
in his letter of initiation: '. . . I was born in Parga but because
of the invasions and poor circumstances (there) I have been
forced to abandon my most sweet *patrida* and emigrate here to
Corfu where I am without work. . . . I hope that I will return so
that I can enjoy our longed-for *patrida*.' Among the most
interesting letters of initiation was that written by Ioannis
Kavvadias. He expressed a sense of tradition for his occupation
as well as his birthplace:

> It is known to you that for a long time I lived in my *patrida*
> Preveza of Rumeli. I was born there, and always carried arms,
> which was for me a paternal tradition (*patroparadota*). It is
> however nearly twenty years since I was forced to flee by the
> tyrants and was exiled by them from the fatherland of our
> race (*tis phylis imon patridos*).[18]

The fragility of the *Etairia*'s success in recruiting Peloponnesian
notables is evident in the society's agreement with the leading

clans of the Mani, the remote and mountainous region in the southern part of the Morea which enjoyed a high degree of autonomy from the Porte. Khristophoros Perraivos, an agent of the society, had been assigned the task of uniting several rival clans and bringing them into the *Etairia*. The text of the final agreement displayed a curious mixture of traditional and modern views in regard to national identity and political authority:

> We, the three families, that is to say, Mavromikhalis, Grigorakis and Troupakis, as the most powerful and most worthy of all the other families of our fatherland (*patrida*) Sparta, swear by the aforementioned frightful oath, that from now in our bodies only one soul, one passion, and one will shall rule. And never will any domestic or foreign issue ever cause this holy bond to be broken or weakened.[19]

The word *patrida* was used here in its traditional sense and the family-based political authority of the signatories was made quite clear. Yet, in the next sentence, *patrida* was employed to mean the entire nation of Greeks, and the united families agreed to abide by the wishes of that nation's leaders:

> The main and universal purpose of this sacred bond is viewed and has been made for no other reason but the common benefit of our fatherland (*patrida*), and we shall be ready, in agreement and eagerness, to put into action all that the distinguished leaders of our Race (*Genos*) order us to do for the common benefit of our fatherland Hellas (*tis patridos mas Ellados*).[20]

The first regional usage of *patrida* was even more distinct and had a political meaning that was absent when employed by the expatriate merchants who had joined the society outside their native areas. It referred to a region that had been recognised by the Ottomans from the start of their second occupation of the Peloponnese in 1715 as a separate and semi-autonomous area; a native, clan-based oligarchy had been given the power to rule the *patrida* in return for annual tribute. The second usage of *patrida* was less distinct and referred to a people rather than to a boundaried area. The word *Genos* or race, which occurs throughout the document, clearly indicates a less traditional view that had rarely been expressed in the letters of initiation. It is unlikely, however, that these modern expressions of national identity originated from the Maniote leaders themselves. Perraivos was responsible for the agreement and probably for a good portion of its wording as well. That they were aware of the double meaning of fatherland and that there was a need for clarifying the distinction is evident from the frequent use of the phrases 'the general fatherland' (*geniki patrida*), 'common fatherland' (*koini patrida*), and 'our own fatherland' (*i diki mas patrida*), rather than 'fatherland' alone.

A bargain had been struck: the Maniotes would acknowledge and come to the aid of the 'general fatherland' in return for the recognition of their traditional political and social position in their particular 'fatherland':

> Just as we have accepted the burden of maintaining the good governing of our fatherland (*patrida*), in the same manner we will accept and act upon all other commands of our Race (*Genos*) . . .[21]

The risk of rising up against the Ottomans and loosing the position they already enjoyed was mitigated by the promise of Russia's firm support. Perraivos undoubtedly assured them of this:

> Whatever command we receive, whether Royal (*Vasiliki*) or from our Race (*Genos*), whose purpose is the benefit of the common fatherland (*koini patrida*), will be considered and acted upon with eagerness and passion by us, without, however, being unjust to any of the military officers of our fatherland, that is to say, the so-called *Kapetanioi* . . . [22]

The agreement between three families, and the oath they swore to, was different from the *Etairia*'s oaths of initiation: they swore not as individuals but as clan chiefs. Their oath also acknowledged the authorities they were responsible to in the event of betrayal – a revealing hierarchy of allegiances:

> Therefore with one voice, one soul, and heart, in an un-breakable bond, we swear to uphold the above agreements completely and steadfastly. If one of us (which we believe will never happen!) reaches such a degree of criminality and

impiety that he appears a transgressor and perjurer of these agreements, which are beneficial to our fatherland (*patrida*) we shall first commit him to the hands of God; second to the curses of our own fatherland (*i diki mas patrida*); and third to the just and impartial laws of our general fatherland Hellas (*geniki patrida Ellada*); may the name of his family remain eternally in dishonour, cursed and hated by the entire fatherland (*patrida*) and Race (*Genos*).[23]

The interesting feature of the *Etairia*, and other secret societies similar to it, is that although its leaders did not fully understand their dilemma, that is to say, the problem faced by all men who seek to create a national body within a highly traditional and rural society, the ceremony and ritual of initiation which the society adopted reflected a primitive awareness of it; perhaps because they themselves had not been fully converted. They employed traditional oaths and ceremonies (e.g., the ritual of *adelphopoiisis* or blood-brotherhood) in an attempt to guarantee the conversion. The initiates were threatened with terrible punishments to assure that they fulfilled the obligations of the new alliance:

> ... reflect that all the other bonds and responsibilities that he has in the world from now on are nothing before the bond of the *Etairia* ... Once he enters the *Etairia*, he must keep death within his view, death with all its harsh torments. If the occasion arises he must be able to murder a betrayer of the *Etairia*, even if it is his closest relative.[24]

In what was called the 'Great Oath', the Fatherland was deified and new members were asked to swear to it with extraordinary passion:

> Finally I swear upon your holy name, oh sacred and wretched fatherland. I swear upon your lengthy sufferings, upon the bitter tears of your imprisoned and persecuted people, shed for so many centuries until this moment by your wretched children. I devote my entire self to you. Henceforth, you will be the cause and the purpose of my thoughts. Your name will be the guide of all my actions and your happiness the reward of all my efforts. If ever I should, even for a moment, become oblivious to your sufferings and fail to fulfil my duty to you,

may divine justice exhaust upon my head all the thunder of its righteousness; may my name, inherited by my heirs, be detested; may my person become the object of curses and anathema of my compatriots; and may my death be the inescapable punishment and reward for my sin, so that I may not infect the purity of the *Etairia* with my membership.

The modern vision of the *Etairia*'s founders failed to survive the Greek revolt of 1821. For the revolt was, in fact, devoted not to a social transformation in which all Greeks would be equal in the eyes of the nation, but to the enrichment and preservation of a traditional oligarchy. The Greek Revolution, in this sense, was not a revolution at all. But this is not to say that all the participants were void of national feeling. Each possessed his own nationalism – either in the form of a concern for the preservation and development of the modern Greek language, or in the resurrection of a Helleno-Byzantine Empire. The Peloponnesian notables sought an extension of their authority but also an extension of the autonomy and eventually the independence of the community that they represented, which was, after all, Greek. However, the fact remains that these motives were not truly revolutionary in any modern sense. It should also be borne in mind that a large portion of the Greek-speaking Orthodox Christians of the Ottoman Empire never took part in any phase of the war for Greek independence. Broad segments of the upper clergy, the Phanariots and the Asia minor Greeks saw their fortune and well-being not only within traditional society, but within the Ottoman State.

The *Philiki Etairia*, without a doubt, played a role in the events that led to the Greek revolt. For one, it spread the belief that the Russian Tsar would not abandon the Greeks in their hour of need. In fact, several years later, but unrelated to the *Etairia*'s boast, the Russians did come to the aid of their Orthodox brothers and set the stage for the granting of national independence. However, the *Etairia* was not a party of national unity that organised the Greeks to resist the Turks. Its membership reflected the deep divisions of Greek society which eventually led to open civil war during the struggle for independence. The *Etairia*, as it was conceived by its founders, was born too soon.

NOTES TO CHAPTER 4

The study resulting in this publication was made under a fellowship granted by the Foreign Area Fellowship Program. However, the conclusions, opinions, and other statements in this publication are those of the author and are not necessarily those of the Fellowship Program.

1. The list employed in this study was collated from three primary lists, a published secondary collation and a list compiled by the author from letters of initiation into the society and other correspondence. The three primary lists are: the so-called Philimon list of 692 individuals, attached to the Ypsilantis archive published by Ioannis Philimon, *Dokimion Istorikon peri tis Ellinikis Epanastaseos*, 4 vols. (Athens, 1859–61) I, pp. 387–416; the Panagiotis Sekeris list of 520 individuals, recently published by I. A. Meletopoulos (ed.), *I Philiki Etaireia, Arkheion P. Sekeris* (Athens, 1967) pp. 98–165; the Emmanouil Xanthos list of 133 individuals, collated together with the Sekeris list by V. G. Mexas (ed.), *Oi Philikoi, katalogos ton melon tis Philikis Etaireias ek tou Arkheiou Sekeri* (Athens, 1937) pp. 1–80. These, together with 60 individuals not included in the primary lists, were collated by the author to produce a total of 1093 entries with a maximum of 24 characteristics for each one. The Crosstabs II computer programme, which was developed by Cambridge Computer Associates, Cambridge, Massachusetts, for operation on the IBM system/360 under the IBM Operating System, was employed in an extended quantitative analysis of the data contained in the author's final list of the *Etairia*'s membership. For the complete analysis upon which a portion of this article is based and a full critical discussion of the reliability of the data as well as the definition of the categories of analysis, see the author's 'The Philike Etaireia, 1814–1821: A Social and Historical Analysis' (unpublished doctoral dissertation, Columbia University, 1971).

2. Out of a total of 1093 entries, 910 reported their occupation.

3. For example, see T. Kh. Kandiloros, *I Philiki Etaireia, 1814–1821* (Athens, 1926), p. 207; and more recently E. G. Protopsaltis (ed.), *I Philiki Etaireia, Anamnistikon tefkhos epi ti 150eteridi* (Athens, 1964) p. 84.

4. Giannis Kordatos, *I koinoniki simasia tis Ellinikis Epanastaseos tou 1821* (Athens, 1924); T. Stamatopoulos, *O Esoterikos Agonas kata tin Epanastasi tou 1821*, 2 vols. (Athens, 1957) I, pp. 57–105; Tasos Vournas (ed.), *Philiki Etaireia* (Athens, 1965) p. 17.

5. The major figures of the Serbian 'awakening', Dositej Obradović and Vuk Karadzić, travelled widely throughout Europe and did their work in Germany and Austria; the first Serbian newspaper was published in Vienna in 1791. Bulgarian merchants in Odessa were responsible for the first schools to teach their native language, and Fan S. Noli, a leader of the Albanian awakening, did much of his work in Boston, Massachusetts, at the beginning of the twentieth century. See L. S. Stavrianos, 'Antecedents to the Balkan Revolutions of the Nineteenth Century', *Journal of Modern History*, XXIX (1957) 335, 343–4; Stavro Skendi, *The Albanian National Awakening 1878–1912* (Princeton, New Jersey, 1967) pp. 145–64. The Greek 'enlightenment' is treated authoritatively by Konstantinos Dimaras,

Istoria tis Neoellinikis Logotekhnias (4th rev. ed.; Athens, 1968). A summary of recent Greek scholarship on the subject is by G. P. Henderson, *The Revival of Revival of Greek Thought, 1620–1830* (Albany, New York, 1970 and Edinburgh, 1971).

6. H. A. R. Gibb and Harold Bowen, *Islamic Society and the West*, vol. I, part I (Oxford, 1950) pp. 159–61, 208–16; L. S. Stavrianos, 'Antecedents to the Balkan Revolutions of the Nineteenth Century', 336–7; see also L. S. Stavrianos, *The Balkans since 1453* (New York, 1959) pp. 89–90; Theodore H. Papadopoullos, *Studies and Documents relating to the History of the Greek Church and People under Turkish Domination* (Bibliotheca Graeca Aevi Posterioris) (Brussels, 1952) pp. 1–39; G. G. Arnakis, 'The Greek Church in the Ottoman Empire', *Journal of Modern History*, xxiv (1952) 235–50.

7. Dankwart A. Rustow provides a useful definition of modernisation as well as an illuminating analysis of its relationship to nationalism: *A World of Nations, Problems of Political Modernization* (Washington, D.C., 1967) pp. 1–71. 'Modernization ... denotes rapidly widening control over nature through closer cooperation among men. ... It implies an intellectual, a technological and a social revolution. It transforms three of man's most fundamental relations: to time, to nature and to his fellowman' (p. 3). See also, Boyd C. Shafer, *Nationalism: Myth and Reality* (New York, 1955) pp. 3–56; Louis Snyder, *The Meaning of Nationalism* (New Brunswick, New Jersey, 1954).

8. T. Kolokotronis, *Diigisis symvanton tis Ellinikis phylis apo ta 1770 eos ta 1836*, narrated to Georgios Tersetis (Athens, 1846) p. 71.

9. Traian Stoianovich, 'The Conquering Balkan Orthodox Merchant', *The Journal of Economic History*, xx (1960) 234–313.

10. Nestor Camariano, 'L'organisation et l'activité culturelle de la compagnie des marchands grecs de Sibiu', *Balcania*, vi (1943) 201–41. This useful article contains a detailed summary and description of the company's register found in the Arhivele Statului din Sibiu, nos. 975–87. Dimitru Limona, a Rumanian archivist of Greek extraction, has compiled and edited an invaluable catalogue of Greek merchant documents found in the Sibiu and Braşov state archives with informative summaries of each document: *Catalogul Documentelor referitoare la viaţa economică a ţărilor Române în sec. XVII–XIX*, 2 vols. (Bucharest, 1966) and *Catalogul Documentelor Greceşti din Arhivele Statului de la Oraşul Stalin*, 2 vols. (Bucharest, 1958).

11. Stoianovich, *The Journal of Economic History*, 295; for a contemporary account of these international commercial families, see Henry Holland, *Travels in the Ionian Islands, Albania, Thessaly, Macedonia, etc. during the Years 1812 and 1813* (London, 1815) pp. 148–9.

12. Georgios Laios, *Anekdotes Epistoles kai Engrapha tou 1821: Istorika Dokoumenta apo ta Austriaka Arkeia* (Athens, 1958) pp. 39–40. Cf. pp. 16–17 above.

13. Mexas, *Oi Philikoi*, number 3.

14. Philimon, *Dokimion istorikon peri tis Ellinikis Epanastaseos*, I, 333–5.

15. Ioannis Philimon, *Dokimion istorikon peri tis Philikis Etaireias* (Nafplion, 1834) p. 179.

16. E. J. Hobsbawm, *Primitive Rebels: Studies in Archaic Forms of Social*

Movement in the 19th and 20th Centuries (New York, 1965 [originally published in London, 1959 under the title *Social Bandits and Primitive Rebels*]) pp. 2–12. On the Decembrists, see Anatole G. Mazour, *The First Russian Revolution, 1825: The Decembrist Movement, Its Origins, Development, and Significance* (Berkeley, California, 1937). See also relevant material in Norman Mackenzie (ed.), *Secret Societies* (London, 1967).

17. Rare exceptions were letters written by the relatively well-educated members, especially those of Phanariot or Constantinopolitan origin. Unlike the Society's letters of initiation, letters of inauguration, which marked a member's elevation to a higher degree, were prescribed in form as well as content; they were probably composed by the authors of the oaths of initiation. In these letters, the word *sympolitis* (fellow-citizen) rather than *patriotis* (fellow-countryman) was used to note a fellow of one's own region.

18. The three letters in the above were published together with other *Etairia* documents from the *Genika Arkheia tou Kratous* (Athens) in facsimile edition as well as in transliteration by Protopsaltis, 253–5.

19. Philimon, *Dokimion Istorikon peri tis Ellinikis Epanastaseos*, i, p. 158.

20. *Ibid.*

21. *Ibid.*, p. 159.

22. *Ibid.*, p. 161. In a note appended to the document Philimon points out that *Vasiliki* (Royal) refers to the Russian Tsar.

23. *Ibid.*, p. 160.

24. This passage is from the *Didaskalia* or *Teaching* which was the manual for initiating members into the *Etairia*. Several manuscripts have survived and have been published in numerous editions. Both passages below are from the version found in the Bucharest State Archive, published by Andrei Oţetea *et al.* (eds.), *Răscoală din 1821. Eteria în Principatele Romîne*, vol. IV of *Documente Privind Istoria Romîniei. Răscoală din 1821* (Bucharest, 1960) pp. 32–46.

The oaths, rituals of initiation and organisation of the *Etairia* bear a striking resemblance to those of the Carbonari, Freemasons and other secret societies of the period. Some have argued that the *Etairia* was, in fact, directly linked to them (see, for example, P. G. Panagiotis, 'Philiki Etaireia kai Tektonismos: Symvoli eis ton apeleftherotikon agona tou ethnous', offprint from *Tektonikon Deltion*, n.v. [1956]. The view that they were all connected in some grand conspiracy has been rightly discredited. Individual connections did exist (at least one of the founders of the *Etairia* claimed to have been a Freemason) and doubtless account for many of the similarities. The important point, however, is that these groups, especially the Carbonari and the Decembrists, all faced to some degree the problem of competing traditional allegiances: each borrowed from the other what it needed. Though both the Italian and Russian societies were far more politically developed in the expression of their aims, their oaths and rituals were immersed in pre-modern or 'primitive' idioms. M. Saint-Edme (pseud.), *Constitution et Organisation des Carbonari, ou documents exacts sur tout ce qui concerne l'existence, l'origine et le but de cette société secrète* (2nd ed.; Paris, 1822) p. 62; Marc Raeff, *The Decembrist Movement* (Englewood Cliffs, New Jersey, 1966) pp. 159–60.

5 Kapodistrias and the *Philiki Etairia*, 1814–21

C. M. WOODHOUSE

It seems unlikely that any conclusive evidence will ever come to light on Kapodistrias' relations with the *Philiki Etairia*. There is no doubt, of course, that he knew a great deal about its membership and activities. Equally there is no doubt that he was never a card-carrying member, to use a modern idiom; for if he had been, it is improbable that the secret records of the Society, which were kept with punctilious accuracy and which record the date of enrolment and membership number of his brother Viaro among others, should have entirely omitted him. These matters are not in question. The question is rather this: was Kapodistrias a conscious and committed accomplice in the conspiracy which led to the risings in the Danubian Principalities, in the Peloponnese and elsewhere in Greece in March 1821? If he was, did he act on his own initiative or with the knowledge and consent of the Tsar?

The answers to these questions can only rest on evidence that is circumstantial, fragmentary, and to some extent speculative. Obviously no documents are ever going to emerge which would completely acquit Kapodistrias and the Tsar of complicity in the plot: such negative proof is not in the nature of historical evidence. It is scarcely more likely that either of them would have allowed evidence to survive which would prove their complicity. A fairly imposing mosaic can be built up of circumstantial fragments, but in the last analysis the verdict can only be a matter of judgment. Counsel has been darkened over the last century and a half by the conjunction of two inconvenient facts. On the one hand, Kapodistrias' enemies, headed by Metternich, wanted to prove that he was implicated in the conspiracy in order to undermine his position as the Tsar's joint Foreign Minister. On the other hand, his admirers wanted to prove that he was involved in the nationalist movement as a true Greek patriot. His friends and his enemies, in fact, had a common interest for opposite reasons. These influences still persist among some historians, though I know of only two – Makris[1] and Oţetea[2] – who believe that there was actual collusion on the part of Kapodistrias and the Tsar in the rising of March 1821.

On this particular point I range myself with the sceptics. The documentary sources have been very thoroughly examined in recent years. Many Greek scholars – too many to mention individually – have studied and published the personal papers of Kapodistrias, his family and friends and contemporaries in the greatest detail. Other scholars have worked in the Russian archives: I would particularly mention G. L. Arsh,[3] Mrs Patricia K. Grimsted,[4] and A. Oţetea.[5] The work is not complete, but it is already voluminous. So far as the crucial question which I have defined is concerned, the results range only from the negative to the inconclusive. Those who wish to believe in Kapodistrias' complicity are reduced to highly special pleading. The keen eye of Greek patriotism would hardly have missed any fragment of truth which escaped the no less keen eye of Metternich's hostility; and it is scarcely to be expected that further research will alter the verdict of 'not proven'. But this does not minimise the significance of the evidence, which deserves to be summarised and assessed.

Since the evidence is so largely circumstantial, it is right to call witnesses to Kapodistrias' own character. This involves going back earlier than the year 1814, when the *Philiki Etairia* was founded. For it was not the first such secret society among the Greeks, nor even the first of which Kapodistrias had knowledge. The poet, Rigas Velestinlis, whom the Turks executed in 1798, was reputed to have founded an *Etairia*; and even if that is doubtful, he was certainly the ring-leader of a conspiracy which included many Greeks living in the Hapsburg Empire. Some, who were familiar with the drama of Rigas at first hand, were still living in Vienna when Kapodistrias took up his first diplomatic post there in 1811. Among them were the priest and schoolmaster Anthimos Gazis, who founded the Greek periodical *Logios Ermis*; the wealthy merchant Ioannis Stavrou; and his son Georgios, who later founded the Bank of Greece. All of them became close friends of Kapodistrias.[6] He had other friends already who were committed to the liberation of the Greeks, particularly those with whom he had served on Levkas against Ali Paşa in 1807, such as Bishop Ignatios, the ex-Metropolitan of Arta, and Khristophoros Perraivos, another associate of Rigas Velestinlis. There were also numerous guerrilla chieftains like Kolokotronis, Botzaris, Tzavellas and Odysseas Androutsos.[7] All these associates of Kapodistrias were later *Philikoi*. Although the *Philiki Etairia* had not yet been founded, Greek conspiracies do not have to have a formal constitution to exist. It is arguable that this conspiracy, with Kapodistrias as part of it, had existed since the day in 1807 when he and his friends drank a toast to the liberation of Greece at the 'place called Magemenos' during the siege of Levkas.[8]

Nevertheless, once he entered the Russian service in 1809, Kapodistrias adopted an extremely cautious attitude towards the Greek nationalist movement. It has been suggested that he played a part in founding a Masonic lodge in Moscow; and there were certainly many such lodges formed among the Greeks abroad, and the *Philiki Etairia* itself was based on some of the principles of Freemasonry, though with important differences.[9] But apart from the fact that the evidence for Kapodistrias' role is extremely nebulous, there was nothing very sinister about Freemasonry in Russia at this date. It was tolerated by the Tsar; his brother, Constantine, was himself a Freemason, and the movement was not banned until August 1822 – the very month, by a significant coincidence, in which Kapodistrias had to quit his post in the Russian government.[10] So far as Greek nationalism proper was concerned, he resolutely refused to take part in any clandestine activity because it would have been incompatible with his loyalty to the Tsar. This is testified by Ioannis Philimon, the first historian of the *Philiki Etairia*, who had most of its records at his disposal. He wrote that in 1813 (though the year is doubtful) Kapodistrias rebuffed an approach by a group of Greek intellectuals and merchants in Vienna who were planning 'active measures', his response being that the Greeks must rely first on education before independence could be contemplated.[11] Education was always his sovereign remedy for the grievances of his fellow-countrymen, but he was never very clear how education alone could lead to independence without some more forcible action at the crucial time.

At least he practised what he preached. During his first five years in the Russian service, from 1809 to 1814, he devoted much of his spare time, which was ample, to the study of Greek, both classical and modern. Whereas his early letters were all written in Italian, from 1808 onwards he made strenuous efforts to improve his written Greek, and many of his friends were chosen with a view to intellectual self-improvement. Chief among them were the Stourdza family. Alexandros Stourdza became his junior colleague and devoted supporter, and his sister Roxani was the only woman with whom Kapodistrias ever contemplated marriage. One or two examples out of many may be given of his cultural patriotism. He wrote to Bishop Ignatios in February 1811 urging that they should correspond exclusively in Greek: 'Any Greek who writes to another Greek in a foreign language should be declared a foreigner', but unfortunately he had to admit at once that his own Greek was scarcely good enough to submit to such a rule.[12] Another Greek in St. Petersburg, Spyridon Destounis, recorded in his memoirs that Kapodistrias had formed a small group for conversational practice, it being forbidden to talk other languages among them.[13] And it was under Kapodistrias' influence that the wealthy Epirote merchant, Ioannis Dombolis, long resident in St. Petersburg, left his fortune forty years later to the University of Athens.[14]

These examples are cited to emphasise the innocence of Kapodistrias' contacts with the Greeks during these years. Equally innocuous were the many memoranda which he submitted to his superiors on the state of Greece and the Ionian Islands. Those which have survived, whether published or found in the Russian archives, were essentially factual and contained no suggestion or hint of revolutionary action.[15] In Vienna the attempts of Metternich's spies to incriminate Kapodistrias, whether by trailing his Greek contacts or rifling his waste-paper basket, were uniformly unsuccessful. Since Metternich did not scruple in later years to present to the Tsar what he called his 'evidence' of Kapodistrias' complicity in Greek plots, and since none of it amounted to anything but trivial gossip, it may be taken as certain that there was no real evidence at all.[16] As in other cases as well, the vast archives of the Austrian state police form a cast-iron monument to Kapodistrias' innocence.

Matters took a somewhat different turn, on the surface at any rate, when he was posted as head of chancery to the Army of the Danube under Admiral Chichagov in 1812. He arrived too late to take part in the negotiation of the Treaty of Bucharest, which he regarded as an unmitigated disaster. It was perhaps at this date that he arrived at the conclusion that nothing could be done with the Ottoman government except by force or the threat of force; and this conviction dominated the advice which he gave to the Tsar for the next ten years. It also to some extent influenced his immediate conduct. His new post entailed several duties which would have revived Metternich's suspicions, however Kapodistrias had conducted himself. For example, he was responsible for the organisation of Bessarabia, which had a large Greek population; for communications with the Serbs, who were in a semi-permanent state of revolt; and for the appointment of Russian consuls in the Danubian Principalities and other parts of the Ottoman Empire.[17] Many of the consuls appointed were Greeks, a notable case being Ioannis Vlasopoulos at Patras. Vlasopoulos' official interpreter, Ioannis Paparrigopoulos, an indefatigable intriguer, made many trips to Ioannina to visit Ali Paşa;[18] and one of Kapodistrias' friends in Vienna, Ioannis Stavrou, was also reputed to be in correspondence with Ali Paşa.[19] Metternich would have had no difficulty in assembling such circumstantial fragments into a Balkan conspiracy with Kapodistrias at its centre. What he was in fact aiming at is perhaps best summarised in the words of a memorandum from Chichagov to the Tsar, which Kapodistrias probably drafted:

> The primary aim is to prepare the spirits of the oppressed, so as to promote by their enthusiasm the Porte's good intentions in the event of an alliance, or to declare openly in our favour if a decision is eventually made to break the Porte's resistance.[20]

In other words, Kapodistras wanted to be able to say to the Turks on behalf of their Balkan subjects: 'Heads we win, tails you lose.' But in saying this he was happily conscious of a perfect identity of interest between Greek patriotism and Russian policy.

However, the chance of destroying the Treaty of Bucharest had not yet come, nor did it come during his Russian service. In the course of the war against Napoleon, the Army of the Danube moved north under Admiral Chichagov, then west under General Barclay de Tolley; and Kapodistrias moved with it. For two years his contacts with the Balkans almost entirely lapsed. His main task in the years 1813–14 was to bring about the re-organisation of the Swiss Confederation, and he had little more than occasional correspondence with Greek friends like the Stourdzas and his relatives in Corfu.[21] He naturally developed a keen interest in the disposition of the Ionian Islands once Napoleon's grip on them began to be broken. But he did not associate their fate at this date with that of mainland Greece, and there was nothing conspiratorial about his concern. Clearly there had to be a Russian policy for the islands, and naturally the Tsar turned to Kapodistrias for advice. He was largely responsible for the decision to establish a British protectorate over the seven islands in 1814. It was not until he became bitterly disillusioned over the manner in which the British protectorate was administered that his conduct began to attract the suspicions of British as well as Austrian ministers.

Up to the end of 1814, therefore, there was nothing in Kapodistrias' career that would have justified the charge that he had entered the Russian service with a Machiavellian purpose of distorting Russian policy to support a Greek conspiracy. He frequently and candidly asserted his Greek patriotism, of course; but it was his sincere belief that there was a natural affinity of purpose between the Russian people and his own, grounded in religion and sustained by political interest.[22] There was, therefore, no need for him to play a conspiratorial role, since the tide of history was flowing in the direction he desired. All he had to do was to persuade the Tsar of the correctness of his analysis. The opportunity to do so was offered by the Congress of Vienna and its aftermath, which made of Kapodistrias the most influential figure in Russian foreign policy for more than five years. The month of September 1814, when Kapodistrias set out for Vienna, was, therefore, a turning-point in his career. It was also probably the month in which three unknown Greeks – Skouphas, Tsakalov and Xanthos – founded the *Philiki Etairia* in Odessa.

When Kapodistrias first became aware of the existence of the *Philiki Etairia* is unknown. One historian states that Tsakalov met him in Vienna before the end of 1814, but of this there seems to be no evidence.[23] Metternich believed, because he wanted to believe, that Kapodistrias was involved in the conspiracy from the first. He was helped by an unlucky coincidence. During the Congress of Vienna Kapodistrias proposed to the Tsar, in default of anything better to help and encourage the Greeks, the formation of an educational and cultural organisation to be called the *Philomouson Etairia* or Society of Friends of the Muses.[24] He took the idea and the name from a similar society already founded in Athens under the presidency of Frederick North, a younger son of the Prime Minister who lost the American colonies. Kapodistrias suspected that the Society in Athens was an instrument of British policy, though North, like all the philhellenes, had no connection with the British government; this lovable eccentric was Orthodox in religion but heterodox in everything else. Kapodistrias was, therefore, almost certainly mistaken in thinking that he was counteracting a pre-existing British policy when he founded his own *Philomouson Etairia*. However, whatever Kapodistrias' motives, his initiative prospered, and it therefore reinforced the suspicions of Metternich, who mercilessly harried the *Philomouson Etairia* and all its Greek members in Vienna. When Metternich eventually heard of the *Philiki Etairia*, which was truly a conspiracy, he assumed that they were one and the same thing, the one being a cover for the other, and that Kapodistrias was at the centre of the sinister web.

In fact, Kapodistrias was much too cautious to involve himself in rash conspiracies just at the moment when he was gaining the Tsar's confidence. Nevertheless, he unavoidably met many Balkan personalities in Vienna who took a less sophisticated view of the prospects of liberation. They included his old friends Bishop Ignatios and Anthimos Gazis; a Serb delegation led by Matthew Nenadović; the rebel paşa from Vidin, Pasvano-ğlu; the Ionian Greek, Count Valsamakis, who took the place of a delegation from the Ionian Senate which was prevented from attending; and several Greeks in the Tsar's entourage, among them his romantic young A.D.C., Alexandros Ypsilantis. Metternich's spies watched them all like hawks; and since they expected the worst, they had no difficulty in finding it.

Kapodistrias' actual conduct at this date was, in fact, impeccable. He was, of course, sympathetic to all his Greek and Balkan friends, who naturally looked to him for guidance; and he contrived to put their cases to the Tsar in the most favourable light and circumstances. But he did so without subterfuge, and he consistently warned them all against revolutionary activities. His motive was not one of mere timidity, for he was convinced that eventually Russo-Turkish relations would come to a violent crisis from which the Balkan peoples were bound to benefit indirectly; whereas if they tried to precipitate such a crisis themselves, the Tsar would be bound to react against them. The only case in which he resorted to a clandestine manoeuvre on behalf of the Greeks at Vienna was in using Count Valsamakis to submit a proposal on the Ionian Islands to the Powers, which he had himself drafted.[25] This was a long way short of the kind of plotting that Metternich suspected.

The Congress ended with Kapodistrias' appointment as Secretary of State, jointly with the German Count Nesselrode. Although Nesselrode had much the longer tenure of office, Kapodistrias was the more influential of the two for the next five years. Perhaps unavoidably, it was assumed by foreign diplomatists that while Nesselrode was responsible for the outward and public routine, Kapodistrias was in charge of all the secret and unacknowledged activities of Russian policy.[26] In fact, the Tsar conducted a great deal of clandestine policy himself, often very clumsily, behind the backs of his ministers; and Kapodistrias' reputation suffered thereby. When he wrote his autobiography in 1826 for the benefit of the new Tsar, Nicholas I, he discreetly passed over many of Alexander's eccentricities in order to protect his reputation. For example, the name of Mme de Krüdener, who dangerously influenced Alexander in 1815 and claimed to have inspired the Holy Alliance, is never mentioned in Kapodistrias' autobiography; nor was he frank about Alexander's intrigues in Spain through his ambassador Tatishchev and other agents, which caused Kapodistrias himself much embarrassment. Such tactful silences about the Tsar naturally tend to attract suspicion

towards the corresponding silences of Kapodistrias' autobiography about his own role. For example, he never mentioned
that during his first year as Secretary of State he made a private
visit to Vienna, ostensibly for medical consultation but probably
also on business of the *Philomouson Etairia*. Even in his letters to
his father, which were frequent and regular during these years,
there is no mention of the reason for the gap between April and
June 1816. The reports of the Austrian police, which are the
only evidence for this visit, readily enabled Metternich to put
the worst construction on it.[27]

So far as circumstantial evidence goes – and no other evidence
exists – there is nothing to connect Kapodistrias in any way with
the *Philiki Etairia* during the years 1815–16, nor even to show
that he had heard of it as such. Circumstantial evidence indeed
rather points in the opposite direction. He was still establishing
himself in the Tsar's confidence and gaining immense responsibilities. Policy towards France, Spain, Germany, Italy, the
Americas and the great-power alliance all passed through his
hands; so did questions of internal organisation in Poland and
Bessarabia, and most important of all, relations with the
Ottoman Empire and its Balkan dependencies. Kapodistrias
would have been foolish indeed to risk sacrificing such a position of power. He used his position to help his fellow-countrymen indeed, but he was at the same time both open and discreet
in doing so. For example, on the one hand he instructed the
Ambassador in Constantinople, Baron Stroganov, to help the
Ypsilantis family in a claim over property confiscated by the
Turkish authorities;[28] on the other hand, he refused to allow his
brother Viaro to take a post in the Russian service.[29] He helped
to found Greek schools in Russia, but avoided contact with
habitual conspirators, even old friends like Perraivos. He
rebuffed an attempt by Greeks in Vienna to involve him in yet
another secret society, of which evidence duly came into the
hands of Metternich.[30] The *Philomouson Etairia* was forced to
migrate from Vienna to the more philhellenic climate of
Munich; and Anthimos Gazis also left Vienna to found a
school on its behalf in Mount Pelion. Gazis, in fact, joined the
Philiki Etairia in 1816, but Kapodistrias remained uncompromised except in Metternich's eyes.

Early in 1817, however, Kapodistrias was brought face to

face with the conspiracy for the first time. A young man from Ithaki, called Nikolaos Galatis, arrived in St. Petersburg on 20 January 1817. He had applied for a passport in Bucharest five months earlier, and Kapodistrias had authorised it after consulting the Tsar, though he knew nothing more of Galatis' purpose than his own statement that he had an important communication to make 'concerning our nation'.[31] At his first meeting with Kapodistrias, Galatis revealed the existence of the Society and claimed to have authority to offer him the leadership of it. It would be wearisome to describe in detail the subsequent course of this episode, and fortunately it is also unnecessary because the facts are clear. Kapodistrias wrote his own account of it in his autobiography, which recent researches in the Russian archives have confirmed without any significant discrepancy.[32] The gist of the story is that Kapodistrias was horrified by what he heard, and rebuffed Galatis peremptorily; but the Tsar, who was fully informed, took a more relaxed view of the affair.

Galatis certainly behaved with extreme imprudence in St. Petersburg. He lived ostentatiously on borrowed money, he consorted with notorious conspirators (including Perraivos), and he boasted that he had a thousand men under his command, who were so determined that they would even assassinate the Tsar if he gave the word. It says much for Alexander's tolerance that he declined to take these follies seriously. After a brief spell under arrest, Galatis was sent back through Bessarabia to Ottoman territory, under an escort carrying written instructions from Kapodistrias to the Governor-General in Kishinev and the Russian Consul in Jassy. Galatis' indiscretions continued to cause great embarrassment both in Jassy and in Bucharest. He spent eighteen months in the Principalities, recruiting members wholesale into the *Etairia*. Some of his recruits were valuable, but some were undependable; and one of the indirect results of his freelance activities was to shift the apparent centre of gravity of the conspiracy from mainland Greece to the Principalities, with very important consequences when the day of revolution came. Nor had Kapodistrias heard the last of him, for towards the end of 1818, while he was attending the Tsar at the Conference of Aix-la-Chapelle, he received a request from Galatis for the return of a document

issued by the British Consul in Bucharest confirming that as an
Ionian islander he was under British protection.[33] Without this
document (which had been confiscated in St. Petersburg) he
could not travel back to Ithaki. Kapodistrias ordered its
release, and Galatis set out for Greece, where he was murdered
early in 1819 by agents of the *Philiki Etairia*.[34]

The Galatis affair left Kapodistrias in a state of extreme
nervous tension, but uncompromised in the eyes of the Tsar,
who showed his confidence by awarding him a high decoration.[35] It may be argued that this proves the Tsar's complicity
to have been as great as Kapodistrias', but it is more probable
that he simply took a calmer view than his Foreign Minister
and liked to keep his options open. He sympathised with the
Greeks and would do anything short of going to war with the
Turks in order to help them. According to Ypsilantis, he had
known about the *Philiki Etairia* since 1816, though that date
may not be precise; and Ypsilantis later recalled many occasions
when the Tsar spoke vaguely but benevolently about the liberation of the Greeks.[36] During 1817 Perraivos actually submitted
to the Tsar through Alexandros Stourdza a detailed plan of the
insurrection in Greece.[37] The fact that no reaction is on record,
either favourable or unfavourable, suggests that the Tsar's
attitude was not to take the idea either seriously or tragically.
Kapodistrias' attitude, however, was very different.

He wrote to many leading Greeks in Odessa and the Danubian
Principalities to warn them against the conspirators, and he
showed his letters to the Tsar. Later he regretted not having
also written to the Ambassador in Constantinople, so that he
could warn the Russian consuls in the Levant. But he did himself write more than once to the Consul at Jassy, and received
several reports from him on the indiscreet conduct of Galatis
and other conspirators.[38] It was certainly clear to this official
that the *Philiki Etairia* had no support from Kapodistrias. Early
in 1818 he at last sent a warning circular through the Ambassador to the consuls, to the effect that the obligation to protect the
Greek subjects of the Porte must not risk 'placing them under
the threat of danger or inspiring suspicion in the government
under whose yoke they live'.[39] Meanwhile the *Philiki Etairia* was
recruiting members fast and furiously; and many of them
joined it under the misapprehension that Kapodistrias was its

unnamed leader. Among those who made this mistake was Petrobey Mavromikhalis, head of the clan which dominated the Mani in southern Peloponnese.

As a result many more indiscreet approaches were made to Kapodistrias. A group of *kapetanioi*, who had served with him in Levkas, visited him in St. Petersburg early in 1818. He warned them against the *Philiki Etairia*, of which they pretended to have no knowledge; and he gave them a letter of introduction to the ambassador at Constantinople, asking him to treat them as Russian officers.[40] Later in the same year, when he was visiting Odessa and Kishinev with the Tsar, he met other members of the Society, one of whom claimed to have given him the secret sign and to have received the appropriate response, which he believed Kapodistrias must have learnt from Galatis.[41] The story hardly seems probable, especially since one of the consequences of the visit of the Tsar and Kapodistrias to southern Russia was that the headquarters of the *Philiki Etairia* was moved to Constantinople for fear that it would be expelled from Odessa by the Russian authorities.[42] Legends sprang easily to the minds of Greeks, then as always, and they passionately longed to believe that their most celebrated fellow-countryman was at the heart of their movement. The fact is that Kapodistrias kept the Tsar fully informed of his contacts and never acted contrary to his master's policy.

That is not to say that he did not seek to influence Alexander's policy in directions which would promote Greek as well as Russian interests. A certain ambivalence was beginning to develop between them, though without any conscious subterfuge on either side. Kapodistrias was responsible for advising the Tsar on the whole scope of foreign policy, which he had to mould into a consistent whole. His personal view was that if, as Metternich feared, Europe was threatened with further revolution, the way to forestall it was to move towards constitutional government based on popular consent. The Tsar shared this view so far as to grant a constitution in Poland, as well as helping to promote constitutions in France, Switzerland and elsewhere. But gradually bitter experience and the awful warnings of Metternich convinced Alexander that the risks of constitutionalism were too great. At the same time it was clear that the treatment recommended by Kapodistrias could not possibly be applied in the Ottoman Empire. On the contrary, in that quarter Kapodistrias was constantly urging the Tsar to threaten force, even at the risk of war, with the scarcely concealed hope that independence for the Balkan peoples would be the inevitable by-product. It was because he was sure that eventually he could carry the Tsar with him in this policy that he consistently urged his Greek friends not to engage in revolutionary conspiracies. But the prospect of success grew more and more remote. As the Tsar became increasingly alarmed by the revolutionary state of Europe, and even by the threat of revolution in Russia itself, he became correspondingly more reluctant to risk war with Turkey.

Kapodistrias' Greek contacts became equally more and more impatient. In Kishinev, during his tour of southern Russia with the Tsar in 1818, two representatives of the Greek *hospodars* of the Principalities came to pay their respects.[43] One of the two was Alexandros Mavrokordatos the younger, later a prominent leader of the revolution and a bitter antagonist of Kapodistrias. In a private conversation, he told Kapodistrias that 'as Greeks they longed to hear that the Russian armies were about to cross the River Pruth'. But Kapodistrias' reply – of which only his own account survives – gave him no encouragement. Later in the same year, at about the same time as the Conference of Aix-la-Chapelle was assembling, a crucial meeting of the leaders of the *Philiki Etairia* took place in Constantinople, at which it was decided that Xanthos should go to St. Petersburg to make a formal offer of the leadership to Kapodistrias.[44] More than a year was to pass before this decision was actually put into effect, for various reasons. As Xanthos did not know Kapodistrias personally, and as it was socially impossible for a mere merchant's clerk, such as he was, to approach a great aristocrat unintroduced, he went first to Mount Pelion to obtain a letter of introduction from Anthimos Gazis. Then a series of crises in the organisation of the Society in Bessarabia obliged him to spend much of the year 1819 in straightening things out. An additional cause of delay was that Kapodistrias was absent from the capital. Before Xanthos finally reached St. Petersburg in January 1820, Kapodistrias' relations with his fellow-countrymen had passed through another agonising crisis.

After the Conference of Aix-la-Chapelle, Kapodistrias

obtained the Tsar's leave to re-visit Corfu, where his ageing parents were approaching the end of their days. It was a painful visit, coinciding as it did with the final cession of Parga, the former Venetian dependency on the mainland of Epirus, by the British government to Ali Paşa. Kapodistrias formed the most unfavourable impressions of the administration of his native islands by Sir Thomas Maitland, who was variously known as King Tom and the Abortion. Later in the year Kapodistrias remonstrated vainly with the British government, both on a personal visit to London and in a long drawn-out correspondence. More significant in the present context were his contacts with Greeks in the islands and with the *kapetanioi* and others who flocked to see him from the mainland. Among those he met, with or without the knowledge of Maitland, were Kolokotronis, who had served with him in Levkas in 1807, and Paparrigopoulos, the interpreter from the Russian consulate in Patras.[45] The meeting with Kolokotronis was quite open, though he and Kapodistrias also had a private conversation about which nothing was ever divulged. Paparrigopoulos chose to make a considerable mystery of his visit, although as an official employee of the Russian government there was no reason why he should not call on his eminent superior. The fact that Paparrigopoulos' visit to Corfu was both preceded and followed by visits to Ali Paşa in Ioannina naturally excited Maitland's suspicion. But Kapodistrias was, as usual, extremely cautious. When his visitors told him that they hoped to hear 'that soon Russia would again place them under her powerful aegis', he replied that the Tsar would never risk war with Turkey or a quarrel with Britain for their sakes. They must therefore concentrate on education and leave the rest to time and providence. To ensure himself against misrepresentation, he embodied his advice in a written memorandum, which was soon afterwards published.[46] Neither his admirers nor his detractors were ever able to prove that any more suggestive words crossed his lips.

Inevitably, however, his visit to Corfu not only prompted widespread speculation but also accelerated recruitment to the *Philiki Etairia*. His brother Viaro was initiated early in 1819, and Kapodistrias presumably knew it.[47] The Society was virtually ceasing to be secret, and the assumption that Kapodistrias himself was intimately involved came to be taken for granted.

When Kapodistrias rejoined the Tsar in Warsaw in the autumn of 1819, after a separation of nine months, he found his master in a greatly changed mood. Alexander was convinced that Europe was on the brink of revolution again, and therefore by no means inclined to take such a relaxed view as in the past of the restlessness of the Greeks.[48] Terrified by a series of crises which had led to the Carlsbad Decrees in Germany and the Six Acts in Britain, the Tsar had convinced himself that there was a 'directing committee' of international revolutionaries established in Paris, with its tentacles spread everywhere, including even Russia and the Ottoman Empire. Kapodistrias was, therefore, more than ever anxious that the recklessness of his fellow-countrymen should not compromise his own position. Unfortunately that was exactly what it was about to do.

Early in 1820, soon after his return to St. Petersburg, Kapodistrias learned of the conspiratorial activities of Xanthos and others in the Principalities. He also heard that they were associating his own name and that of the *Philomouson Etairia* with their activities. He wrote to the Consul at Jassy on 15 January instructing him to summon the leading conspirators to him and order them to desist.[49] But things were already getting out of hand. Xanthos was at last on his way to St. Petersburg to carry out the fateful mission entrusted to him over a year before. So was an emissary from Petrobey Mavromikhalis, by name Kyriakos Kamarinos.[50] The latter arrived first, bearing two letters from Petrobey which had been written on the assumption that Kapodistrias was, in fact, the leader of the *Philiki Etairia*. Kapodistrias drafted a long reply to Petrobey with his customary caution, a copy of which survived in the Russian archives and was published in 1868.[51] He also took pains to disabuse Kamarinos of the delusion that he was the leader of the Society. Kamarinos was so shocked to learn the truth that when he returned to Constantinople he complained bitterly to the other leading members of the Society, and caused so much trouble that they murdered him as they had earlier murdered Galatis.[52] As a result Kapodistrias' letter never reached Petrobey. He assumed, when he eventually learned of the murders, that the motive for them was to conceal from other members of the Society that he himself had nothing to do with it.

While this embarrassing visitor was being disposed of, there came the still more embarrassing visit of Xanthos. This is the crucial episode in the story of Kapodistrias' relations with the *Philiki Etairia*. It should be stated at once that absolute certainty about what took place is unattainable; one can do no more than establish a balance of probabilities. The fact that Kapodistrias made no mention of the episode, nor even of Xanthos' name, in his autobiography is itself suspicious. But what to suspect is another question. Again one faces the dilemma that Kapodistrias' friends and enemies both wanted to believe the same thing, though for opposite reasons, and were, therefore, equally inclined to bend or stretch the evidence. The following is the most plausible reconstruction I can offer.

After a halt in Moscow to make contact with fellow conspirators there, Xanthos arrived in St. Petersburg on 27 January 1820. He had with him the seal of the Society, which bore round the circumference the initials of the principal leaders – among them 'I' for Ioannis, Kapodistrias' first name, in the central position. This small detail is significant as a symptom of the conspirators' habit of compromising Kapodistrias behind his back. Two days after his arrival, Xanthos met Kapodistrias and handed over Gazis' letter, which recalled conversations they used to have in Vienna:

> Remember, Count, when we were at Vienna, talking of the pitiful condition of our people, you said: 'Have we no Thrasyboulos among us?' See how many Thrasybouloi present themselves before you today.[53]

Here again is an example of the conspirators' habit of compromising Kapodistrias by drawing extreme conclusions from the casual effusions of romantic rhetoric which come naturally to the Greek tongue. Without beating about the bush, Xanthos then appealed to him to accept the leadership 'either directly or through some suitable arrangement'.[54] Kapodistrias replied that as the Tsar's Minister he could not accept, 'and much else'. Undeterred, Xanthos had a second meeting with him, which was arranged by a Greek secretary of Kapodistrias' who was a member of the Society. This time, while again refusing the leadership, Kapodistrias said that 'if the leaders know of any other ways to achieve their object, let them use them, and he prayed to God to help them'.[55] No doubt Kapodistrias meant no more than his customary reference of the problem to educational progress, moral improvement, time and providence. But Xanthos leaped to the conclusion that he was being cryptically advised to seek another leader, who might command equal respect.

The obvious alternative was to turn to Alexandros Ypsilantis, a gallant soldier, a favourite A.D.C. of the Tsar, and son of a former *hospodar* of Wallachia. He was not yet initiated into the *Philiki Etairia*, though two of his brothers were; and one of them (Nikolaos) later wrote that Alexandros was already spoken of in Constantinople 'on an equal footing with Count Kapodistrias as leader of the *Philiki Etairia*'.[56] To him Xanthos duly went, although he had no authority to do so. The decision taken by the leaders in September 1818 had referred only to Kapodistrias; and Xanthos' colleagues in Moscow, with whom he was in correspondence throughout, expressly charged him to stay in St. Petersburg only for so long as was necessary to persuade Kapodistrias, but if that proved finally impossible, to return forthwith.[57] The fact that Xanthos disregarded their advice has been interpreted to suggest that he was explicitly advised by Kapodistrias to turn to Ypsilantis, which he would not otherwise have done without reference back; and this would account for Ypsilantis' bitterness when the Tsar and Kapodistrias later disowned him. It is impossible to be sure, but the argument seems far-fetched. Xanthos, as one of the founders of the *Etairia*, was capable of acting on his own discretion; and he was also capable of hinting to Ypsilantis that he had Kapodistrias' support even if he had not. His memoirs are silent on the point. Others placed it on record that Xanthos always intended to 'knock on both doors' and offer the leadership to whichever might open.[58] All that is certain is that he next contrived to meet Ypsilantis through an introduction by Ioannis Manos, a Greek employed in the British Embassy and a cousin of the Ypsilantis family.

There were two crucial meetings between Xanthos and Ypsilantis. At the first, Xanthos began by being non-committal. He said that he had come to St. Petersburg on business, but gradually brought the conversation round to the condition of the Greeks.[59] Ypsilantis was shocked by what Xanthos told him, which was worse than anything he had known. He de-

clared that he would do anything and make any sacrifice to
serve them. Xanthos was convinced of his patriotism and
sincerity. He then admitted that he had another purpose in
mind in approaching Ypsilantis, but he would not reveal it to
him until the following day. Impatiently Ypsilantis demanded
to know at once, but Xanthos insisted on a night for reflection.
The next day he returned and made the same offer to Ypsilantis
that he had already made to Kapodistrias. Another crucial
doubt now enters the story, again involving the role of
Kapodistrias. Was he informed or consulted before or after
Ypsilantis accepted the proffered leadership?

All accounts of these historic days rest necessarily on the
recollections of Kapodistrias, Xanthos or Ypsilantis. Kapodistrias was tight-lipped to the end of his life, though by implication he always denied having played any part in Ypsilantis'
fateful decision before it was taken. It must be remembered
that Kapodistrias never knew what Ypsilantis told the other
witnesses, so he had no opportunity to rebut explicitly the story
Ypsilantis put into circulation, for all the relevant memoirs
were written after both men were dead. In his autobiography
Kapodistrias mentioned two private meetings with Ypsilantis
'in the winter of 1820', which in the context must mean
February or March.[60] He implied that the meetings took place
after Ypsilantis' application for leave from the Tsar's service to
travel abroad, which means after he had accepted the leadership of the *Etairia*. On the first occasion, Ypsilantis told him that
he was going to France and asked for an introduction to the Duc
de Richelieu, who might be able to help him over the recovery
of the confiscated family mansion in Constantinople, which had
at one time been used as the French Ambassador's residence.
The story was not wholly implausible, though it was only one of
several that Ypsilantis used for his plan to travel abroad. For
the Tsar's ears, his purpose was to restore health; for the leaders
of the *Etairia*, it was to appeal for funds in France and even
from the U.S.A. In any case Kapodistrias gave him the letter he
requested. Nothing more compromising seems to have been
said at their first meeting, according to Kapodistrias' account:
but things went much further at the second.

At their farewell meeting, Kapodistrias recorded that
Ypsilantis 'spoke of the desperate situation in which the Greeks

were placed as a consequence of the political system of Russia and England, and of the war which the Porte was about to wage against Ali Paşa, who had been proclaimed a rebel at this date'. His account of the further discussion between them is explicit but not wholly frank. He wrote that he told Ypsilantis these matters were beyond their competence. Ypsilantis should be on his guard against 'intriguers representing themselves without authority as spokesmen for the Greek nation'. By further calling them 'miserable merchants' clerks', Kapodistrias clearly showed that he knew they were talking about Xanthos. Ypsilantis replied that some of them were respectable people. He tried to show Kapodistrias a paper relating to the formation of a society for raising funds for the liberation of Greece, but Kapodistrias refused to look at it. Ypsilantis must not be led astray by such conspirators, he warned him again, for they would bring ruin on Greece. 'And what will become of the poor Greeks?' asked Ypsilantis. 'Are they to be forever massacred by the Turks, and will no policy do anything for them?' Kapodistrias replied that those Greeks who had arms would fight as they had always fought. The rebellion of Ali Paşa might help them; so might the passage of time and other events; 'but they will demand nothing of European policy'. To try to provoke disturbances in order to force the Tsar's hand would be disastrous for the Greeks. It would 'precipitate this unhappy nation into an abyss of troubles from which no power on earth will be able to extricate them'. With a final warning to Ypsilantis to be careful, 'because his language had made me suspect that he was surrounded by dangerous men, more astute than himself', Kapodistrias sent him on his way and thought no more about it. Such was Kapodistrias' own story, written six years later.

There is nothing of substance in Xanthos' account which directly contradicts Kapodistras. But Ypsilantis was more loquacious, and a number of versions have survived of what he said to different friends in his last years. Xanthos' memoirs, Ypsilantis' own letters, the reminiscences of his friends (particularly his brother Nikolaos, the Countess Lulu Thürheim[61] and the Comte de la Garde Chambonas[62]), and the first history of the *Philiki Etairia* by Ioannis Philimon, all recorded partial and sometimes incompatible accounts of Ypsilantis' recollections of these momentous meetings. It must be remembered that many of these sources were more or less prejudiced against Kapodistrias. Nikolaos Ypsilantis was later at the centre of an intrigue, based in Paris, against Kapodistrias when he was President of Greece. Lulu Thürheim, one of two Austrian sisters who moved much in Russian circles during the Congress of Vienna, was deeply in love with Alexandros Ypsilantis and blamed Kapodistrias bitterly for his tragic fate. So did the Comte de la Garde Chambonas, a French playboy and gossip-writer, who had likewise known both men at Vienna in 1815. Some of their stories need to be read with caution. The accounts of Xanthos and Philimon, on the other hand, though certainly not disinterested, are more dependable.

Some points are common ground and beyond dispute – for instance, that Kapodistrias would not allow Ypsilantis a formal interview with the Tsar – but others are more uncertain. Philimon, who had access to the documents of the *Etairia* as well as the recollections of many participants, was in no doubt that Kapodistrias absolutely rejected any personal involvement with the *Etairia*, whose existence he regarded as 'untimely'.[63] He was equally definite that Xanthos approached Ypsilantis solely on his own initiative. He accepted Xanthos' story that Ypsilantis agreed to accept the leadership on the spot at their second meeting, and only told Kapodistrias afterwards. In fact, Philimon says that a week passed after his acceptance before Ypsilantis was able to invite Kapodistrias to dinner at the cavalry barracks where he lived, because he had been ill; and this detail is confirmed by the reminiscences of his brother, Nikolaos.[64] But Ypsilantis himself told the Countess Lulu Thürheim on his deathbed in 1828 that he had asked Xanthos for three days to reflect and to consult Kapodistrias, in whom, she wrote, he had 'blind confidence'.[65]

Both accounts – the one more deeply involving Kapodistrias, the other less so – are derived from first-hand recollection, and it is impossible to reconcile them. But both accounts agree that whether the meeting between Ypsilantis and Kapodistrias took place before or after Ypsilantis had accepted the leadership, he used the occasion to inform Kapodistrias of his plans; and in that respect they imply that Kapodistrias suppressed the truth in his autobiography. In the version preserved in Philimon's

Historical Essay on the Greek Revolution (a later work than his book on the *Philiki Etairia*), Kapodistrias is reported to have 'opposed no contrary opinion' to Ypsilantis' plans, to have 'supported his decision' and commented that 'the appearance of a few thousand rebels in Greece is enough for Russia to help to the utmost of her ability'. Substantially the same words were recorded by Ypsilantis' brother, Nikolaos. But Philimon also wrote that Kapodistrias refused to allow Ypsilantis to see the Tsar, and no account contradicts that version. He knew that the Tsar must refuse his consent to Ypsilantis' plans; but Ypsilantis insisted on his wish to see the Tsar, and Kapodistrias therefore asked him to submit a request in writing. On receiving it the next day, Kapodistrias asked for a week's delay. During the interval, Ypsilantis finally committed himself by signing a document accepting the leadership of the *Etairia*. The text survives, dated 12 April 1820 in the Old Style. At the end of the week Kapodistrias told him definitely that there could be no question of an interview with the Tsar, 'who was in no way disposed to face war with Turkey or complications with England'. On the other hand, wrote Philimon, 'he added no further word of discouragement'. Plainly he knew that the die was about to be cast.[66] Such was Philimon's account.

Philimon also recorded that when he was writing his earlier history of the *Philiki Etairia*, Kapodistrias' surviving brother Viaro wrote to beg him 'for the sake of our country to safeguard the reputation of my brother Ioannis'.[67] He obligingly did his best. In fact, Philimon categorically denied the claim which Ypsilantis repeatedly made to his colleagues and friends, that he had the agreement of both Kapodistrias and the Tsar to his plans.[68] Ypsilantis made this claim, according to Philimon, without authority for psychological reasons. When it is remembered that Ypsilantis was also a party to the murder of Kamarinos, for having revealed that Kapodistrias had denied all connection with the *Etairia*, it is not difficult to accept Philimon's account. Yet the historian also contrived to suggest doubts of his own by hinting at another version of the relationship between the two men. After recording that Kapodistrias disapproved of Ypsilantis' venture, he went on to say that 'Kapodistrias spoke to other people in this way because he was the Tsar's minister and did not want futile demonstrations';

but that Ypsilantis 'recognised his meaning, accepted his instructions, and adopted a system of paying no attention to the faint-hearted among his companions, who vaguely counselled waiting for more favourable circumstances at some future date before embarking on the task'.[69] The natural inference is that Kapodistrias had connived at Ypsilantis' initiative, but Philimon was protecting him as he had promised Viaro he would.

Certainly Ypsilantis had no doubt that Kapodistrias explicitly encouraged him. Early in the year 1828, shortly after his release from Austrian imprisonment and shortly before his death, he wrote to the new Tsar, Nicholas I:

Count Kapodistrias, whom I consulted, agreed with my judgement, found my plans and preparations sound and appropriate, and advised me to act, to take the initiative in putting them into effect, and not to hesitate about the prospect of success.[70]

Apart from this letter to the new Tsar, he gave a long account of his last days in the capital to the two Austrian sisters, Lulu and Constance Thürheim, on his deathbed in January 1828. While they tended him lovingly in his last illness, they heard a detailed account of the drama of 1820-1 from the lips of its principal victim, and the elder sister, Lulu, wrote it all down in her memoirs. She even added a corroborative detail of her own.[71] Kapodistrias himself told her at Geneva (some time between 1822 and 1827), that when Ypsilantis told the Tsar about his plans and asked to be released from the Russian army, the Tsar jumped for joy, clapped his hands and exclaimed: 'Bravo, young man! That's what I call what's needed!' The utter improbability of this incident is plain. Even if the Tsar had behaved as Lulu Thürheim described, which is unbelievable, Kapodistrias could hardly have been so foolish as to tell her the story. Yet, when she was reporting Ypsilantis' own account, her story carries conviction. Beyond doubt it was what Ypsilantis himself believed.

Ypsilantis was unaware of the heavy strain under which Kapodistrias was suffering at the time of their meeting. He was engaged in drafting his reply to Petrobey; Kamarinos was behaving indiscreetly in St. Petersburg, to the annoyance of the

Tsar; many Greeks were actively intriguing in St. Petersburg, including many members of his own staff. There is no trace of these tensions in Ypsilantis' account to Lulu Thürheim. Kapodistrias, he told her, was 'fully informed and enthusiastically approved his patriotic desire to sacrifice his life for the happiness of his country'.[72] He went even further, saying that 'even if the Tsar's European policy did not permit him to declare himself openly in support of the Greek cause, nevertheless his heart was absolutely on the side of Greece'. Once more the Tsar was implicated. According to Ypsilantis' version, as recorded by Lulu Thürheim, the Tsar repeated 'at every opportunity' that although he could not act himself, 'the cause of Greece was also the cause of Russia'. Kapodistrias himself, by the same account, was so delighted when he saw Ypsilantis' plans that 'he jumped for joy, embraced Ypsilantis and showered him with praise'. It is plain that once more the Countess's imagination carried her away: jumping for joy on such an occasion was even more out of character for Kapodistrias than for the Tsar. Her story, written with a lover's devotion for a dying man, is impossible to take as literal truth.

The myth of the Tsar's complicity, nevertheless, dies hard. It has even been suggested that the plans and the timing of the Greek rising were concerted with the Russian government.[73] The assumption is made that Ypsilantis would not have dared to accept the leadership of the *Etairia* without the Tsar's express approval; that the object was to create a disturbance in the Principalities in order to justify a Russian intervention there; and that only Ypsilantis' folly in publicly claiming Russian support caused the plot to break down, by compelling the Tsar to make an equally public disavowal of it. The argument is far-fetched, on every count. General indications of the Tsar's mood at the time suggest that he was determined, under the growing influence of Metternich, to avoid war with Turkey at almost any cost.[74] None of the known exchanges between Kapodistrias, Ypsilantis and the Tsar implicates the last in any way. It is not necessary to doubt that the Tsar at one time or another used the words attributed to him. He did, indeed, frequently talk in terms of general affection about the Greeks. But it does not follow that the words quoted were uttered on this specific occasion to encourage a Greek rising. In any case they constitute no challenge to the statement that Kapodistrias would not allow Ypsilantis even to meet the Tsar. Whatever Ypsilantis may have said to Lulu Thürheim on his deathbed, his written testimony virtually acquits the Tsar of complicity.

Neither at the time nor later did Ypsilantis claim more in writing than that he thought he was acting in accordance with the Tsar's general line of policy. In the three letters which he wrote to Alexander and his successor from Austria (at the end of 1821, in 1826, and in January 1828), he never so much as hinted at any complicity on Alexander's part, though he categorically implicated Kapodistrias. His last letter, dated 14 January 1828 and addressed to Nicholas I, was equally revealing about Alexander's mentality and his own. After describing Kapodistrias' role in the passage quoted above, he went on to say that he was convinced, from his earlier conversations with the Tsar, that he would approve:

> It is true that his Majesty always spoke vaguely, but with such benevolence that my hopes were kindled even more and turned into a certainty about the future. I still seem to hear him saying to me with his habitual kindness: 'I could not die happy without doing something for my poor Greeks. I await only a sign from heaven, and I should recognise it as soon as the Greeks point it out to me, for they deserve their happiness. Then I could say: You see these men; they demand their liberty; they deserve it; help them.' But he would prudently add: 'I must think of it in my personal capacity. One shot near the Danube will set the whole of Europe in flames.'[75]

It is impossible to doubt either the authenticity or the implications of this account. The words attributed to the Tsar were wholly characteristic, and so was Ypsilantis' interpretation of them. The Tsar, as always, was displaying a sentimental good will towards an oppressed people whose religion he shared; but as always, too, he was keeping his options open, and even pursuing two rival policies at once – that of Kapodistrias and that of Metternich, supported by Nesselrode. He had committed himself to nothing. But Ypsilantis assumed that he wanted only an excuse for intervention, which might be provided by a spontaneous rising of the Greeks. His letter went on to say that he could not tell whether the Tsar's 'vague expressions' similarly convinced Kapodistrias, who had 'considered it useless to warn the Tsar of the detailed content of my plans'. Kapodistrias had also, in the words of Ypsilantis, 'committed the error of preventing me from personally informing the Tsar, and it is to that error that all my misfortunes are due'. Ypsilantis' judgment was almost certainly at fault, since the Tsar was in no mood to sanction such a venture as he planned; but his testimony reinforces the presumption that the Tsar was innocent.

One further episode completes the exculpation of the Tsar. It rests again on Ypsilantis' recollection, as recorded by his brother Nikolaos.[76] It appears that despite Kapodistrias' precautions, Ypsilantis did, in fact, have a brief meeting with the Tsar in June 1820, before leaving St. Petersburg, but only by accident. He had gone in person to the Tsar's country palace at Tsarskoe Selo to obtain his leave of absence, undoubtedly in the hope that they might meet. And so it happened: he encountered the Tsar walking in the garden, and had a brief conversation.

But despite his efforts to introduce the burning subject in his mind, he was unsuccessful. When he tried to talk about the Greeks, the Tsar cut him short, saying: 'You are young and eager, as always, my friend, but you can see that Europe is at peace.' Ypsilantis did not dare to continue. Such testimony from a source so close to him, and so hostile to Kapodistrias, must be regarded as conclusive. If Ypsilantis could tell his own brother nothing more compromising about the Tsar's role, there was nothing to tell.

The exculpation of the Tsar, however, seems only to implicate Kapodistrias more deeply. It is easy to find clues pointing to his complicity, since veiled language and insinuation, which were the order of the day, can be interpreted or misinterpreted to taste. But his own story never varied. He denied all knowledge of the plot, both in 1821 and in his autobiography; and none of his colleagues hinted at any suspicion against him. Metternich, who claimed to have proofs of his complicity, made the mistake of producing them, and so destroyed his own case, for the evidence was worthless. Perhaps even more persuasive than Kapodistrias' denials in 1821, or his silence in 1826, are his emphatic remarks after he became President of Greece; for by that time it was not only less compromising to have been associated with the *Philiki Etairia*, but almost unheroic not to have been. Yet his denials continued. A journalist who knew him in his last years reported after his death that Kapodistrias had often said in his hearing 'if he had known of the coming outbreak, which was untimely in relation to his diplomatic plans, he would have sent Ypsilantis in chains to Siberia'.[77] A more circumstantial account was given by his secretary, Nikolaos Dragoumis, of a conversation with Kapodistrias on Poros in 1828. After talking suspiciously about secret societies in their own time, Kapodistrias went on to attack the *Philiki Etairia* in the severest terms.

> He summarised the whole course of its history, referred to the invitations to himself and his own negative replies, and ended by exclaiming in passionate terms these actual words: 'Yes, that's what you did – you tore your own eyes out!'[78]

The young Dragoumis, then in his twentieth year, was dumbfounded by Kapodistrias' denunciation of men whom he had learned to look upon as national heroes. From his vivid description of the shock, there can be no doubt of the authenticity of his story. There could be no reason, either, for Kapodistrias to lie to his private secretary so many years after the event. Such is the circumstantial evidence on which the assessment of Kapodistrias' role must rest.

The course of events between Xanthos' visit to St. Petersburg and the outbreak of the revolution a year later is consistent with this account, though a more compromising construction can also be put on it. Ypsilantis' movements after he accepted the leadership were public knowledge. He visited Germany, where by chance he met his friend Chambonas and told him that the rising was imminent and that it had the Tsar's support. This would have been a crazy imprudence – for Chambonas was a notorious gossip – were it not for the fact that Chambonas was able to tell him in reply that he had already heard about it from another Russian friend.[79] Ypsilantis next travelled through Russia with Xanthos to his estate near Kishinev, where Greeks congregated to join him with the connivance of the local Governors-General (Langeron and Inzov) in Odessa and Bessarabia.[80] He carried a passport signed by Nesselrode and a letter from the Tsar's mother to a local senior officer, so there

was no secret about his movements.[81] He corresponded freely
with leading Greeks, and also with Serb and Rumanian leaders,
and he drafted many heroic proclamations.[82] It is hard to
believe that none of these activities came to the knowledge of
Kapodistrias between April 1820 and March 1821, yet that is
what Kapodistrias explicitly asserted in his autobiography;[83]
and the Russian archives have so far yielded no document that
would contradict him. The most reasonable explanation is that
the Governors-General in southern Russia tacitly assumed that
the right policy was a blind eye and a conspiracy of silence, so
they neither sought instructions nor sent reports of what was
going on under their noses.

For this they were severely rebuked by Kapodistrias and
Nesselrode after Ypsilantis crossed the River Pruth on 6 March
1821. Kapodistrias' reactions cannot have been feigned when
the news reached him during the Conference at Laibach
(Ljubljana). Even Metternich described him as 'like a man
struck by a thunderbolt'.[84] He drafted the Tsar's denunciation
of Ypsilantis in deep sorrow; and on learning that Stroganov
in Constantinople had already disowned Russian support for
the rising, he wrote to congratulate him.[85] All his statements
and letters at this date – to his colleagues at Laibach, to
Stroganov, to the Governors-General, to Greek friends, to
Roxani Stourdza (now the Countess Edling) – without exception repudiate, explicitly or tacitly, any hint of complicity.[86]
Yet his policy had not altered, and he still hoped that out of the
'criminal enterprise', as he called it, some good result might
providentially emerge.[87] One cannot say whether it was due to
providence or calculation that Kapodistrias' letter to Ypsilantis
and Nesselrode's rebuke to Langeron did not reach them with
the fastest possible despatch, so that the headquarters of the
Greek rising were allowed to continue functioning on Russian
soil and Ypsilantis could persist in his fraudulent claim to have
the Tsar's support for a few more weeks. But it is a matter of
history that in the event it did him no good.

The conclusion is that it must remain uncertain how deeply
Kapodistrias was involved in Ypsilantis' plans. That he knew
what was going on between Ypsilantis and the *Philiki Etairia* is
virtually certain; that he told the Tsar is highly improbable;
whether he approved Ypsilantis' plans is the most problematical

point of all. Almost certainly Ypsilantis was already committed before he saw Kapodistrias in March 1820. On that point, the version of Philimon must be preferred to that of Lulu Thürheim, although both rest on Ypsilantis' word, because the story which is less creditable to Ypsilantis' judgment is the more likely to be true. Not less certainly, whatever plans Ypsilantis may have revealed to Kapodistrias early in 1820 were not those which he eventually carried out in 1821, for many changes took place in the intervening twelve months, with disastrous results.[88] Probably the truth about Kapodistrias' position lies somewhere between tacit acquiescence and explicit approval. He heard but did not want to know, what Ypsilantis intended; perhaps he actively forgot. There was undoubtedly some measure of misunderstanding, which was inherent in the character of the two men. Alexandros Ypsilantis was a romantic extrovert, simple-minded, volatile, and, in the most literal sense, quixotic. Kapodistrias was introverted, subtle, cautious, and accustomed to devious and diplomatic language which Ypsilantis was ill-equipped to construe. Kapodistrias was also overwhelmingly preoccupied with other problems, particularly the state of central Europe and the preparations for the conferences at Troppau and Laibach. More important psychologically, he was suffering from an agony of divided counsels. It would not be surprising if in the circumstances the two men simply misunderstood each other. When Ypsilantis declared that Kapodistrias 'agreed with my judgement and advised me to act', and when Kapodistrias declared that 'there piled on my head a weight of responsibility which I had done nothing to incur by my conduct', both men were deeply convinced that they were telling the truth.[89] Both suffered bitterly from the consequences, Ypsilantis dying in exile in 1828 of the effects of seven years' imprisonment, and Kapodistrias in 1831 from an assassin's bullet. But the Greeks ultimately gained their independence from the fateful mistake. It seemed plain to the Greeks that Kapodistrias was behind Ypsilantis, and the Tsar behind Kapodistrias. They put two and two together and made *eikosi-ena*; and no one can say how or when it would otherwise have come about.

NOTES TO CHAPTER 5

This chapter is also being published in *Neo-Hellenika II* (1972), the publication of the Center for Neo-Hellenic Studies at the University of Austin, Texas, U.S.A.

1. Theodoros S. Makris, *O Ioannis Kapodistrias* (Kerkyra, 1964) esp. pp. 152–64.

2. A. Oţetea, 'L'Hétairie d'il y a cent cinquante ans', *Balkan Studies*, VI (1965) 255–64.

3. G. L. Arsh, *Etairistskoe dvizhenie v Rossii* (Moscow, 1970) esp. chs. 4–8.

4. Patricia K. Grimsted, *The Foreign Ministers of Alexander I* (Berkeley-Los Angeles, 1969), esp. ch. 7.

5. Oţetea, loc. cit., and in 'Les Grandes Puissances et le mouvement Hétairiste dans les Principautés Roumaines', *Balkan Studies*, VII (1966) 379–94.

6. P. K. Enepekidis, *Rigas-Ypsilantis-Kapodistrias* (Athens, 1965) pp. 187–9, 195–6.

7. Makris, *Kapodistrias*, pp. 30–43.

8. K. Mendelssohn-Bartholdy, *Graf Johann Kapodistrias* (Berlin, 1864) pp. 398–9.

9. P. G. Kritikos, 'O Ioannis Kapodistrias tekton kanonikos', *O Eranistis*, III (1965) 136. (See also Chapter 4.)

10. Hugh Seton-Watson, *The Russian Empire 1801–1917* (Oxford, 1967) p. 185.

11. I. Philimon, *Dokimion istorikon peri tis Philikis Etairias* (Nafplion,1834) pp. 127–8.

12. Makris, *Kapodistrias*, p. 17, quoting S. M. Theotokis.

13. Arsh, *Etairistskoe dvizhenie v Rossii*, p. 161, quoting Russian State Archives.

14. Makris, *Kapodistrias*, p. 49, quoting A. Andreadis.

15. Arsh, *Etairistskoe dvizhenie v Rossii*, pp. 50, 64–5; P. K. Grimsted, 'Capodistrias and a New Order for Restoration Europe: The Liberal Ideas of a Russian Foreign Minister, 1814–1822', *Journal of Modern History*, XL (1968) p. 169 footnote.

16. Enepekidis, *Rigas*, pp. 177–80.

17. Kapodistrias, *Aperçu de ma carrière*, in vol. III of *Sbornik imperatorskogo russkogo istoricheskogo obshchestva* (St. Petersburg, 1868) pp. 171–2.

18. Makris, *Kapodistrias*, p. 136.

19. Enepekidis, *Rigas*, p. 189.

20. C. G. Lahovary, *Mémoires de l'Amiral P. Tchitchagof* (Paris, 1909) pp. 387–9.

21. S. Lascaris, *Capodistrias avant la révolution grecque* (Lausanne, 1918) esp. ch. III.

22. *Sbornik*, III, p. 166; Grimsted, *Foreign Ministers*, pp. 231–3.

23. *Megali Elliniki Enkyklopaideia*, XIII, s.v. Tsakalov.

24. *Sbornik*, III, p. 195.

25. Mendelssohn-Bartholdy, *Graf Johann Kapodistrias*, pp. 28–9.

26. *Sbornik*, CXIX, p. 208.

27. Enepekidis, *Rigas*, pp. 186-90 and *Ioannis Kapodistrias - 176 anekdotes epistoles pros ton patera tou (1809-1820)* (Athens, 1972) p. 227.

28. Arsh, *Etairistskoe dvizhenie v Rossii*, pp. 156-7.

29. A. Papadopoulos-Vretos, *Mémoires biographiques-historiques* (Paris, 1837) I, pp. 37-9.

30. Enepekidis, *Rigas*, pp. 200-7.

31. Arsh, *Etairistskoe dvizhenie v Rossii*, pp. 177-8.

32. *Sbornik*, III, pp. 215-20; Arsh, *Etairistskoe dvizhenie v Rossii*, ch. v.

33. Arsh, *Etairistskoe dvizhenie v Rossii*, pp. 197-9.

34. Xanthos, *Apomnimonevmata* (Athens, 1845) p. 13.

35. *Sbornik*, III, p. 220.

36. Philimon, *Peri tis Ellinikis Epanastaseos* (Athens, 1859) II, p. 226.

37. *Ibid.*, I, pp. 134-7.

38. Arsh, *Etairistskoe dvizhenie v Rossii*, pp. 187-92.

39. *Ibid.*, p. 227.

40. *Sbornik*, III, pp. 224-6; Arsh, *Etairistskoe dvizhenia v Rossii*, pp. 204-7.

41. N. Botzaris, *Visions balkaniques dans la préparation de la Révolution Grecque (1789-1821)* (Geneva-Paris, 1962) p. 92 footnote.

42. E. G. Protopsaltis, *Philiki Etairia* (Athens, 1964) p. 45.

43. *Sbornik*, III, pp. 228-9.

44. Protopsaltis, *Philiki Etairia*, p. 66.

45. Makris, *Kapodistrias*, pp. 128-33, 138-42; Gatopoulos, *Ioannis Kapodistrias* (Athens, 1932) pp. 45-8.

46. George Waddington, *A Visit to Greece in 1823 and 1824* (London, 1825) pp. xxxiv-xlv.

47. Makris, *Kapodistrias*, p. 134.

48. *Sbornik*, III, pp. 250-1.

49. Arsh, *Etairistskoe dvizhenie v Rossii*, pp. 231, 238.

50. *Sbornik*, III, pp. 253-4.

51. *Ibid.*, pp. 297-303.

52. Philimon, *Philiki Etairia*, p. 267.

53. Philimon, *Elliniki Epanastasis*, I, p. 29.

54. Xanthos, *Apomnimonevmata*, p. 16.

55. Philimon, *Elliniki Epanastasis*, I, p. 30.

56. N. Ypsilanti, *Mémoires*, pp. 65-6.

57. Texts in Xanthos, *Apomnimonevmata*, pp. 61-80.

58. Mendelssohn-Bartholdy, *Graf Johann Kapodistrias*, p. 58.

59. Xanthos, *Apomnimonevmata*, pp. 17-18.

60. *Sbornik*, III, pp. 255-7.

61. Lulu Gräfin Thürheim, *Mein Leben* (Munich, 1913), quoted by Enepekidis, *Rigas*, pp. 108-50.

62. A. de la Garde Chambonas, *Fêtes et Souvenirs* (Paris, 1901) pp. 415-22.

63. Philimon, *Philiki Etairia*, p. 253.

64. Philimon, *Elliniki Epanastasis*, I, pp. 30-2; N. Ypsilanti, *Mémoires*, p. 86.

65. Enepekidis, *Rigas*, p. 125.

66. Philimon, *Elliniki Epanastasis*, I, pp. 32-4.

67. *Ibid.*, pp. 129–30.

68. Philimon, *Philiki Etairia*, pp. 275–6.

69. *Ibid.*, p. 267.

70. Philimon, *Elliniki Epanastasis*, II, p. 226.

71. Quoted in Enepekidis, *Rigas*, p. 129.

72. *Ibid.*, p. 125.

73. Oţetea, *Balkan Studies*, VI, 249–64; refuted by A. Despotopoulos, 'La Révolution grecque, Alexandre Ypsilantis et la politique de la Russie', *Balkan Studies*, VII (1966) 395–410.

74. See, for example, *Sbornik*, III, p. 257; Grimsted, *Foreign Ministers*, pp. 263–5.

75. Texts in Philimon, *Elliniki Epanastasis*, II, pp. 216–17, 221, 224–8.

76. N. Ypsilanti, *Mémoires*, p. 116.

77. I. Vlakhogiannis, *Istorika Anekdota* (Athens, 1927) p. 4.

78. N. Dragoumis, *Istorikai Anamniseis* (Athens, 1874) pp. 89–90.

79. Chambonas, *Fêtes et Souvenirs*, p. 419.

80. Xanthos, *Apomnimonevmata*, pp. 19–23; Arsh, *Etairistskoe dvizhenie v Rossii*, ch. VIII.

81. Oţetea, *Balkan Studies*, VI, 264.

82. Philimon, *Elliniki Epanastasis*, I, p. 188 ff.

83. *Sbornik*, III, pp. 263–4.

84. C. K. Webster, *The Foreign Policy of Castlereagh* (London, 1925) II, p. 338.

85. Oţetea, *Balkan Studies*, VII, 389.

86. Grimsted, *Foreign Ministers*, pp. 260–1; Makris, *Kapodistrias*, pp. 196–7, 213–15; Arsh, *Etairistskoe dvizhenie v Rossii*, pp. 295, 304–6; Waddington, *A Visit to Greece*, pp. xii–xiii.

87. *Sbornik*, III, p. 263.

88. Protopsaltis, *Philiki Etairia*, pp. 72–83.

89. *Sbornik*, III, p. 263.

6 The 1821 Revolution in the Rumanian Principalities

E. D. TAPPE

Until the last months of the year 1820 the Rumanian Principalities do not seem to have figured in the plans of the *Philiki Etairia* as a field of military operations, although in the event they were used as such after a sudden change of plan. But they were obviously a very promising source of recruits and of money. Being vassal states and not Turkish territory they offered to anti-Turkish activists a certain immunity from interference. In addition, the Greek presence there was very strong and had been so for a hundred years. Indeed, even in the early seventeenth century the Greek presence in the Principalities had been strong enough to provoke outbursts of xenophobia. In the second half of that century the Kantakouzinos family may be said to have dominated the scene in Wallachia. Greek scholars came to teach in the Principalities; Greek books were printed there. And then uninterruptedly from 1715 the two thrones had been occupied by Phanariots. In both Principalities the language of the court and of higher eduction came to be Greek.

The groundwork for the action of the *Etairia* had first become known by the visit of Nikolaos Galatis to both Principalities in 1816–17.[1] General Pini, the Russian Consul at Bucharest, was at the centre of its activities in Wallachia. The reigning Prince there, Alexandros Soutsos, was not one of its supporters. When in 1806 Napoleon's ambassador, Sebastiani, had persuaded the Porte to depose Konstantinos Ypsilantis for his pro-Russian attitude, Alexandros Soutsos had been appointed to succeed him as Prince of Wallachia. But just as he was about to enter Bucharest, Soutsos had received a *firman* deposing him, Russia and Britain having combined to put pressure on the Porte. It was not till 1819 that he actually reigned in Wallachia. In

Moldavia, on the other hand, the reigning Prince, Mikhail Soutsos, was an active supporter of the *Etairia*. In any case, the administrations of both Principalities were filled with the nominees of the Russian Consuls, and the guards of both Princes were similarly infiltrated.[2]

In the spring of 1820 Alexandros Ypsilantis had been declared supreme chief of the *Etairia*. He was the eldest son of the pro-Russian Konstantinos Ypsilantis, who had reigned in Wallachia from 1802 to 1807, and then taken refuge in Russia. Alexandros held the rank of general in the Russian army. In the autumn of 1820 he met other leaders of the *Etairia* for a conference at Ismail. It was decided that he should go across Austrian territory to Trieste and there embark on a Greek ship for the Peloponnese. In the Peloponnese he would give the signal for revolution.

This plan, however, was quickly changed to that of raising an insurrection in the Principalities. Various explanations have been given. The *Etairia* may have felt that it would be easier to draw the Serbs and Bulgars into a general insurrection against the Turks if a start was made in the Principalities. Lt.-Col. Liprandi, an officer in the Russian Intelligence, whose accounts of these events were written within ten years of their occurrence and who had very good opportunities for investigation, believed that the real reason was this: Ypsilantis wanted his campaign to be near a frontier across which he could seek asylum in case of disaster.[3]

Two other Greeks were to play prominent parts in the insurrection in the Principalities. Ypsilantis had given the chief command of the hoped-for 'armies of the Danube' to Iordakis, known as Olympiotis because his native village was at the foot of Mount Olympus. Beginning his career as secretary to the local band of brigands, he had later fought against the Turks in Serbia. In the Russo-Turkish war of 1806–12 he had been with the Pandours, a corps of volunteers formed in Oltenia under Russian command, and had received a Russian decoration. It was the protection of the Russian Consulate which had saved him when he was implicated in a plot against the reigning Prince of Wallachia, Ioannis Karatzas. Later, the dragoman of the Russian Consulate, Georgios Levendis, induced Alexandros Soutsos to favour Iordakis. In fact, Soutsos made him com-

mander of part of his Albanian guard. From this position
Iordakis could work on the guard to further the cause of the
Etairia.⁴ Binbaşı Savvas was a Greek from Patmos. He had
served in the guards in Wallachia, had fought on the Turkish
side in the war of 1806–12, and had become commander of
Prince Skarlatos Kallimakhis' guard in Moldavia. Returning to
Bucharest at the end of Kallimakhis' reign, he had been
initiated into the *Etairia*.⁵

The *Etairia*'s new plan was for Iordakis and Savvas to overthrow Alexandros Soutsos and to set up a provisional government in Bucharest. Simultaneously Vasileios Karavias was to
appear at Jassy, where, as we have seen, Prince Mikhail
Soutsos was a supporter of the *Etairia*. This plan in its turn was
revoked when Prince Miloš of Serbia refused to join the insurrection. Savvas believed that Miloš' participation was
indispensable; but Iordakis maintained that the Serbs could be
drawn in through his own old comrades in arms.⁶ Nevertheless,
the longer the rising was to be postponed, the more chance the
Turks had of discovering the ramifications of the plot. The
sickness of the Prince of Wallachia contributed to hastening the
outbreak. Alexandros Soutsos fell ill in December. Whether he
was poisoned, as rumour has it, one cannot decide; his son in his
memoirs declines either to confirm or to deny the report.⁷
Towards the end of January the Prince was on his deathbed.
The interval that must elapse between his death and the arrival
of the *kaymakams*, his successor's representatives, from Constantinople would be a very favourable time for an uprising. So
it was that on 29 January 1821 Tudor Vladimirescu left
Bucharest with a band of Albanians from the Prince's guard
and with a supply of cash provided by the *Etairia*.

Why Tudor Vladimirescu? What were his qualifications for
the role he was called upon to play? Born about 1780 in
Vladimiri, a village in Oltenia, probably a free peasant, he
entered in his 'teens the service of a *boyar* of Craiova, Ioan
Glogoveanu. Here he received some education and became
administrator of some of Glogoveanu's estates. In 1806 he was
appointed *vătaf de plai*, an officer in the county police. During
the ensuing Russo-Turkish war, he was a company commander
in the Pandours; for his bravery he was promoted and decorated
with the order of St. Vladimir. He also became a Russian

subject, closely connected with the Russian Consulate. He spent most of the year 1814 at Vienna, engaged in a law suit on Glogoveanu's behalf. How far he came under the influence of the Greek colony there is matter for speculation. He is even said to have been presented to Tsar Alexander during the Congress, by Kapodistrias and Strogonov.[8]

The same source says that Tudor was initiated into the *Etairia* by Iordakis and Savvas, taking the oath in the church of St. Sava in Bucharest. He was no doubt given a strong recommendation by Constantin Samurcaş, in whose house the *Etairia* carried on much of its activity. As governor of Oltenia, Samurcaş had in 1807 organised the corps of volunteers, the Pandours already mentioned, to fight under Russian command. He had had plenty of opportunity to know Tudor's capabilities both as a commander and as a police official. An Austrian despatch has preserved in translation a bond signed by Tudor, Iordakis and Pharmakis. They agreed that each must be free to pretend to provoke disorders . . . and to use any cunning which may lead to attaining the common end. There is also a provision against anyone sowing discord by insisting, for instance, that the native Rumanian should not be subject to the Albanian.[9]

Liprandi indicates Ilarion, Bishop of Argeş, as the chief link between Tudor and the pro-*Etairia* party among Wallachian *boyars*. Liprandi's analysis of the political factions in Wallachia is interesting. He says that there were at this time three parties among the Wallachian *boyars*. The first wanted restoration of Wallachian rights (which meant, in particular, that the Prince should be chosen from among the native *boyars*). They hoped to win over the other two parties to make a common appeal to the Porte. The second party only required that the Metropolitan and the Bishops should not be Greeks. The third party, much the strongest, favoured Phanariot princes. It was the first party that saw in the *Etairia* a movement which could be used for its own purposes. But in Liprandi's view this group did not suppose that the Greek revolution would succeed; it merely felt that the Phanariot princes would be discredited by it in Turkish eyes and that a Rumanian rising directed against the Phanariot oppressors would add to their disgrace. Prominent in this group was Grigore Brîncoveanu.[10]

On 27 January the dying Alexandros Soutsos set up a committee consisting of the Metropolitan Dionisie Lupu and six great *boyars*, which, in fact, on his death became the caretaker government. On the same day three of these, Grigore Brîncoveanu, Barbu Văcărescu, and Grigore Ghica (who next year came to the throne of Wallachia as the first native Prince for over a century) gave Tudor a written promise of aid. They had chosen him, they said, to raise the people with arms and to proceed as he had been instructed. If the signatories broke their promise, they were to be judged by the brethren and punished.[11]

This group knew that the brothers Dimitrie and Pavel Macedonschi had great influence among the Pandours. So, fearing that they might be dangerous if they were not participants in the rising, the group got Tudor to bring the Macedonschi brothers in.[12] Thus it was that the Macedonschis accompanied Tudor and his twenty-seven picked Albanian guards when he left Bucharest on the night of 29 January, ostensibly to re-restablish order in the part of Oltenia where he was *vătaf*. The news of Soutsos' death reached Tudor at Piteşti. When he arrived in his own bailiwick at Padeş, he issued a proclamation to all Wallachia, calling on the inhabitants to assemble with guns, if they had any – otherwise, with forks and spears – at a place which would be announced later. No one was to touch any property other than the ill-gotten wealth of those *boyars* who would not support the movement. The rising was justified as directed against the government – justified because the Sultan himself wished his loyal subjects to prosper.[13]

This proclamation does not voice the aspirations of the *Etairia*. Nor does the petition which Tudor despatched to the Porte, assuring the Sultan of the loyalty of his followers and asking for a commissioner to be sent to investigate their complaints.[14] Both these documents had, in fact, been drawn up in Bucharest; they contain references to 'the present Prince', meaning Alexandros Soutsos. As a contemporary put it: 'If Tudor had told the Oltenians the aim of the revolution, namely that it was against the Turks in favour of the Greeks, he would not have succeeded; but being a good politician, he knew where to touch them.'[15] Only a call to arms against their immediate oppressors would bring them out; hence references in the proclamation to 'the dragons who swallow us alive' and to leaders in church and state 'sucking our blood'. This was calculated to lull Turkish suspicions too. Finally, by making the property of the *boyars* who did not support the movement an exception to the general immunity, the proclamation was intended to put pressure on such *boyars* to join the movement. The plan of deception is in fact spelled out by Ypsilantis' subordinate, Konstantinos Doukas, in a letter to Pancu Haci Khristo, who had a similar mission to that of Tudor, namely to assist Ypsilantis' passage of the Danube by organising resistance around Zimnicea and Sistov. 'Lull the Turks,' says the letter, 'into thinking that nothing is the matter and tell them that you are the Sultan's most loyal subject.'[16]

The provisional government, which had been arranged by Soutsos just before his death, found itself at once faced with the problem of Tudor's rising. They sent him an ultimatum, promising that if his submission were handed to their courier within two hours, they would intercede with the future prince to overlook his actions.[17] Tudor did not bother to reply for some days; he then rebutted their charges of stirring up the people and appealed to the *boyars* to be 'true patriots'.[18] To this the government replied in a conciliatory tone, and announced that the Pandours would henceforth be exempted from taxes.[19] Meanwhile they sent reinforcements to their own troops in Oltenia. Since such men as Iordakis were among the leaders of these reinforcements, it is not surprising that the troops either went over to Tudor or at most made ineffective resistance. The chief command of these reinforcements had been given to Nicolae Văcărescu, but he was soon recalled and replaced by Samurcaş, of whom there can be no doubt that he was acting on behalf of the *Etairia*. On 12 March Tudor struck camp and crossed the Olt on his way to Bucharest. Presumably he had waited to hear of Ypsilantis' arrival in Moldavia.

On 6 March Ypsilantis, in the uniform of a Russian general, had crossed the Pruth into Moldavia accompanied by about twenty people. Arriving in Jassy, he assured the Prince, Mikhail Soutzos, that 70,000 Russians would be following him. He told the Austrian vice-consul Raab that his object was to free Greece from the Turkish yoke and that the Tsar hoped that his effort to raise up the Greeks would be supported by Austria and the other allies.[20] To Iakovakis Rizos Neroulos, who held the office of *postelnic* (Minister of Foreign Affairs), he confided that he intended to proclaim the abolition of class privileges in the Principalities. Rizos persuaded him that this would stir up formidable opposition, because such a very large number of people possessed privileges. Accordingly it was dropped.[21] Ypsilantis' proclamation stated that he was merely passing through the Principalities on his way to Greece; the inhabitants need not fear the Turks, who would, as he put it, be chastised by 'a tremendous power'.[22] Next day he announced that all Greece was in arms and appealed for volunteers to go to her rescue.[23] He and Mikhail Soutsos wrote to the Tsar to ask for his support. Soutsos convened the *boyars* in Jassy and asked them to sign addresses to the Tsar, to Strogonov and to Wittgenstein, the commander of the Russian forces in Bessarabia, calling for Russian intervention. Meanwhile, on the night before Ypsilantis crossed the Pruth, Vasileios Karavias with his Greeks and Albanians in Galatz had massacred all the Turks in the town. Two nights later a similar massacre took place at Jassy.

Although, in their confident expectation of Russian intervention, the Moldavian *boyars* contributed generously to the *Etairia*'s funds, the volunteer army could not be supported on voluntary contributions alone. They spread over the countryside requisitioning. Nor could the army be brought up to the required strength with volunteers, although Greeks and Albanians in the Principalities enlisted, and bands of volunteers came from Odessa. When on 13 March Ypsilantis started to lead his troops towards Bucharest, they numbered less than two thousand. Mikhail Soutsos continued to enlist volunteers, but on the very day of Ypsilantis' departure he heard that three or four thousand Turkish troops had already reached Brăila, and that a larger force was on the way. The Russian Consul, Pisani, could not bring himself to communicate to the Moldavian *boyars* the reply which Wittgenstein had made to their appeal for intervention: namely, that he could only await instructions from St. Petersburg.[24]

What those instructions would be was being determined far away in what is now Ljubljana. The Congress of Laibach had assembled early in January to deal with troubles in Italy. A series of extracts from Metternich's letters reveals the outlines of a change in the Tsar's outlook and in Kapodistrias' standing, which was to be disastrous for the course of the insurrection in the Principalities.

4 January. Do you know an English novel called *Anastasius*? In it there is a description of the Greek character . . . which is very good and accurate. You will find there Capo d'Istria word for word, exactly as he is . . .

10 January. Capo d'Istria twists about like a devil in holy water, but he is in holy water and can do nothing. The chief cause of our activity today arises from my thorough agreement with the Emperor Alexander . . .

7 February. This evening I spent three hours with the Emperor Alexander. I cannot rightly describe the impression which I appeared to make on him. My words sounded like a voice from the other world. The inward feeling of the Emperor has, moreover, much altered, and to this, I believe I have much contributed . . .

12 February. The star of the Russian Premier begins to decline. The breach between Capo d'Istria and the Emperor constantly increases; in a team, if one horse pulls to the right and the other to the left, the carriage will not reach its destination till the stronger has dragged off the weaker of the two. The Emperor is the stronger, and for transparent reasons.

23 February. No one believes that the Emperor Alexander and I understand one another thoroughly, and yet it is so. The influence of the last four months has been effectual; the stronger has carried off the weaker, according to all the laws of mechanics, physics, and morals. The Russian Premier lies on the ground. Will he ever get up again?[25]

From this last extract it would seem that Kapodistrias had fallen a week or so before Ypsilantis crossed the Pruth.

We left Tudor crossing the Olt on 12 March on his way to Bucharest. On 7 March the *kaymakams* designated at Constantinople by the newly appointed Prince, Skarlatos Kallimakhis, had reached that city. Although empowered by the Porte to ask for the entry of Turkish troops into Wallachia, their consultations with the *boyars* led to no such action. The fact was that they, too, were members of the *Etairia* and made no secret of it. But the *boyars* were in a very unpleasant position. The Russian Consul, who had a finger in every pie, was now holding himself aloof. On 2 March he had written a letter to Samurcaş, intended for publication, in which he said that according to instructions received from Strogonov, he must regard Tudor's movement as a revolutionary disturbance. On the other hand he wrote to Tudor himself, telling him to count on his support. His diplomatic colleagues found Pini's attitude incomprehensible.

The forces which Tudor had sent on ahead under Iordakis and Pharmakis continued to plunder, in spite of the severity with which Tudor had repressed such acts in Oltenia. When on 11 March it became known at Bucharest that Ypsilantis was at Jassy, an exodus of *boyars* began, mostly for Transylvania. On the fifteenth Pini's wife left for Braşov. On the twenty-third the Prussian Consul reported that the town was deserted; everyone who could flee had fled, and the lower classes were left without work. The *kaymakams* departed for Giurgiu a few days later, and Pini himself for Braşov on the twenty-eighth. That was the day on which Tudor's main body of troops reached the outskirts of Bucharest. At that moment Ypsilantis had not crossed the border into Wallachia.

On the evening of 17 March a courier had arrived from Laibach with despatches for the Russian Consul and the Austrian agent. They had been written before the Tsar and the Austrian Emperor knew of Ypsilantis' exploit, and were concerned with Tudor's. The Tsar declared Tudor degraded from the order of St. Vladimir and no longer under Russian protection. When Pini notified Tudor and spoke of publishing the Tsar's disavowal, Tudor replied that he did not care whether it were published or not.[26] Perhaps he did not believe that the Tsar really meant to leave the insurrection to its fate. In a tête-à-tête with the Austrian agent's chancellor Udritzki, he said:

> The approach of a Greek force commanded by Prince Ypsilantis puts me in the greatest difficulties, because I do not know on what basis such an action rests, and I should not like to frustrate certain secret plans of a higher Power.[27]

On 4 April Tudor had a meeting with the Metropolitan of Wallachia, who came escorted by fifty Albanian guards under Iordakis and Ghencea. Evidently the *Etairia* was determined not to let the Metropolitan, who was the chief authority left in Bucharest, out of their sight and their grasp. Not surprisingly, Tudor was begged to collaborate with Ypsilantis. But in the course of the consultation the Metropolitan received from the Russian Consulate two papers which had just arrived from Constantinople that very morning. One was a note from Strogonov telling the Consulate to issue a statement that the Tsar had declared Ypsilantis a rebel; the other was an anathema from the Patriarch. The document from the Patriarch annouced that there would be an amnesty for those who laid down their arms, but persistent rebels would be severely punished. Turkish troops were about to enter the Principalities. The Metropolitan refused to communicate what he had received, but the news could not be suppressed for long.[28] The *Etairia* tried to counter its effect by a public demonstration of Iordakis and his troops, and of Greek civilians and priests, with the flag of liberty and patriotic songs. The demonstration ended with a shout of 'To the gates of Byzantium!'[29]

The result of Tudor's consultations with the caretaker government was an agreement, formulated under oath and accompanied by a proclamation. Tudor undertook:

(a) not to harbour designs on the life or property of any of his fellow-countrymen;

(b) to recognise the caretaker government and to entrust to it the supplying of his troops;

(c) to enforce his orders restraining his troops from outrage;

(d) to persuade the inhabitants of Wallachia to obey the government, provided it protected them from injustice; and

(e) to use his troops in case of need against the enemy of his country's rights.

On their part the Metropolitan, bishops and *boyars* acknowledged the beneficent purpose of Tudor's movement and swore not to plot against his life; they would support all plans made between him and those united with him.[30]

In conformity with this agreement Tudor distributed a manifesto throughout the country, advising the population to submit to the government and to pay up their arrears of taxes, as the Treasury was in great straits.[31] Such a proclamation was not likely to satisfy the peasants who had expected relief from taxes. Within two weeks the Austrian agency was reporting that the peasants had begun to abandon Tudor's 'assembly', because the promises made them had not been fulfilled and Tudor was going to use them in the Greek cause.[32]

There is plenty of evidence that Tudor was hoping to become Prince of Wallachia. Rizos Neroulos says that Iordakis had plied him with the idea, when initiating him into the *Etairia*.[33] The peasants had, from the start of his rising, referred to him as 'Prince Tudor'. At Bucharest he even started wearing the head-dress of a Prince. A British report refers to 'the Usurper Theodore'.[34] Nevertheless, to achieve this ambition he would need to be elected Prince by the *boyars*. Hence his need to come to terms with the caretaker government, even at the risk of losing peasant support.

The day of meeting between the Rumanian and Greek leaders of revolt was now near at hand. Ypsilantis had waited nearly a fortnight on the border between the two Principalities, apparently expecting reinforcements. During this time the Sacred Band was organised, mostly from enthusiastic Greek students. Its commander was Georgios Kantakouzinos, a retired colonel of the Russian army who had never served in a fighting unit.

On 25 March Ypsilantis crossed the border into Wallachia. His was a leisurely progress. At Ploieşti he waited to collect arms and enrol Greeks and Bulgars. It was not till 6 April that he reached the outskirts of Bucharest. The government invited him to enter the city, but Tudor prevented him. In the words of a British despatch:

> Theodore has succeeded in preventing the entry of the army of Ypsilandi into Buccarest (*his* capital), but treats Ypsilandi himself with great respect, has given him a superb house for his residence, and offered him all necessary supplies, upon payment of ready money. This may be a farce of the Russians, but it is well planned and well executed.[35]

It was not of course a farce of the Russians; Tudor, with his pretensions to princedom, was not likely to allow what another British report calls 'this Greek Gustavus' to enter *his* capital.[36]

Such was the suspicion between the two leaders that Tudor required Ypsilantis to send Binbaşı Savvas to him as hostage for his safety during their meeting. The anonymous Greek narrative found in the papers of Thomas Gordon, an account which is very much anti-Ypsilantis and pro-Doukas, states that when Doukas went to Ypsilantis before the meeting to get permission to attack Tudor, the following exchange took place:

Ypsilantis: Well, but we shall lose Savvas, who has been given to Tudor as a pledge.
Doukas: So much the better; we shall be rid of two very suspicious characters.

The two leaders came to the meeting with armed escorts, and Ilarion of Argeş acted as interpreter.[37]

There are no minutes of the meeting, and accounts vary as to what passed. According to Liprandi, Tudor pressed Ypsilantis for proof that he had Russian aid. At length Ypsilantis had to admit that this was not so, and appealed to Tudor to cooperate with him for the common good. Tudor replied that their aims were incompatible; he himself was fighting only against abuses, not against the Turks. Kantakouzinos, who was present, tried to persuade Ypsilantis either to return to Moldavia or to cross the Danube. To this Ypsilantis would not agree. But he took care to conceal the failure of his meeting, and spread the rumour that Tudor had sworn to help him.[38]

It may be felt that the *Etairia*'s operations in the Principalities were doomed as soon as the Tsar had disavowed the risings. In any case, the prospect was made far blacker by the split between Tudor and Ypsilantis. And division went even further; Ypsilantis was suspicious of Savvas. Iordakis did his best to widen this rift. On 12 April Ypsilantis and his forces withdrew from the neighbourhood of Bucharest to Tîrgovişte, the town which had been the capital of those princes of Wallachia in the seventeenth century who had found themselves in a stronger position vis-à-vis the Turks. Here the government was to follow him. But Tudor was determined not to let the government out of his grasp; probably, now that he was sure that the insurrection would not have the support of Russia, he was feeling his way towards an approach to the Porte.

There seems to be significance in the fact that, almost

simultaneously, about Eastertide (Easter Day fell on 22 April), both he and Ypsilantis issued proclamations of a sort of constitution for Wallachia. Ypsilantis, after thanking the 'noble sons of Dacia' for their hospitality, laid down principles for a liberal Wallachian constitution: a native prince who should consider himself First Citizen of the province; one or two legislative bodies elected from all classes; a regular army; no taxation without the knowledge of the deputies.[39] Tudor's is a less coherent document. Tudor was himself to be head and governor, and yet there was to be a prince, who before crossing the Danube into Wallachia, would have to put his signature to the constitution. Its provisions are very conservative; often they only remove abuses which had grown up under the last prince, Alexandros Soutsos, and return to the arrangements of his predecessor, Ioannis Karatzas.[40]

Are we to interpret these proclamations as bids by the two leaders for the throne of Wallachia, with Ypsilantis appealing to the progressives and Tudor to the *boyars* who did not want change? At least, that is very likely what each suspected of the other.

Tudor needed to hold on to the caretaker government. Accordingly, just before the end of April, they were removed from the centre of Bucharest to Dinicu Golescu's house, Belvedere, which was near to Tudor's headquarters at Cotroceni. This move is said by Liprandi to have been engineered by the Treasurer Filipescu, who was in some ways the key figure in the government. A British observer at Braşov, in reporting the flight of the Russian and Austrian consuls from the capital, wrote that it

is to be attributed to their dread of the Wild Wallachians of Theodore – and what is more decisive – Alexander Philippesko (called 'Vulpe' the Fox) . . . who remains at Buccorest in the dangerous post of *Vistiar*, or *Treasurer*. It seems *he* is *not afraid*.[41]

Filipescu had been admitted to the *Etairia* when Nikolaos Galatis visited Wallachia four years earlier. But now that he realised that Ypsilantis was not just passing through to cross the Danube, but had moved north to Tîrgovişte, he needed an excuse for not joining him there. And so Filipescu and Ilarion

of Argeş terrified the Metropolitan by telling him that Binbaşı
Savvas intended to seize him and hand him over to the Turks.
At the same time they persuaded Tudor that it was necessary to
prevent the government from leaving Bucharest. By confining
them at Belvedere, Tudor gave Filipescu and Ilarion the excuse
of force-majeure which they needed. On 9 May Savvas
appeared with a force of cavalry to liberate them, but as Tudor
had ordered that, if Savvas tried to force his way in, the
prisoners were to be murdered, they begged Savvas to go away.[42]

Both Tudor and Savvas were now negotiating with the Turks,
but found themselves required either to lay down their arms or
to fight the forces of the *Etairia*. They had not sufficient confidence in the good faith of the Turks to do the first, and they
could not rely on their troops to do the second. They made a
demonstration of mutual solidarity on 20 May, raising the flag
of liberty. But a few days later Savvas slipped off with part of his
forces to join Ypsilantis at Tîrgovişte. On 25 May at Bucharest
the boom of cannon was heard in the distance; the Turkish
army was at last advancing on the capital. Two days later
Tudor allowed the caretaker government to leave for Braşov,
and in the dusk he set out with his troops in the direction of
Piteşti.

Tudor's strength was based on Oltenia, and it was there that
he now intended to move his force. But Ypsilantis, too, had
shown signs of intending to cross the Olt; his troops were
already deployed between Piteşti and Rîmnic. Here was another
source of friction. It was on 30 May that Tudor, reaching
Goleşti, found his advance towards Piteşti barred by Iordakis
with a force of infantry and cavalry drawn up for battle.
The sight of Tudor and the Pandours preparing to force a
passage, however, induced Iordakis to parley, as a result of
which his forces retired to Piteşti. Tudor's chief officers,
Macedonschi and Prodan, took up their quarters in the manor-
house of the Golescu family, while he himself chose as his
headquarters the little kiosk over the gateway, which gave a
good view round about.

It is probable that Ypsilantis had by now found proof of
Tudor's negotiations with the Turks. But as long as Tudor was
at the head of a loyal force of Pandours, it was difficult to dis-
pose of him. Now, however, his position was fatally weakened.

On the way from Bucharest Tudor had shown remarkable severity in punishing looters. For instance, he had killed with his own hand two young Pandours who had taken two rolls of linen from a peasant's house. He had also demanded that his captains should undertake in writing to answer with their lives for any such act of insubordination in their own companies. All but four signed; the four returned a defiant reply. This was a revolution, they said; what need had he of their signatures, as he was ready to kill them at any moment, signature or no? To this he made no answer. That evening at Goleşti he went out to inspect the posts and when he came to that of Captain Urdăreanu, one of the four, he had him immediately hanged from a nearby willow. Tudor then returned to his quarters.[43]

This, the twenty-fifth execution since Bucharest, proved to be the last straw. Macedonschi quickly consulted his fellow-officers and rode off into the night towards Piteşti. Next morning Tudor found himself faced with Iordakis, Pharmakis and other leaders from Ypsilantis' forces. Iordakis asked him by what right he had executed those men; he replied that he was with his own sword in his own country. Iordakis then showed him captured letters addressed by him to the Turks; Tudor did not deny his own signature. He was removed to Piteşti and, next day, to Tîrgovişte, where Karavias guarded him in the Metropolitan's palace. There does not seem to have been a formal trial; he is said to have been interrogated under torture by Karavias and executed on Ypsilantis' orders.[44]

From the point of view of the *Etairia* Tudor was a traitor, a member of their society who had broken his oath of loyalty. Since his own adjutant, Cioranu, says that Tudor and Savvas were planning to take up positions on the south of the Carpathians and so to catch Ypsilantis' forces between themselves and the advancing Turks, we cannot be surprised that he was put to death. His Pandours now began to melt away, and out of 6000 only 800 crossed the Olt as a military force.

The Turkish troops had entered the Principalities on 13 May; one force in Moldavia, one in Wallachia, one in Oltenia. There was no swift advance in Wallachia; as we have seen, Tudor did not leave Bucharest till 27 May, when the Turks were at last close by. Next day the capital surrendered to the Turkish commander-in-chief. On 6 June he was ready to advance on Tîrgovişte. Greek forces under Kolokotronis and Doukas who tried to bar the way were scattered before Ypsilantis could bring up the Sacred Band and other reinforcements. He now decided to abandon Tîrgovişte and to make for Rîmnic. Before they reached Piteşti, Doukas and some other officers slipped away and made for Transylvania. When on the tenth the Turks appeared before Tîrgovişte, Savvas, who had been with his men in the monastery of Mărgineni, made his submission. He and his force were at once used against the forces of the *Etairia*, their first success being to catch a body of men held up by the flooded waters of the Dîmboviţa. But the main body of Ypsilantis' troops succeeded in crossing the Olt on the twelfth.

At Rîmnic, Ypsilantis found Dimitrie Macedonschi with those Pandours who had not dispersed. Macedonschi reproached him with the murder of Tudor, who, he said, had been entrusted to him by the people's army for judgment by the Divan. Ypsilantis swore that Tudor was alive and had been sent by him to Bessarabia. This was a story which gained popular belief.[45] Macedonschi tried to persuade Ypsilantis not to fight a pitched battle with the Turks, but to wage guerrilla warfare. But though his advice was accepted, it came too late.

The Sacred Band, the artillery and other troops gathered at Drăgăşani on the night of 18 June. Their chief commander was Iordakis. Karavias and some Albanians, with the Sacred Band behind them, formed an advance guard. Iordakis, inspecting on the morning of the nineteenth, told Karavias on no account to start a battle before he himself returned with his own detachment. He then went off – it is said, to despatch all his money to his wife – leaving the Greek forces without a supreme commander. Meanwhile, Ypsilantis, in the words of Tudor's adjutant, Cioranu, 'played the generalissimo or fieldmarshal, standing at a very great distance from the scene of battle, lest by any chance a shell or bullet might reach him'.[46] When, after hearing Macedonschi's advice, he wrote instructions to Iordakis, he tactlessly included the phrase 'following the advice of our friend Macedonschi, who knows the district'. In Iordakis' absence this message was handed to Karavias, who, with the words 'I don't need another man's advice', sent it after Iordakis.

When Iordakis read it, he threw it on the ground in a rage, saying 'If that's so, let Macedonschi be in charge of everything'. Such were the jealousies of the Greek commanders.[47] Presently some 200 Turkish cavalry provided a tempting target for the Greek advance guard. Karavias (who is said to have been drunk) ordered them to fire. The enemy charged and drove the Albanians before them. Then turning round, they attacked the Sacred Band. The artillery was almost useless for lack of matches. Nikolaos Ypsilantis, who was in command of the Sacred Band, galloped to the Albanians, but they fled the field, saying that nobody had paid them. Of the 800 youths who composed the Sacred Band, about 100 escaped into the woods, and many of those perished later. Alexandros Ypsilantis, hearing the news, rode towards the battlefield, but was unable to make the fugitives turn. Nor had he better success at Rîmnic, where other fugitives overtook him. No one had any confidence in him. For the four days during which he stayed in the monastery of Cozia, he feared that he would be roughly handled by them. To cover his escape, he spread the rumour that Austrian troops had crossed the frontier and ordered rejoicings; then by night he slipped out of the monastery and crossed into Transylvania. Thence he issued his final proclamation, beginning 'Soldiers! No, I will not profane this holy name . . .', in which he consigns Savvas, Doukas, Karavias and others to the hatred of mankind, the justice of the laws and the curse of their fellow-countrymen. His next few years were spent in Austrian prisons.[48]

Meanwhile, in Moldavia, too, the situation had worsened. The Prince, Mikhail Soutsos, who had done much for Ypsilantis' cause, soon found his position untenable. Once it was realised that Russian support would not be given, he was left alone to face the *boyars* who wanted to show their loyalty to the Porte. Moreover, he was powerless to keep order in his realm against those who, in the name of the *Etairia*, were plundering and committing acts of violence. On 10 April he abdicated and left for Russia. The government, in its hostility to the *Etairia*, now armed a hundred Turks who were in hiding. But Ypsilantis, who had heard of Soutsos' intention of abdicating, sent two of his captains, Pendedekas and Athanasios, back to Moldavia. Pendedekas succeeded in establishing control of the government at Jassy. Athanasios had not been long at Galatz when Turkish forces emerged from Brăila and he had to retreat to the bank of the Pruth.

Georgios Kantakouzinos had persuaded Ypsilantis to appoint him commander-in-chief in Moldavia. But when he arrived at Jassy he found that Pendedekas would not admit his authority. He soon left the capital and established himself on the bank of the Pruth at Sculeni, opposite the quarantine station. When the Turkish forces drew near, he crossed into Bessarabia. This left Athanasios in command at Sculeni. With some 450 others he took an oath to die for liberty. When he and other captains crossed to the quarantine to say goodbye, their friends and relations begged them to stay in safety on the Russian shore, but Athanasios replied: 'I know we shall die here; that is our duty. It is a question of the whole people's honour.' And so on 29 June they fought heroically to the end.[49]

Iordakis had parted from Ypsilantis after Drăgăşani, and made for Curtea-de-Argeş, where his detachment still was. When he heard that Ypsilantis had crossed into Transylvania, he realised that the cause was lost. He could not himself take refuge on Austrian territory, as he had twice been condemned as a criminal in that empire. With Pharmakis he decided to make for Moldavia in the hope of crossing into Russia. They kept close to the Austrian frontier. Eventually they occupied the Moldavian monastery of Secu. The Turks brought up a gun to shell it and flung burning tow on to the thatched roofs. The thatch caught fire, and while the defenders were occupied in resisting an attack on the gateway, Iordakis and others were burned to death in a little tower which was suddenly isolated by the flames. Pharmakis held out for twelve days. When supplies were nearly exhausted, he was induced to surrender by the statement that the Sultan had sent a *firman* pardoning them. This was guaranteed by the Austrian vice-consul from Bacău, Wolf. But when they laid down their arms, they were massacred, only Pharmakis and a few others being reserved for execution at Constantinople.[50]

Savvas, after joining the Turkish side, had used his position to delay the pursuit of Iordakis and Pharmakis. When he had the chance to cross into Austrian territory at Timiş, he refused to save just himself and a few, saying that he hoped to return with his whole detachment. But he had a taste of Ottoman perfidy at

Cozia. The Turkish commander obtained the surrender of the Albanian Diamandi Djuvara and his sixty men by pointing to the immunity of Savvas, who was more guilty than Diamandi. When they surrendered, the men were massacred and Diamandi sent to Constantinople for execution. Savvas still would not seek refuge across the border. As he approached Bucharest, to which he had been summoned to receive another honour bestowed by the Sultan, his detachment began to melt away. His captains besought him not to enter Bucharest. But telling them characteristically that they were a lot of old women, he went and was graciously received by the *Kehaya Bey*. Next day (19 August) he and his two colleagues, Ivancea and Ghencea, went again, but this time they were shot down before reaching the audience chamber. There followed eight days of horror in Bucharest, during which not only the Albanians were hunted down; the janissaries, in their zeal to produce heads for the *Kehaya Bey*, did not care much whose heads they were. Nevertheless, apart from these eight days in Bucharest, the Turks behaved with much more restraint during the mopping-up process in Wallachia than they did in Moldavia. The massacre perpetrated by Karavias at Galatz may account, at least in part, for the Turkish ruthlessness in Moldavia.[51]

Some of the causes of the failure of this insurrection in the Principalities have been mentioned already. First and foremost was the lack of support from Russia. But it may be asked why, when this became apparent, a guerrilla resistance could not have been organised, sufficient to distract a large Turkish force from other parts of South Eastern Europe. Presumably this was impossible because the inhabitants found the depredations of the *Etairia* bad enough, and would have refused to expose themselves to a guerrilla war in which the Turks would have shown them no mercy. We have also to remember the rivalries of the *Etairia*'s leaders on Rumanian soil, their selfish ambitions and their jealousy of one another. It would have needed an exceptional chief to keep them together. And Ypsilantis appears to have been a fundamentally frivolous man without deep convictions or practical ability.[52]

The events of 1821 had the important result in the Principalities of ending Phanariot rule, because they destroyed Turkish confidence in the loyalty of the Greeks. In 1822

Grigore Ghica was appointed Prince of Wallachia and Ion Sandu Sturza Prince of Moldavia, both being native rulers in the sense that they were born into families long-established in the Principalities. With the restoration of native rule, it was easier for Rumanian national consciousness to find expression in the use of Rumanian as the official language.

NOTES TO CHAPTER 6

Many of the primary sources have been collected in the five volumes of *Răscoală din 1821*, edited by A. Oțetea and others (Bucharest, 1962) and referred to below as *R.1821*. Others are in N. Iorga, *Izvoarele contemporane asupra mișcării lui Tudor Vladimirescu* (Bucharest, 1921). Foreign Office papers in the Public Record Office, London, are referred to as F.O. The chief secondary work is A. Oțetea, *Tudor Vladimirescu și mișcarea eteristă în Țările Românești 1821–1822* (Bucharest, 1945), referred to below as *T.V.* and to which this chapter is deeply indebted.

1. Liprandi in *R.1821*, v, p. 418.
2. *T.V.*, p. 129.
3. *R.1821*, v, p. 281.
4. Liprandi in *R.1821*, v, pp. 414–18.
5. *Ibid.*, p. 419.
6. *T.V.*, p. 130.
7. P. Rizos (ed.), *Mémoires du Prince Nicolas Soutzo* (Vienna, 1899) p. 37.
8. Ion Ghica, *Opere*, I (1967) p. 170.
9. A. Oțetea, 'Legămîntul lui Tudor Vladimirescu față de *Eterie*', *Studii*, IX (Bucharest, 1956) 2–3, 126.
10. *R.1821*, v, p. 265.
11. In *Revista istorică română*, XVI (1946) 3.
12. *R.1821*, v, p. 269.
13. *T.V.*, pp. 144–5.
14. *Ibid.*, pp. 146–7.
15. S. S. Dăscălescu, quoted in *T.V.*, p. 147.
16. Quoted, *ibid.*, p. 148.
17. *R.1821*, I, pp. 212–13.
18. *Ibid.*, pp. 228–30.
19. *T.V.*, p. 161.
20. I. Rizos Néroulos, *Histoire moderne de la Grèce* (Geneva, 1828) p. 289.
21. *R.1821*, I, p. 295.
22. *R.1821*, IV, p. 132.
23. *Ibid.*, pp. 134–5.
24. *T.V.*, p. 186.
25. *Memoirs of Prince Metternich 1815–1829* (London, 1881) III, p. 486 ff.
26. *T.V.*, p. 227.

27. *Ibid.*, p. 228.

28. *Ibid.*, p. 229.

29. *Ibid.*, p. 231.

30. *Ibid.*, pp. 236–7.

31. *Ibid.*, p. 237.

32. *Ibid.*, p. 238.

33. I. Rizos Néroulos, *Histoire moderne de la Grèce*, p. 284.

34. F.O.7/159, Wyborn to Lord Stewart, Cronstadt [Braşov], 2 April 1821.

35. Quoted in *T.V.*, p. 242, n. 1.

36. F.O.7/159, Wyborn to Lord Stewart, Cronstadt, 2 April 1821.

37. *R.1821*, IV, p. 248.

38. *R.1821*, V, pp. 288–9.

39. *R.1821*, II, pp. 83–4.

40. *T.V.*, pp. 273–4.

41. F.O.7/159, Wyborn to Lord Stewart, Cronstadt, 2 April 1821.

42. *T.V.*, pp. 269–70.

43. 'Memoriu despre mişcarea lui Tudor Vladimirescu de Chiriac Popescu' in N. Iorga, *Izvoarele contemporane asupra mişcării lui Tudor Vladimirescu* (Bucharest, 1921) pp. 292–3.

44. *T.V.*, p. 299.

45. *T.V.*, p. 301.

46. 'Revoluţia lui Tudor Vladimirescu de Mihai Cioranu' in N. Iorga, *op. cit.*, p. 307.

47. *R.1821*, V, p. 315–16.

48. *Ibid.*, pp. 99–100.

49. *Ibid.*, pp. 325–7.

50. *Ibid.*, pp. 332–4.

51. *Ibid.*, pp. 339–41.

52. See the characterisation of Ypsilantis by Liprandi in *R.1821*, V, pp. 292, 481.

7   The Formation of the Greek State, 1821–33

DOUGLAS DAKIN

If the Greeks of 1821 were not fully fledged Mazzinians, they had, each according to his station and experience, characteristics which gave them, to some degree or other, the sense of nationality. They had a common spoken language which was remarkably uniform; they had a common creed which was free from doctrinal and liturgical dispute; and, despite the relative freedom they enjoyed under a Greco-Turkish regime, they all had a sense of inferiority, each according to his status. Every Greek must have felt that he belonged to a different order from that of the Muslim Turk, no matter whether the Turk was a fellow peasant, a fellow landowner, or a fellow official. As a non-Moslem the Greek paid the *harac*, a capitation tax, in receipt for which he was given an identity card[1] which expressly permitted the bearer as an infidel 'to keep his head upon his shoulders'. This tax was highly objectionable, not only because it was relatively heavy, but because it was a constant reminder of inferior status; and it is surely significant that during the disturbances that heralded the formal proclamation of the Greek revolution in the Peloponnese, one Soliotis and his band attacked a party of Turkish officials who were collecting the *harac*.

Yet another mark of inferiority was the heavier rate of tithe paid by the Christian tenants in respect of their holdings. This was a tax on earnings, whether from land, from commercial enterprise, or from a profession. Levied usually in kind upon the products of the soil, as in eighteenth-century France and Italy, it was particularly onerous in those regions and in those periods where the crops were poor. From the evils of this tax, in the administration of which there was much abuse, the Moslem tenant was not greatly more immune than his Christian neighbour. But although the peasants of both creeds suffered in common at the hands of a ruling class composed of both Turks and Greeks,[2] their common suffering showed no signs of giving rise to a peasants' revolt. When rebellion at length broke out, the Greek peasantry joined their betters in a national revolt against the Turks – a revolt which displayed from its outset all the fanaticism of a religious war. Indeed, the Greek rebellion was primarily the work of a people who, though disunited in many ways, had long achieved a form of nationhood under the aegis of the hierarchy of the Orthodox Christian Church.

In the Ottoman Empire at large the thirteen million or so Orthodox Greek Christians (approximately one-quarter of the total Imperial population) were under the theocratic rule of the Greek Patriarch and the Bishops. In the villages, townships and cities, they formed self-governing theocracies; and under the Turkish system, which hardly distinguished between the temporal and spiritual spheres of government, these theocracies regulated, in accordance with canon and custom, almost the whole of life's activities – indeed, all those activities that were not ruthlessly determined by the routine of the agricultural seasons, by the need to toil to avoid starvation, and by the obligation to perform labour services and to pay tithes and taxes. All things pertaining to the family (marriage, births, death and probate), to holy days and holidays, to religious feasts and name days, came within the province of the Church, which had its own independent legal system. Rather than go to the Turkish courts, the Orthodox Christians would frequently submit their differences to the arbitration of their priests, and, as time went on, almost every conceivable kind of case had come to be dealt with by the Christian clergy.[3] It was the Church, too, that provided a rudimentary education for the young and a way of life for those who reached man's estate. In teaching the time-honoured Christian rites, the Bible and the lives of the saints to the Christian communities, it taught the Greek that he belonged to a nation, a chosen race, whose trials and tribulations would one day pass and which, when God willed it, would regain complete control of the Holy City of Constantinople. In so far as the tolerant Turk allowed the Christian Church a large degree of autonomy, the Orthodox Christian peasant was free – as free, perhaps, as his counterpart in western Europe.

But even where the tentacles of the Turkish state system touched the pockets of the Greeks, those in the higher strata of society enjoyed, besides religious liberty, a considerable degree of secular freedom. In the Peloponnese the Greek primates or landowners (known variously as *proestoi*, *prokritoi*, and *hocabaşıs*) had a hand in the allocation of taxation, both regular and extraordinary, and, as tax farmers, most of the work of collection was done by them. In certain other regions, above all in the islands, the Greeks administered the state and the local taxation completely, fulfilling their communal obligation to raise fixed sums demanded by the Turks and to make provision for local expenditure. Hence it is no exaggeration to say that the numerous self-governing Christian theocracies of Turkish Greece were, in certain aspects, miniature republics, more strictly oligarchies, for the rulers were the well-to-do. More democratic were the *klephtokhoria*, the villages of the *klephts* or outlaws,[4] who had for long defied Turkish rule. Here again, however, the organisation tended to oligarchy, almost to popular monarchy, for the chief *klepht* was usually a man of substance and authority. Much the same is true of the seafaring Greeks of the islands. A few of them were very wealthy, and there were many who were certainly not poor. The shipowners (*noikokyreoi*), like the landowners, were known as primates (*proestoi*, etc.). It was not unusual, however, for the sailors to have shares not only in the ships but in the cargoes they carried. Each vessel was a noisy floating republic (except when all aboard were listening to some yarn told by story-tellers,[5] who were always in much demand). Kinglake travelled in Greek ships shortly after the war of liberation, but conditions had not vastly changed. In his *Eothen* he wrote:

[The crew] choose a captain to whom they entrust just power enough to keep the vessel on her course in fine weather, but not quite enough for a gale of wind: they also elect a cook and a mate. The cook whom we had on board was particularly careful about the ship's reckoning and when . . . we grew fondly expectant of an instant dinner, the great author of pilafs would be standing on the deck with an ancient quadrant in his hands . . . But then, to make up for this, the captain would be exercising a controlling influence over the soup.

Kinglake goes on to say that one of the principal duties of the mate was to act as counter captain, or leader of the opposition: his task was to denounce the first symptoms of tyranny and to protect even the cabin boy from oppression.

No matter whether the Greek was a sailor, a labouring share-cropper, a *pallikari* in a klephtic band, a professional man, a small trader or artisan, a landowner or merchant, he enjoyed considerable freedom. Turkish rule had become inefficient. The Imperial writ, even in those areas of administration where the Sultan had most interest, had ceased to run. The *paşas*,[6] who went to rule the provinces, had to come to terms with local authorities and prescriptive powers, with the result that the whole provincial scene had become one of political intrigue, of frequent truces and treaties, and of marauding and vendetta. It was here that the lawless men of Greece, who among them-selves observed strict codes of honour and duty, learned their patriotism – their loyalty to their locality (*patrida*), faith, families, and patrons; and it was this patriotism that finds expression in the *klephtika*[7] – ballads which tell of the relentless struggle, not against the Sultan, but against the petty tyrant and the infidel. This poetry, like the liturgy of the Church, was a great spiritual force among the Christian masses. It was the basis of their sense of nationality, the force that was to give a kind of unity to their intense local patriotism. Indeed, before they rose in 1821, the Greeks already formed a potential national state within a state, a national state which consisted of a com-plex of authorities within an Empire in which, to a very large degree, local institutions had broken loose from central control. It is true that where Ali Paşa and his sons[8] had usurped the Sultan's power, local institutions were certainly less free. But they existed all the same, and Ali worked through them when it was convenient to do so. He constantly made bargains with the local communities and the *klephts*; he employed Greeks in his administration; and he usually refrained from interfering with spiritual affairs whether Orthodox or Muslim. In his miniature Turkish Empire, the Greeks certainly did not lose their identity. Indeed, it can be argued that it was here precisely that they had the greatest urge to throw off Turkish rule, or at least to usurp the authority which Ali and his sons had themselves usurped. It was within Ali Paşa's orbit that the Greek *klephts* began to roam more widely, to stretch their minds, and to think politically upon a larger scale. Those who were driven to seek asylum in the Ionian Islands[9] came into close contact with the French, the Russians, and the British, all of whom brought them into the arena of the politics of the Napoleonic Wars. By the time of the Congress of Vienna (1814–15) many of them had visions of emulating the Ionian Greeks and of establishing some form of independence or at least autonomies on the Greek mainland. These visions became more pronounced under the influence of a growing intellectual conception of a regenerated Greece[10] – an idea which was not entirely beyond the grasp of many of the unruly warriors. Of perhaps greater importance in the formation of their ideas was the decision of the Congress of Vienna to recognise an independent Ionian Septinsular State, the first Greek state to be created in the modern age. It is true, indeed, that this state was placed under the protection of Great Britain, who was to rule it more or less as a Crown colony; nevertheless, it was in theory an independent state, and its very existence was of some importance (exactly how much it is difficult to say) in the process of the intensification of Greek nationalism.

But although the sense of nationhood in all its various forms and at all its various levels was to be a vital factor in developments leading to the outbreak of the War of Independence in 1821, much more important for the prosecution of the war and for the evolution of the Greek nation state were the apparently conflicting forces of local lawlessness and the entrenched habits of local self-government in the regions of the Turkish empire, which were ultimately to be assigned to Greece. Militarily the war was fought largely in terms of local lawlessness by men who got their hands on the institutions of local self-government and on local funds. But exactly how these local institutions functioned we do not know in any detail. What we do know, however, in a general way, is how the westernised Greeks attempted, under the influence of their political theories, their more refined patriotism, and their wider strategic conceptions, to replace and to improve upon the Turkish governmental superstructure that had been destroyed during the first two months of the Revolution. Roughly speaking, they succeeded in replacing (at least on paper) the higher Turkish officials by a number of committees. What we do not know precisely is the degree of efficiency with which these committees worked – how far, if at all, they were able to assert administrative authority over local bodies and local worthies. What we do know, however, in some detail, is the story of the intense political struggle waged over these central committees and between these committees and the localities. From that story it is evident that the leaders of the major regions of Greece – the Peloponnese, Western Greece, Eastern Greece, and the Islands – were all reluctant to submit to a central authority unless they themselves had a controlling influence in it. What we also know in some detail is the history of the intense rivalries within those four principal regions. Indeed, George Finlay, the British historian of modern Greece,[11] who himself took part in the War of Independence, must be somewhere very near the mark when he said that a whole crop of minor Ali Paşas sprang up on the ruins of Turkish power.

These intense local struggles had the curious and paradoxical effect of providing support for central institutions. Disappointed local worthies – those who had come off badly in the regional struggles for power – not infrequently sought the help of, and gave support to, those engaged in the attempt to create central institutions and to provide a central direction of the war – a task close to the hearts of the westernised Greeks, and above all of the Phanariots[12] who had joined the struggle. Foremost among these during the early stages of the war were Alexandros Mavrokordatos,[13] Theodoros Negris,[14] and Dimitrios Ypsilantis, brother and representative of Alexandros Ypsilantis, the leader of the *Philiki Etairia*.[15] None of them had property or connections in Greece. But all of them quickly became leaders of followers, who wished, not so much to be led, as to monopolise them and to push them from behind. Thus, they soon found themselves in a position to exploit the struggles, not only those between the military leaders (*kapetanioi*) and the primates but also those between the different regions. Their activities gave rise to the idea, though not necessarily to the reality, of central government – an idea by no means outside the ken of certain *kapetanioi* (Theodoros Kolokotronis, for example[16]), much as they detested civilians, and much as they asserted their local independence. Strong local attachments do not necessarily preclude thinking or action on a national scale. One has only to read the local histories of the seventeenth-century civil war in

England to appreciate that national issues were fought over by those whose immediate allegiances were essentially parochial. In early nineteenth-century Greece, strong local attachments, combined with the intense individualism displayed by Greeks of all ranks, merely complicated the picture, making central institutions of government almost unworkable, yet at the same time emphasising the need for them. Certain foreign observers of nascent Greece, George Finlay and Colonel Leicester Stanhope for example,[17] thought that Greece should have been fashioned as a Balkan Switzerland. But this idea was never mooted by any Greek of importance; and the whole history of the Greek War of Independence shows that, so strong were the forces working in their devious ways for the creation of a centralised monarchical state, the chances of establishing a republican federation were very slight indeed.

Already, before the arrival in Greece of the three leading Phanariots, a whole crop of regional authorities had sprung up to assume direction of the war, claiming the right to speak for Greece as a whole and hoping to extend their activities to other regions. Early in April 1821 Petros Mavromikhalis (Petrobey), chief of the district of Mani in the southeast of the Peloponnese, had appealed in the name of the Greek nation to the powers of Europe for assistance and recognition. Having stated that the Greeks were determined to free themselves or perish, he continued:

> We invoke therefore the aid of all the civilised nations of Europe, that we may the more promptly attain to the goal of a just and sacred enterprise, reconquer our rights, and regenerate our unfortunate people. Greece, our Mother, was the lamp that illuminated you; on this ground she reckons on your active philanthropy. Arms, money, and counsel are what she expects from you. We promise you her lively gratitude, which she will prove by deeds in more prosperous times.

Shortly afterwards Petrobey set up a body known as the Senate (*gerousia*) of Messinia, a body which resembled the so-called Directory of Achaia established by Bishop Germanos and the notables of the region of Patras. In May 1821 Petrobey and his partisans invited the islands of Hydra, Spetsai and Psara[18] to send representatives to a general Peloponnesian (Moreot)

Assembly.[19] The islanders, however, did not respond, and when in early June the assembly met at the monastery of Kaltezies, with Petrobey as chairman and Rigas Palamidis as secretary, it was restricted to the Peloponnesian notables. This assembly established at Stemnitsa an elected senate under the presidency of Petrobey. Its task was to co-ordinate the work of a multiplicity of lesser authorities, to centralise funds and military plans, and generally to face Dimitrios Ypsilantis, who had been appointed by his brother Alexandros as the chief representative of the *Etairia* in Greece, with a *fait accompli*.

Dimitrios Ypsilantis[20] had proceeded first to Hydra, where he had attempted to organise the resources of the islands. From Hydra he crossed over to the Peloponnese and early in July entered into discussion with the Peloponnesian primates at Vervena. By the masses and men of intermediate rank he was well received. It was generally thought that he had the support of Russia in whom the wishful-thinking Greeks still had some hopes, and almost everyone was prepared at least to listen to his plans for the prosecution of the national struggle, the *kapetanioi* in particular wanting his blessing in their conflict with the primates. On his arrival at Vervena he proposed that the Peloponnesian Senate should be dissolved, and that his own plan, 'the General Organisation of the Morea', should be adopted – a plan for establishing twenty-four *ephories*, each consisting of five *ephoroi* (ephors) elected by the notables. One out of each of these five *ephoroi* was to serve in a *vouli* (parliament) over which Ypsilantis himself as the chief representative of the *Etairia* was to preside. This central *vouli* was to be divided into committees, each taking charge of a branch of government. In the *ephories* the five *ephoroi* were each to specialise in one of the tasks of administration – supplies, recruitment, communications, finance, and police – but all of them, and their assistants, were to have judicial functions.

To these plans the notables of the Peloponnese objected. They wanted the *ephoroi* to be elected in their districts and, instead of the twenty-four member *vouli*, they wanted the Peloponnesian senate, with Petrobey as president, to continue. They were prepared, however, to admit Ypsilantis to the meetings of the Senate. With this arrangement Ypsilantis was himself ready to fall in, but his strong entourage of *kapetanioi* persuaded him to withdraw to Leondari. Later he established at Trikorfo (near Vitina) his headquarters, which was, in effect, the government of the *Etairia* and which competed with that established by the primates. From this headquarters he sent out circulars to the lesser authorities, hoping to secure their co-operation and allegiance. To Trikorfo he invited Mavrokordatos, who had first gone to Mesolonghi in Western Greece, where he had been well received by both the *kapetanioi* and the primates, it being thought that the funds he carried were an instalment of more to come. Like Ypsilantis, Mavrokordatos hoped to establish a central authority in Greece. What he wished to prevent was a government under the exclusive control of the *Etairia* and the *kapetanioi*, a government which looked towards Russia as the saviour of Greece. Both these Phanariots, however, were anxious to avoid a head-on clash and were prepared (with reservations) to work together, Ypsilantis going so far as to give his blessing to Mavrokordatos' proposal to draw up an instrument of government, which, it was hoped, all parties would accept.

In this task, Mavrokordatos sought the assistance of Negris and eventually presented his plan to the Peloponnesian primates assembled at Zarakova. Briefly, this plan provided for a national parliament of the Peloponnesian primates' nominees, who were to be joined by representatives from other regions; there was to be a senate of twenty-four persons under the presidency of Ypsilantis and district administrative officers (*ephoroi*) who were to serve a four-year term. These proposed arrangements, however, met with resolute opposition from the *kapetanioi*, who even threatened to massacre the primates. The most they would accept was a temporary measure – a senate of five primates to administer the Peloponnese only, a body which, more or less, was the old Peloponnesian Senate of Turkish days. To this arrangement Ypsilantis, Mavrokordatos and Negris, all being powerless, reluctantly agreed.

All this time Ypsilantis had been making further attempts to establish an administration of the islands. But here, as on the mainland, although he found considerable popular support, he soon discovered that the entrenched authorities were not prepared to submit to the *Etairia*. The whole task indeed of setting up an effective central authority in Greece was exceedingly difficult. Everywhere those with local power and influence were determined to slip quietly into the places vacated by the Turks, and all that the Phanariots could do (they had no local roots, no land, no family influence, and, except for Ypsilantis, no following among the masses) was to exploit the fierce conflicts between the primates and the *kapetanioi*,[21] each one after his own fashion. Mavrokordatos, realising that he could make little headway in the Peloponnese, returned to Western Greece where his prospects were somewhat better, while Negris repaired to Salona in Eastern Greece. In November 1821 Mavrokordatos convened an assembly of thirty persons. This body established a senate of ten elected by *ephoroi* and *kapetanioi* for one year, under the presidency of Mavrokordatos. But real authority rested with the *kapetanioi* who administered their own districts, each according to his whim. Much the same happened in Eastern Greece. Here, Negris convened an assembly of seventy-three persons, among whom were representatives of Thessaly, Epirus and Macedonia. This assembly established a senate, the *Areios Pagos*, consisting of twelve members. In theory this body supervised the communal institutions, but in practice these, as in Western Greece, took their orders from the *kapetanioi*.

Each of the three regional governments envisaged the convention of a national assembly or parliament (*vouli*), that of Eastern Greece having gone so far as to contemplate that this assembly should make a formal request to the European powers to arrange for Greece a monarchy – an idea already widely current among the Greek revolutionaries, who wished to appear respectable in the eyes of Europe. But when the so-called National Assembly met at Argos in December 1821, its twenty-four members were nearly all primates from the Peloponnese. Its president was Ypsilantis,[22] but, becoming disgusted with its intrigues, he retired to Corinth to organise the siege of that stronghold which was in Turkish hands. The task of drawing up an instrument of government again fell to Mavrokordatos and Negris, who were assisted by Vicenzo Gallina, an Italian philhellene. Known as the 'Provisional Constitution of Epidavros (Piada)', and dated 1 January 1822, this instrument's basic provision was as follows: primates and respectable citizens were to elect for one year *ephoroi* from each village or township – one to five according to the size of the population; these were, in turn, to elect five representatives from each district (*eparkhia*)[23] to form a senate, to which were to be attached four *kapetanioi* as military advisers. This basic provision, despite the pronouncements of revolutionary and democratic principles, merely confirmed the pre-revolutionary influence of the primates, to whom it gave, in theory at least, the authority relinquished by the Turks.

In no way a slavish imitation of the French Constitution of August 1795,[24] this Greek constitution merged the functions of the executive and the legislative. The executive, a body of five to be elected in a special assembly, could revise legislation, while the legislature was empowered to review all executive action. Both bodies were to be served by eight ministers, who like the departmental civil servants, were to be appointed by the executive. These eight ministers had no independent power and, being debarred from being deputies, they had little or no political influence. They were, in fact, merely heads of department in a rudimentary civil service. Power, if it resided anywhere, resided in the executive of five, four of whom represented the Peloponnese, Eastern Greece, Western Greece, and the islands. The fifth member was the president, Mavrokordatos. Negris was made minister of foreign affairs and president of a ministerial council, which had no power; and he was given the high-sounding but empty title of Chancellor of State. Ypsilantis was likewise placed in a minor position. Although made president of the legislative body (Petrobey was vice-president), he could derive but little influence from that office. Indeed, the constitution as a whole was chiefly the outcome of Mavrokordatos' determination, by throwing in his lot with the primates and by attempting to pacify the *kapetanioi*, to obtain a firm footing in Greece. What it also did, behind a façade deliberately fashioned to impress and deceive Europe,[25] was to organise anarchy, or rather to give a form of legality to the existing regional governments. These, however, were soon to undergo changes. In the Peloponnese effective power passed more and more into the hands of Kolokotronis; in Western Greece first Georgios Varnakiotis and later the Souliot Markos Botzaris,[26] both *kapetanioi*, came to the fore; while in Eastern Greece the famous *klepht*, Androutsos (Odysseas),[27] left the *Areios Pagos* and convened his own assembly.

Owing to the calls of military operations, the provisional constitution was prolonged until April 1823 when a second national assembly met at Astros. No regular elections were held. The assembly was simply a gathering of leaders who chose to attend or who were afraid to stay away. Its main task was to revise the constitution which satisfied no one. The principal revisions were: the substitution of a suspensive veto for the absolute veto of the executive on the resolutions of the legislature; a voice for the legislature in the appointment of higher civil servants; and the replacement of the war and naval ministers by two committees representing regional interests. After further elections (which were irregular) the following appointments were made: Petrobey, president of the executive (Kolokotronis, vice-president); Mavrokordatos, secretary-general; and Ioannis Orlandos, president of the legislature. In theory, the legislature was supreme; in practice, it counted for little, for the chieftains in the executive had their own armies and a tight grip upon provincial administration. Orlandos resigned in disgust. Mavrokordatos succeeded him (July 1823), but he, too, became disgruntled and fled (in danger) to Hydra. Ypsilantis no longer counted, for it had become generally known that Greece could expect no help from Russia. In any case his ideas were not in harmony with the intense nationalist thinking of fellow Greeks. 'The War', he said (and here he was imploring the captains not to massacre the Turks at Tripolitsa), 'is not against tyranny. We are fighting in order to be able to live with the Turks in a state based on law. The cities we conquer are our cities and you should not destroy them.' No wonder then that his place as the leader of the 'military-democratic' factions passed to Kolokotronis who, having become richer than ever from booty from the villages, was able to keep the majority of the lesser Peloponnesian chieftains under his own control.

So disgusted were the members of the legislature with the situation that most of them left Astros and established themselves at Kranidi where they elected a rival executive with Koundouriotis[28] as president. This schism was the result of new political alignments which were based on regional rather than on class division. On the one side were the Peloponnesian chieftains and primates, temporarily in alliance; on the other, were the maritime Greeks, the Greeks of Western Rumeli, and men like Mavrokordatos who were remnants of a national party.

Eventually the two governments found themselves at war. In December, however, the legislative body managed to dismiss Petrobey from the executive (Kolokotronis had already left) and in his place appointed Koundouriotis. This move in some measure reduced the tension. At least it marked a victory for the Peloponnesian primates, now in alliance with the island interest, over the Peloponnesian *kapetanioi*. The executive, thus reconstructed, prolonged its existence until October 1824. Meanwhile, civil strife had continued throughout the summer. All attempts to establish a national congress of conciliation at Salona in Eastern Greece, in which Negris and Androutsos had hoped to play a leading role, had failed completely, and the Peloponnesian chieftains not only drove the executive body from its seat at Nafplion, but also attacked Argos where the members of a newly-elected legislative assembly were beginning to arrive. It was at this juncture, however, that the executive body managed to raise Rumeliot troops under Notaras[29] and Makriyannis[30] to send against the Peloponnesians. It was able to do this because it had every prospect of obtaining the proceeds of the English loan and because it had as a member Ioannis Kolettis,[31] a ruthless, uncompromising politician, who was determined to break the power of the Kolokotronists. In June 1824 Notaras and Makriyannis defeated the Peloponnesians at the mills of Lerna and forced Panos, the eldest son of Theodoros Kolokotronis, to abandon Nafplion.

Here in Nafplion in October 1824 a new assembly was formed. It reappointed Koundouriotis as president of the executive and (later) Mavrokordatos as secretary-general. Within the executive was Kolettis, a rival of both, but indispensable because of his influence with the Rumeliots. These appointments, however, were little to the satisfaction of either the Kolokotronists or of the Peloponnesian primates, who did their utmost to win over Petrobey and Androutsos to their side. But these two remained aloof; and it was Kolettis who ultimately came out best in the political manoeuvres that were taking place. By some means or other he managed to enlist the support of Gouras, who was gaining influence in Eastern Greece at the expense of Androutsos, in whose entourage he had served as lieutenant.[32] In December 1824 and early in 1825 Gouras defeated the Peloponnesians. The primates Sisinis and Deliyannis, and the chieftain Theodoros Kolokotronis were taken prisoner. This political victory, however, was militarily a disaster for Greece. Already the Sultan's Egyptian allies, who had earlier formed a base in Crete, were on the point of building a bridgehead in the southwest Peloponnese. As the threat developed Koundouriotis had the good sense to release Kolokotronis from prison,[33] ignoring the protests of his colleague Mavrokordatos.

Despite the failure of the Greeks to set up a central authority, their constant attempts to do so kept before them the idea of national unity, without which they could never have survived to enjoy independence.[34] These attempts were, however, made less with a view to co-ordinating military operations than with the object of creating a state that would qualify for recognition by the European powers. Military and naval operations could, for the most part, be left to the initiative of individual chiefs and captains of the ships. Turkish strategy was no mystery and needed no Greek general staff to combat it. In the years 1822–4 Moslem armies advanced at their leisure (and the War of Independence as a whole was a most leisurely affair) along predictable routes, traversing the broken coastal plains of eastern and western continental Greece and passing through the gates of Makrinoros in the west and the gates of Thermopylae in the east. The plan was that the western and eastern armies should converge on the Isthmus of Corinth and enter the Peloponnese. Here the Turkish squadrons and transports would land reinforcements and provisions, utilising as salients such maritime fortresses as remained in Turkish hands. Like the land routes, the sea lanes were predictable and there was usually an ample warning of the movements of the Turkish ships. The sea captains, among them Miaoulis, the Tombazis brothers, and Kanaris, needed no direction. Nevertheless, there were occasions when the Greeks made attempts to co-ordinate their military and naval operations and it was on these occasions that the central authority used its none too ample central funds to impart to the Greek campaigns (though not necessarily to their execution) some semblance of a general plan. But once these funds got into the pockets of the *kapetanioi*, there was no knowing what might happen; indeed, most of the proceeds of the first English loan (the raising of which was the work of a central government[35]) were largely dissipated in civil war.

If military efforts could be left for the most part to local enterprise, the long hoped for dealings with the European powers must be the concern of a national government or at least of a government that masqueraded as such. There was, it is true, much private enterprise even in Greek diplomacy. Among Greeks of all parties there was a constant itch to dangle a non-existent Greek crown before the eyes of Europe, and certain individuals and factions became involved in intrigues with agents (often self-appointed) of the European powers, who themselves were disposed within limits to intrigue in Greece.[36] In the course of these intrigues many names were put forward and Greeks of all parties speculated endlessly on the tortuous twists and turns of European diplomacy. There were even plans for making Count Ioannis Kapodistrias king of Greece, and the name of Lord Byron was also put forward. But amidst all these intrigues and individual initiatives, there ran the idea that the Greeks themselves must create a centralised state on western lines. However disruptive his action might be in the field of politics, every Greek of importance had as his political ideal a centralised state which he and his friends would control and a figurehead (a monarch or perhaps even a president) whom he could monopolise. So disposed indeed were all the leading Greeks to distrust one another that it was generally agreed that the head of state should come from outside Greece.

The desire for monarchy (or for a president brought in from outside) gave a form of unity to Greek politics and led to the formation of three parties which were more national, less regional, and less class parties than those that tended to form on other issues. These groupings were not rigid: certain individuals moved from one to another or kept a connection with all of them, hoping to choose the one that promised most at a later stage. Of these groupings the first to attain a definite shape was the Kapodistrian faction, consisting of some six or seven leading[37] figures, who early in 1822 were hoping to bring either Count Ioannis or his brother Viaro Kapodistrias to Greece, it being assumed that he would gain the support of many of the *kapetanioi* with whom he had associated in his Levkas days.[38] This grouping was in no way a pro-Russian party: by 1822 no leading Greek placed any hope in Russia, unless it were Varvakis, one of Orloff's old veterans of 1770.

As a reaction to the Kapodistrian intrigue a so-called French party took shape, the prime movers being the French philhellene Colonel Jourdain and the Vitalis brothers, who were merchants from Zante. Their plan was to place an Orleanist on the throne of Greece, a plan which gained considerable Greek support when General Roche, agent of the Paris Greek committee, arrived in Greece to promote it. But already there had developed an English interest to which greater dimensions were given by the founding of the London Greek Committee, by Lord Byron's arrival among the Greeks, by Edward Blaquiere's efforts to raise a Greek loan in London, by Canning's elevation to the British foreign office, by his policy generally and by his formal recognition of Greek blockades (March 1823). But it was not until 1824 that a definite party emerged from the activities of Lord Guilford,[39] his pupil Spyridon Trikoupis, and a committee of Zantiots which included Count Romas,[40] who managed to win the support of Theodoros Kolokotronis, formerly, if any-thing, a 'Kapodistrian'. With this party Mavrokordatos had some dealing, but he also retained a connection with the French intrigue, hoping, in case it should be successful, to prevent it from being monopolised by his rival Kolettis. From the outset Mavrokordatos had seen that the acceptance by Europe of a Greek national state might be best promoted by the rivalry of France and England for influence in a regenerated Greece – a rivalry which would activate the European concert, of whose mysterious workings he had some inkling. By way of contrast neither Kolokotronis nor any of the leading *kapitanioi* had a clear picture of European diplomacy, but in the hour of danger (the Egyptian advance in the Peloponnese in 1825) they began to look to England or to France – a development which led to more intense thinking on a national scale and to groupings which cut across the earliest regional and personal groupings which we have examined.

Encouraged by the British Naval Commander, Commodore Hamilton, the pro-English Greeks circulated for signature a petition requesting for the Greek nation the sole protection of Great Britain. This petition, the so-called Act of Submission (30 June 1825), was sent to England. It was subsequently approved (1 August) by the Greek Legislative Assembly and a further copy was sent to London in a Greek ship, much to the

annoyance of Kolokotronis who resented its becoming a
governmental act. He had envisaged the petition, which he had
signed, as an anti-governmental measure: he had had visions of
monopolising the English connection. (It was at this time that
he was hoping to prevail upon his old friend General Sir Richard
Church[41] to appear in Greece.) Later he signed, along with
Ypsilantis, Nikitas,[42] and others, an act of submission to Russia,
having been persuaded, no doubt, that under Nicholas I the
policy of Russia towards Greece had changed. Shortly afterwards (February 1826) other Greeks signed an address to the
Duke of Orleans, asking him to accept, on behalf of his son the
Duke of Nemours, the Crown of Greece.

The years of crisis (1825–6) brought about in Greek political
life many other subtle changes which increased the trickles from
the pools of localism into the growing catchment (or quagmire)
of central institutions. Ibrahim Paşa's[43] campaign in the
Peloponnese revealed the limitations of klephtic military
tactics and the military organisation based upon the *kapetanioi*
and their bands.[44] The idea of a regular army and of the
introduction of western military science gained adherents,
especially among those lesser *kapetanioi* who had been thrown up
by the war and who had no connection with the old fighting
families of the Peloponnese and Rumeli – men like 'Captain'
Makriyannis, who joined Colonel Fabvier's regulars as a private,
and like Karatzas, the shoemaker from Patras. The new
captains operated, for the most part, according to governmental orders and were kinder to the local populations, whereas
the traditional *kapetanioi* simply lived upon the country, levying
taxes and stealing animals. Nevertheless, the principal resistance
to the Turks and Egyptians still depended on the old system.
Kolokotronis, on being released from prison, went back to the
Peloponnese and raised fresh bands, which inflicted on the
enemy heavy casualties. Karaiskakis (Georgios Karaiskos), a
former *armatolos* leading an army of 11,000 Rumeliots, kept the
war going in continental Greece.

During the winter of 1825–6 the three Greek 'national'
parties prepared for the third National Assembly which met at
Epidavros in April 1826 and which consisted principally of
those Peloponnesian primates and *kapetanioi* who had been
defeated in December 1824. This assembly appointed a

governmental committee of eleven members and a legislative body of thirteen. The governmental committee 'created', or rather recognised, certain existing local committees through which it attempted, though without much success, to co-ordinate the war effort. The legislative body was to concern itself with the expected negotiations with the European powers and to continue the attempts to find a western military commander. Already in August 1825 Lord Cochrane's services had been secured in principle and a decision had been taken to use the second London loan (of February 1825) chiefly for the provision of a steam fleet for this prospective commander of the Hellenic navy.

Upon the National Assembly and new government the fall of Mesolonghi in April 1826, after a long siege, had a sobering effect and momentarily led the leading Greeks to close their ranks. It was not long, however, before Kolokotronis was at loggerheads with certain Peloponnesian primates. He joined forces with Koundouriotis who was in conflict with fellow primates of Hydra. Reinforced by the primate Sisinis these two called in February 1827 their own assembly at Kastri (Ermioni). As a counter move the old government convened its supporters at Aegina. This division was a reversion to the old personal and regional divisions of the years 1822 to 1824. There was no division on policy. All factions, having learned of the St. Petersburg protocol of April 1826 (the decision of Russia and Great Britain to work together for the creation of a Greek tributary state of unspecified size), fully realised that the probable outcome would be a settlement of the Greek question by Great Britain, France and Russia – a settlement which would eventually be accepted by Prussia and Austria, in other words a settlement made by the concert of Europe. What each Greek faction was out to do was to dominate the government that would negotiate the details of that settlement. Kolokotronis, for example, saw that his own interests (and the interests of the nation) might best be served if Count Kapodistrias could be brought to Greece. He realised, however, that this could be done only with the concurrence of the English 'party' and to strengthen his hand in that quarter he made renewed, and this time successful, attempts to bring General Church to Greece, hoping thereby to counter the combined influence of

Mavrokordatos, of certain primates, and of Lord Cochrane whose services had at long last been secured.

Church and Cochrane arrived separately in Greece in March 1827. The two principal factions at Aegina and Kastri respectively attempted to monopolise them. But Church and Cochrane seized the opportunity to form an alliance between the Kapodistrian and English interests. Following their mediation the two rival assemblies came together on 'neutral' ground at Damala (Troezene). Here the Greek deputies appointed Kapodistrias as president of Greece for a period of seven years and a provisional committee of three to carry on the government until his arrival. They appointed Cochrane as chief admiral and Church as generalissimo.

Although the deputies at Damala had decided to vest the executive function in one man, they designed a constitution to limit his powers. His ministers, who were made liable to impeachment, were to countersign all decrees. To the legislative body the president was denied access except at the opening and closing of each session. He had no right of dissolution and no absolute veto on legislation. Indeed, the new constitution, to which was attached a bill of rights, showed a greater aversion to a strong executive power than did its predecessors: it was the work of men (foremost among them was Mavrokordatos) who had their gaze firmly on the future – men who probably had grave doubts of the wisdom of intruding an ex-minister of Russia into the affairs of Greece.

Of this constitution Kapodistrias, although in accepting office he implicitly subscribed to it, was certainly not enamoured. By this time (his earlier political thinking was extremely vague) his own ideal was a nation of small farmers and peasants under his own paternal rule and a version of the French civil code, in other words, a democratic society but not a democratic state. Shortly after his arrival in January 1828, he transferred the powers of the legislature to a council (*panellinion*) chosen by himself and later to an even more docile senate. He filled many offices with those whom he considered to be the more worthy Ionian Greeks; he appointed non-local men as *ephoroi* in the provinces; and, when in July 1829 he belatedly convened a National Assembly, he packed it with his nominees. Although all these measures aroused the opposition of factions which

called themselves the constitutional party, he enjoyed considerable popularity among lesser Greeks and the *kapetanioi*. Indeed,
he led a national party which was not identified with any particular region or class and which survived into the reign of King
Otho. As a consequence, the opposition, although largely based
on regions and class, had, nevertheless, some of the characteristics, too, of a national party.

To what extent Kapodistrias created for Greece a centralised
machine of government that really worked is not an easy
question to answer. We can read the blueprints of the Kapodistrian regime, but we do not know precisely how the administration worked at the extremities. What is important, however,
is that the effort to create a centralised state continued and that
the principle of centralised government was generally accepted.
What is equally important is that the administrative system of
the Kapodistrian period survived into the period of the
Bavarian regency and throughout the remainder of the nineteenth century. The same is substantially true of the ecclesiastical system, the legal code, taxation, and education.

Kapodistrias had gone to Greece at a time when the creation
of a Greek state of unknown dimensions had been assured. The
treaty of London of July 1827 had affirmed the monarchical
principle. It had provided at least a threat of international
force to impose a settlement on Turkey. This threat had
issued in the battle of Navarino (October 1827), with the result
that, when Kapodistrias arrived in Greece, the dangers to the
Greek nation were no longer so great as in the years 1825–6.
Kapodistrias was, therefore, able to introduce a military
organismos based upon the ideas which Dimitrios Ypsilantis had
put forward in 1821. Gradually he reduced the independent
military power of the *kapetanioi* by recruiting their followers
into first *khiliarkhies* and later *tagmata*[45] and by inviting the more
amenable old leaders to enrol in the *taxiarkhia*, which gave them
high sounding titles and honourable retirement. Not all the old
warriors responded to this treatment: many became brigands
and even left Greece for Turkey where they were more at home.
Nevertheless, a fair proportion joined the *typikon* (a model
battalion), which became a kind of training school for the
regular army.

Kapodistrias's more immediate task, however, was to

negotiate with the European powers,[46] whose diplomacy continued to follow its tortuous course. At a conference of ambassadors held at Poros he worked for as large a Greek state as the powers would allow; and it was he who proposed that Leopold of Saxe-Coburg should be made king of Greece in the hopes that this nomination would reconcile the Duke of Wellington to the idea of a relatively large Greek state embracing all regions that had risen in 1821. When, however, on 3 February 1830 the powers offered Leopold the Greek crown, they abandoned the Arta-Volos line on which they had earlier reached provisional agreement, and substituted the more southerly, less favourable Aspropotamos-Zitouni frontier. They excluded Crete, Samos and Chios from the proposed Greek kingdom. Leopold withdrew his candidature. Kapodistrias bravely soldiered on in face of a growing national, regional and personal opposition to his regime. His brave struggle was cut short by his assassination in October 1831. Civil war ensued and once again, as in 1824, Kolettis sent the Rumeliots into the Peloponnese. Eventually, however, a government commission of seven and a cabinet of five ministers were appointed – an arrangement under which most factions were represented. Once again it was shown that the Greeks, though always prone to fly at one another's throats, could, when need be, arrive at a compromise. The labels they gave themselves were highly misleading. No Kapodistrian was absolutely opposed to a constitution and no self-styled constitutionalist despised naked power when he got the chance to wield it. The great need at this juncture was to preserve at least the semblance of nationality in face of the European powers who had chosen Otho of Bavaria to be king of Greece.

The new-found unity was apparent when on 26 July 1832 a national assembly met at Pronia. This assembly abolished the senate, proclaimed an amnesty, approved Otho's nomination, and declared itself a constitutional body. But its work was cut short by the Rumeliot soldiery. Chaos again reigned, and in the confused struggle of the factions the great question was who should have places of honour when Otho should arrive to govern his kingdom (which, by the treaty of May 1832, had been granted the Arta-Volos frontier). Eventually French troops were called in by the European agents (the residents) to restore order, but it was not until 6 February 1833 that the scene was quiet enough for Otho to step ashore at Nafplion. He was the idol of the moment and the symbol of Greek nationhood – at least of 750,000 Greeks, the remaining 2,000,000 being still under Turkish and British rule. The state that had emerged was centralised in form, but local ties, which were to dominate Greek politics for many a decade, remained strong and disruptive. Moreover, the state was based upon conflicting principles – the unconstitutional power of Otho implicit in the treaty of May 1832, and the constituent power of the Greek nation, which was implicit in its recent history and which had, indeed, been recognised in a proclamation of the powers in August 1832. These conflicting principles, along with the regional and personal divisions in Greek society, were to dominate Greek politics throughout most of the nineteenth century.

NOTES TO CHAPTER 7

For this subject the following works of G. Dimakopoulos are most important: *I doiikitiki organosis kata tin Ellinikin Epanastasin, 1821–1827* (Athens, 1966); *I doiikitiki organosis tis Ellinikis Politeias, 1827–1833*, 1 (*1827–1829*) (Athens, 1971); *O Kodix ton Psiphismaton tis Ellinikis Politeias*, 1 (*1828–1829*) (Athens, 1970), 11 (*1829–1832*) (Athens, 1972); *To Ethnikon Nomisma tis Ellados 1821–1833* (Athens, 1971); 'Ai kyvernitikai arkhai tis Ellinikis Politeias, 1827–1833', *O Eranistis*, IV (1966) 117–54. Other valuable works are N. Kaltchas, *Introduction to the Constitutional History of Greece* (New York, 1940); J. A. Petropulos, *Politics and Statecraft in the Kindgom of Greece, 1833–1843* (Princeton, 1968), a work which, though dealing chiefly with the reign of Otho, contains a good bibliography and important material on the origins of the Greek monarchical state; A. Vakalopoulos, *Ta ellinika stratevmata tou 1821* (Thessaloniki, 1948); K. A. Alexandris, *Ai naftikai epikheiriseis tou yper anexartisias agonos 1821* (Athens, 1930); E. G. Kyriakopoulos, *Ta syntagmata tis Ellados* (Athens, 1960); A. Lignadis, *To proton daneion tis Anexartisias* (Athens, 1970); G. P. Nakos, *Ai 'Megalai Dynameis' kai ta 'Ethnika Ktimata' tis Ellados, 1821–1832* (Thessaloniki, 1970); N. Pantazopoulos, *Ellinon syssomatoseis kata tin Tourkokratian* (Athens, 1958); E. Protopsaltis (ed.), *Istorikon Arkheion Alexandrou Mavrokordatou*, 3 vols. (Athens, 1963–70); T. Stamatopoulos, *O esoterikos agonas prin kai kata tin epanastasi tou 1821*, 2 vols. (Athens, 1957); D. Zakythinos, *I Tourkokratia* (Athens, 1957). The standard collection of state documents is that edited by A. Z. Mamoukas, *Ta kata tin anagennisin tis Ellados, itoi syllogi ton peri tin anagennomenin Ellada syntakhthenton politevmaton, nomon, kai allon episimon praxeon, apo tou 1821 mekhri telous tou 1832* (Athens-Piraeus, 1839–52).

1. The distribution of these cards was a black market business. Tax collectors, who included Greeks, bought them and peddled them at a profit.

2. In the Peloponnese the Greeks outnumbered the Turks by roughly 400,000 to 40,000. Out of one million acres, they held about 350,000 much of this acreage being held in large estates. The Greek upper classes, however, enjoyed a position out of all proportion to the land they held. Much of the business of raising taxation was in their hands and, as these taxes were usually levied in kind, the Greeks, who owned warehouses and animals of burden, amassed capital and became wealthy merchants and moneylenders. They often lived as *paşas*, and not infrequently had their own armed retainers (*kapoi*).

3. The Orthodox Christian was subject to three legal systems, Turkish law, the Ecclesiastical (Roman Law) and the customary law, which in some regions was codified. Between these three systems there was always some conflict. Gains made by the Ecclesiastical law courts at the expense of the Turkish were not infrequently lost to the tribunals administering customary law. On this intricate subject, see N.J. Pantazopoulos, *Church and Law in the Balkan Peninsula during the Ottoman Rule* (Thessaloniki, 1967).

4. The *klephts* (literally, robbers) were bands of outlaws who, in the early days of the Turkish occupation, had taken to the mountains. (In the Slav regions these outlaws were known as *haiduks*.) Sometimes the Turks found it expedient to employ the *klephts* as *armatoloi* (guards) in outlying fortresses or frontier passes. *Armatoloi* were not unknown in Byzantine and Venetian Greece. They were taken over by the Turks who increased their number by recruiting *klephts*. There were, however, no *armatoloi* in the Morea. Here there were only *klephts* and *kapoi*. These *kapoi* were employed, however, not by the Turks but by the Greek primates. See G. Vlakhogiannis, *Klephtes tou Morea* (Athens, 1935) and T. Vournas, *Armatoloi kai klephtes*, (3rd ed.; Athens, 1963).

5. Their fabulous stories were often in the style of the *Arabian Nights*.

6. The Turkish lands which were eventually to be incorporated in Greece consisted at the time of the outbreak of the Greek War of Independence of six major *paşalıks* or provinces – Morea (Peloponnese), Negropont (the island of Evia and the mainland opposite), South Albania (including Western Greece), Selanik (Thessaloniki and most of Macedonia), Crete, and the Aegean Islands. These Aegean islands formed the *paşalık* of the *kaptan paşa*, who was at the head of the Turkish navy.

7. See C. Fauriel, *Chants populaires de la Grèce moderne*, 2 vols. (Paris, 1825).

8. Born in 1744, Ali, an Albanian, became a *klepht* at the age of fourteen. He amassed wealth, formed a strong band of marauders, and became the most powerful chief in a locality ever growing in size. In 1786 he was appointed *paşa* of Trikkala, to which *paşalık* the *sancak* (district) of Ioannina was added in 1788. Leaving one of his sons, Veli, in charge of Trikkala, he devoted his own attention to Epirus. As a reward for his victory in 1799 over the Christian Albanian Souliots, he was appointed to the high office of *beylerbeyi* of Rumeli (which included Bulgaria, Macedonia, and Thrace). Veli became *paşa* of Morea, where he began a relentless war against the *klephts* and eventually drove hundreds of them to take refuge in the Ionian

Islands. Ali's other sons were Mouktar and Salih. Much is known of the activities of the so-called Lion of Ioannina, but we are still without a detailed study of this famous man whose history is so closely linked to the history of Greece.

9. These seven islands had not been Turkish except for a very brief period in the fifteenth century. Until the Treaty of Campo Formio (1797) by which they passed under French control, they had been ruled by Venice. From 1799 to 1807 these islands were under first a Turco-Russian condominium and later exclusively under Russian rule. Following the treary of Tilsit, they passed once more under the control of France. In 1809 a British force captured Zante. By 1814 all the seven islands were occupied by British troops. In theory they had come to form a separate state, known as the Septinsular Republic.

10. See Chapter 3.

11. Finlay's *History of the Greek Revolution* was first published in two volumes in 1861. An enlarged and revised edition was published in 1877 as volumes VI and VII of H. R. Tozer's edition (Oxford) of Finlay's *History of Greece*. These two volumes, bound in one, were reprinted and published in 1971 in London. Finlay's vigorous and well-informed work is very good reading. Unfortunately, although he has much to say in a general way about local Greek institutions (and he must have had first-hand knowledge of their working), he obviously did not think it incumbent on him to explain them in detail for the enlightenment of posterity.

12. See Chapter 2.

13. Descended from a famous family which had provided dragomans to the Porte and governors in the Danubian Principalities, in 1818 he had gone into exile with his uncle Ioannis Karatzas, the governor of Wallachia, to whom he had been secretary. He had settled down in Pisa along with another exile from the Principalities, Ignatios, formerly bishop of Oungro-Vlakhia. On 10 July he had left Marseilles in a ship carrying French, Italian and Greek volunteers, along with military supplies and funds provided by Prince Karatzas. It was probably intended that he should prepare the way for his patrons Ignatios and Karatzas, both of whom imagined that they would attain dominating positions in liberated Greece.

14. Negris had left the Principalities to take an appointment in the Turkish Embassy in Paris. On his way to France by ship he had heard of the outbreak of the Greek Revolution and had disembarked in the Peloponnese, arriving there before Mavrokordatos.

15. See Chapters 4 and 5.

16. A *klepht* from Leondari in the Peloponnese, he had been employed as *kapos* (a retainer) by the wealthy Moreot family of Deliyannis. When in exile in the Ionian Islands he had served as captain in the Duke of York's Greek Light Infantry.

17. Lieutenant-Colonel Leicester Stanhope (later fifth Earl of Harrington) was a philhellene and Benthamite. He was sent to Greece towards the end of 1823 by the London Greek Committee to assist Lord Byron in arranging for employment of officers sent to Greece by that committee and in establishing an arsenal.

18. These three islands, which had joined the revolution shortly after the revolt of the Peloponnese, were to provide the principal naval forces for the prosecution of the war at sea.

19. Already the etairist Papaphlessas (Dikaios) had made attempts to organise an *ephoria* (administration) to include the whole of the Peloponnese (Morea).

20. On his career, see the excellent study of K. A. Diamantis, *Dimitrios Ypsilantis, 1793–1832* (Athens, 1966).

21. The war had given the *kapetanioi* greater power and prestige than they had enjoyed under the old order. Kolokotronis, for instance, upon whom the primate Deliyannis had spent a fortune, had found war so profitable that he ceased to be a docile retainer: he imposed contributions on the villages; he took lesser captains into his pay; and he soon became a man of great political importance.

22. Already in October he had sent out invitations for an assembly at Tripolitsa, but, as the primates resented his initiative, there had been no response.

23. In fact, the old Turkish *kaza*.

24. There are some features which ressemble the pre-French Corsican Constitution. Nothing seems to be known of Gallina or, for that matter, of the way in which the three constitution makers worked.

25. In July 1821 Count Kapodistrias advised Mavrokordatos and the primates to satisfy the European powers by setting up a strong central government based on existing local institutions. Little did Kapodistrias then realise that this was a contradiction in terms.

26. The change came in October 1822. Varnakiotis, an *armatolos*, had made a *kapaki* (accommodation) with the Turks.

27. He had formerly served Ali Paşa of Ioannina.

28. A primate from Hydra, he represented the island interest, although it would not be true to say that he represented all the islanders.

29. Ioannis Notaras, who was nephew of the aged primate, Panoutsos Notaras.

30. Yannis 'Makriyannis' (Triantaphyllos), later a general, began life as a small trader in Arta. Like Ioannis Notaras he favoured the creation of and was prepared (probably with certain reservations) to obey a strong central government.

31. He had served as a physician at Ali Paşa's Court.

32. Gouras later captured Androutsos and held him prisoner in the Akropolis. Here Androutsos was murdered. Thus perished a man whose enmity with Kolettis dated from the time they had both served the tyrant Ali Paşa.

33. Kolokotronis was given the rank of field-marshal. Following the failure of Koundouriotis and Mavrokordatos to save the fortresses of Navarino for the Greeks, he mustered strong forces for the defence of the Peloponnese.

34. This point is well brought out by Dimakopoulos (see various works cited above).

35. See the thorough and important study, A. Lignadis, *To proton daneion tis Anexartisias* (Athens, 1970).

36. On the diplomacy of the Greek revolution, see C. W. Crawley, *The Question of Greek Independence, 1821–33* (Cambridge, 1930) and on certain of the intrigues of Greek parties, see my *British Intelligence of Events in Greece* (Athens, 1959).

37. This adjective is relative. The scene of the Greek War of Independence is crowded with minor characters.

38. See Chapter 5.

39. This was Frederick North. An old philhellene, he had been received into the Orthodox Church and had founded an academy (university) at Corfu.

40. His *Istorikon Arkheion*, ed. D. G. Kambouroglou, 2 vols. (Athens, 1901; 1906) is a most important source.

41. On Kolokotronis's relations with Church, see my *British and American Philhellenes*, (Thessaloniki, 1955) *passim*.

42. 'Nikitas' or 'Nikitaras' was Stamatelopoulos, a former Peloponnesian *kapos* who was one of the great warriors of the war of independence.

43. Ibrahim was the son of Mehmet Ali, the viceroy of Egypt.

44. On this subject, see the excellent study, A. Vakalopoulos, *Ta ellinika Stratevmata tou 1821* (Thessaloniki, 1948).

45. That is, regular regiments. The *khilarkhies* (thousands) were not regular regiments in the strict sense.

46. For this subject the well-documented monograph, D. C. Fleming, *John Capodistrias and the Conference of London, 1828–1831* (Thessaloniki, 1970) is essential.

8 Church, State and the Greek War of Independence

PHILIP SHERRARD

In 1798 a document appeared in Constantinople entitled *Paternal Teaching (Didaskalia Patriki)*. It was signed by Anthimos, Patriarch of Jerusalem, and may well have been written by him; but it has also been attributed, perhaps unjustifiably, to the Patriarch of Constantinople, Grigorios V. The document is a warning against revolutionary ideas, and calls on Orthodox Christians 'to note how brilliantly the Lord, infinite in mercy and all-wise, protects intact the holy and Orthodox faith of the devout and preserves all things'. It points out that the new western 'system of liberty', which at that time was being imported into the Orthodox world, not only contradicts the Scriptures but is really no more than a bastard freedom, allowing each individual to pursue his own most selfish interests and appetites. Thus, it is not true freedom at all but simply anarchy and disorder in which each exploits the other for his own gain.[1]

A few years after this in 1807, when the English fleet under Vice-Admiral Sir John Duckworth appeared off Constantinople, in the reign of the Sultan Selim III (who had foolishly been persuaded into entering into a war against Russia and Britain), the Patriarch Grigorios V, with his pastoral staff in hand, led 1000 Greek workers to help the Turks construct fortifications against the western invaders. It was, it has been said, an impressive display of loyalty to the Turkish rulers at a time when the spirit of western liberalism was as alien to the Church at Constantinople as to the Sultan himself.[2]

On 4 April 1821, a few days after the outbreak of the Greek War of Independence, an encyclical was posted in all the Greek churches in Constantinople signed by the Patriarch Grigorios, Polykarpos of Jerusalem and 21 other prelates, excommunicating all those taking part in the revolution against the protector of Christians and lawful sovereign of the Ottoman Empire, the Sultan. A similar encyclical, addressed to all Orthodox Christians living within the Ottoman Empire and excommunicating all those who raised arms against the Ottoman government, was issued by the Patriarch Evgenios in August 1821.[3]

In 1821, Adamantios Korais published in Paris his commentary on Aristotle's *Politics*. Among other things, he wrote in this commentary:

> From this hour the clergy of the liberated parts of Greece no longer owe recognition to the ecclesiastical authority of the patriarch of Constantinople. . . . It must be governed by a Synod . . .[4]

On 15 July 1833, a Synod was, in fact, summoned by the Greek government. It consisted of 22 prelates (9 were native bishops, and the other 13 were refugee prelates) and was presided over by Spyridon Trikoupis. Its purpose was to discuss and vote on the government's proposals to bring the Church in Greece under the control of the state. One of the proposals was that the Church in Greece should separate itself from the patriarchate of Constantinople and establish its autocephaly. By 4 o'clock that same afternoon, after the Synod had met for barely seven hours, it voted in favour of this proposal and so severed a connection which had lasted for eleven centuries.[5]

Some days later, on 23 July 1833, the Greek government issued the new ecclesiastical constitution, largely the work of the Regent, Georg von Maurer, a German protestant heavily dependent on legal training obtained in Napoleonic France, ably assisted by Theoklitos Pharmakidis, a priest who derived his views on ecclesiastical matters largely from German protestant thought and the works of Korais. Article one of the new ecclesiastical constitution read:

> The Orthodox Eastern Apostolic Church of the Kingdom of Greece in spiritual matters recognizes no head other than the founder of the Christian faith, Our Lord and Saviour Jesus Christ, while in secular affairs it recognizes the authority of the King of Greece. It is autocephalous and independent of all other authority. . . .

Article Two read:

> The highest ecclesiastical authority is entrusted, under the
> authority of the King, to a permanent Synod, entitled 'The
> Holy Synod of the Kingdom of Greece'. The King will
> determine by an organic decree of the Secretary of State who
> will exercise this authority and under whom, as regards this
> authority, the Synod will act. . . .[6]

The year was 1833, which happened to be the 300th anniversary of Henry VIII of England's *Act in Restraint of Appeals*,
enunciating the theory of a Church and State that found their
point of union in the king, who was to be head of both Church
and State. The Henrician changes, which formed the basis of
the English Reformation and denied the Papacy all rights of
jurisdiction over the Church in England, disrupted the mediaeval idea of the Church and State as two aspects of one
community. In the place of this idea, they established the State
as the dominant partner in the alliance. The Greek form of
Erastianism (doctrine of the ascendancy of the State over the
Church), established by the Church settlement of 1833, did
much the same: it reduced the Church in Greece to a department of the State and its officers to little more than office boys
in the governmental bureaucracy. It is not surprising that only
the intervention of the Tsar prevented the Patriarch of Constantinople from excommunicating the whole Greek Church
which had acted in total disregard of the canons of the Orthodox
Church and had established the rule of a government-supervised
Synod subject to an heretical or at least schismatic king. As it
was, it was not until 1850 that the Patriarch could be persuaded
to recognise the new status of the Greek Church; and even then
he only granted this recognition with certain conditions which,
in fact, have never been fulfilled by the Greek Church.

It is quite clear that these incidents and events represent a
clash of interests or attitudes, to say the least. On one level, this
clash could be explained by pointing to certain obvious and, so
to speak, local motives operating on the parties concerned. It
could be said, for instance, that the attitude and actions of the
Patriarch of Constantinople were due to the fact that he had to
do what he could to prevent any revolt on the part of the Greeks
because such a revolt would lead the Turks to take reprisals

against the Sultan's Christian subjects for whose good order he was responsible – or even to take reprisals against the Patriarch himself, as they did in the case of Grigorios V. Or it could be said that the policy of the Greek government itself was dictated by the need to consolidate a national state, this consolidation being impossible so long as the jurisdictional authority over the Greek Church resided in a Patriarch who, in so many ways, was the instrument of the Porte and compelled to serve its interests. But these are contingent reasons, and behind this clash and behind the more local reasons which may be said to have contributed to it, lie deeper causes. What, in fact, is coming to the surface here and manifesting itself on the historical plane is ultimately a clash in principles; and the true significance of the changes in the relationship between the Church and the State in this period, as well as of the conflicting positions taken up by the Patriarch and the Greek authorities, ecclesiastical and civil, can only become clear if they are referred back, not to politics or statesmanship or expediency, but to a much larger frame-work of theory and practice. Indeed, they presume a series of developments, intellectual and other, which reach right back up the mainstream of European history to at least the new era in Church–State relationships initiated by Constantine the Great in the fourth century. They will only become properly intellig-ible, therefore, when set within a perspective which includes the Constantinian settlement and so, by implication, what comes before that.

With Constantine the Great or, it might be better to say, through his actions and beliefs, a new conception of things enters into the mainstream of European history. It is from this conception of things, through a series of modifications, that the whole pattern of Church–State relationships in the mediaeval and post-mediaeval world has gradually unfolded. What happened in 1821 in Greece is but a phase in this pattern and may be said to have been determined by it. What was this new conception of things that has so vitally affected the course of European history?

Until the time of Constantine, Christians, broadly speaking, had the idea that the Church's activity among mankind was directed towards its individual members and not towards the salvation or christianisation of society as a whole. The Church manifested itself, not through the State, but solely through the local communities of Christians who formed as it were an independent society, a new kind of society, a state within the state. In this view, although Christians were obedient to the State in all things lawful, there was no idea that the State might or should cooperate in the realisation of the Kingdom of God. There was no idea that society as a whole should be an area submissive to the divine revelation of the Gospels where the will of God is actualised in the rule of its governors and administrators and their laws. Indeed, in certain ways the opposite might be said to have been the case. It could be argued that through these early centuries the Church survived, certainly not in cooperation with the State and society, but in spite of the State and society. The Christian Saviour Himself had shown what the attitude of the Christians should be towards the civil powers and their laws. He had consistently rejected all this-worldly authority in achieving His mission. He had proclaimed that His Kingdom was not of this world and that the peace and unity He brought were not the peace and unity of society or of any this-worldly establishment. Insofar as society and any this-worldly establishment were concerned, He said He had come to bring not peace but the sword. And by and large Christians had followed the example of the Christian Saviour. They did not revolt against the State. In fact, they were willing to be obedient to the State in all matters that did not concern their faith; and where it was a question of having to choose between revolt or suffering when the State did interfere with their faith, they consistently chose suffering. The early history of the Church is full, not of social agitators or revolutionaries, but of martyrs.

At the time of Constantine, however, and through his conversion to Christianity, this pattern in the relationship between Church and State was changed. It was changed by the introduction of what is virtually a new idea into history, a new idea even for Christians. This idea is that of the Christian State or the Christian society. Constantine was the representative of the old theocratic ideology. He was the representative, that is to say, of the idea that the State, with the god-like figure of the absolute and autocratic ruler at its centre, was a divine institution. And the revolution which his conversion initiated consisted in the forming of an alliance between this old non-Christian theocratic idea, inherited from Rome and the classical world, and the Christian Church.

Here it is important to remark upon an anomaly in the circumstances which led to the forming of this alliance that vitally affected its whole future development. This anomaly lay in the manner in which Constantine became a Christian. The legend is that a few days before the battle in which he was to defeat one of his rivals, Maxentius, he was told in a dream to put a new sign on his weapons. It was later said that this sign was the Christian Cross. Whatever the truth about this, it is clear that from this time forth Constantine went into battle under a Christian sign and counted himself a Christian. I say 'counted himself a Christian' rather than 'was a Christian' because, technically, the only way a person could become a Christian and a member of the Church was through baptism; and Constantine was not baptised until he was on his deathbed. And it is in this apparently minor technical discrepancy that the whole future fundamental paradox of the relationships between Church and State in the Byzantine world lies.

In Constantine's mind – and so by extension in the minds of his successors – the Christian faith or, rather, faith in Christ, did not come to him through the Church. It came to him, rather as it had come to St. Paul on the road to Damascus, by direct and personal intervention on the part of God so that he could win his battle over his rival. This meant that the victory he had won with the help of the Christian God had placed the emperor – and so the whole empire as well – directly under the protection of the Cross and in direct dependence on Christ. Christ Himself had sanctioned Constantine's power as emperor. He had elected Constantine to be His representative; and through Constantine He had put the empire, the Roman empire, under His immediate care and charge. And He had done all this, not through the Church and its hierarchy, but outside the Church and its hierarchy.

It is because of this that Constantine's conversion did not lead him or his successors to surrender or even fundamentally to modify the idea or structure of the theocratic empire. On the contrary, the reverse was rather the case. Christians and the Church itself became convinced that the emperor had received God's special benediction and that the empire was now a consecrated kingdom, chosen by God and dedicated to His service.

The empire was a worldly instrument in the hands of God for carrying out His purpose. The citizens of the empire, of the Christian empire, were now a people chosen under God, the patriarchs of a new age, a new chosen nation. The emperor was to rule on earth as God's vice-regent and representative; and his task was to achieve the corporate salvation of his chosen people by knitting them together into this new Christian theocracy, a universal Christian society. All the subsequent history of the relationships between the Church and the State in the Christian world, both Orthodox and non-Orthodox, has been vitally coloured by this fact: that the first Christian emperor was a Christian *outside* the Church and independent of the Church; that he had received his authority directly from God; and that the Church recognised him and accepted the whole empire and the whole theocratic conception of the State that went with him.

In practice, this meant that for Byzantium and for the Orthodox states which issued from Byzantium the whole political Roman inheritance – the whole establishment of the theocratic state with its laws and institutions and ceremonies – had to be accepted by the Church and given a Christian benediction. It had, in fact, to be christianised. Instead of the Church standing apart from the State, or forming a state within the state, it now entered into alliance with the State. Instead of the Church breaking drastically with the old Roman ideals of theocratic absolutism, this absolutism was now included as part of the Church's programme for establishing and maintaining a Christian society and for christianising the world. For Byzantium and, generally speaking, for the Orthodox countries that issued from Byzantium, religion now became and continued to be a state matter because the Church itself had accepted the State as a divine institution.

This in its turn meant something else. If religion is a state matter and if, in terms of the theocratic idea, the unity of the State must be based on the unity of the faith of its members, it at once follows that the State cannot tolerate any freedom of conscience or expression in matters of faith or religion. It has to impose a single faith, a single religion on its subjects. Correspondingly, insofar as the Church has accepted the State as a divine institution and allies itself with the State in the task of creating and maintaining a Christian society, the Church, too, becomes involved in this process of imposing a uniform religion – Christianity – on all the subjects of the State. This is what happened in Byzantium and this is the legacy that Byzantium left to later Orthodox countries, including Greece: this willingness of the Church to cooperate with the State because the State is regarded as having a sacrosanct status.

There must be no misunderstanding on this point. Neither in Byzantium nor subsequently in Orthodox countries did the Church become simply a state church and nothing more. One has to distinguish, in a way that many historians fail to distinguish, between the State's idea of itself and its relations to the Church, and the Church's idea of itself and its relations to the State. Sometimes these ideas are radically opposed and yet the opposition is concealed from either side and only becomes clear in times of crisis. Thus, although the theocratic absolutism of the State must lead logically to the subordination of the Church to the State, the Church by definition must claim that a whole sphere of its interests and activities are beyond and superior to state control. If the Church renounces this claim, it ceases to be the Church. By definition there cannot be a *Christian* Church which is simply a state church and nothing more. But there can be, and frequently is, a situation in which the Church cooperates with the State in making people Christian not only by grace but also by law and believes that in this manner it is helping to form or advance the Kingdom of God, while the State's purpose in making a Christian society and invoking the assistance of the Church is not really for the sake of the Kingdom of God but simply for its own aggrandisement and absolutism. There is, that is to say, a situation in which Church and State cooperate for radically different reasons; and each may be unaware that the reasons differ until it is too late.

The Church, once it has agreed to recognise the State as a sacrosanct institution and so to accept that its religion should become the religion of the State, is particularly vulnerable in a situation like that outlined above. Once it cooperates with the State on these terms it becomes not only a community of believers, but also a community of those who are obliged to believe in order to be citizens of the State. This is what happened in the Byzantine period. From the time it entered into an alliance with the State in the person of Constantine the

Great and his immediate successors, down to the fall of Constantinople in 1453, the Church never succeeded in freeing itself from the illusion that now the emperor was a Christian emperor he must in some way be working for the Kingdom of God, so that it was the Church's duty to assist him by allowing its faith and organisation to back and support the imperial structure. In fact, so deeply had this idea of the inherent sanctity of the State and its laws eaten into the consciousness of the Church that, provided its own dogma was not disturbed, it could still feel it was its duty to back and support the imperial structure even when the emperor ceased to be a Christian.

That this was the case is illustrated by the way in which the Patriarch of Constantinople accepted his new role after the fall of the city in 1453. His agreement to become the *ethnarch* (*millet başi*) of the Sultan's Orthodox Christian subjects, uniting in his office an ecclesiastical and civil authority greater than any he had possessed during the Byzantine period, was again not a matter of expediency or mere statesmanship. It was implicit in the Church's original acceptance of the emperor and the State as divine institutions at the time of Constantine and his successors. In accepting the emperor and the State in this way the Church had also acknowledged that the emperor derived his authority not from the Church but directly from God independently of the Church. His office was a sacred one in its own right. And this principle could be applied equally as well to the Sultan as it could to a Christian emperor.

In any case, the recognition by the Patriarch of the Sultan as the temporal power in the society in which the Church had to function after the fall of Constantinople, and his decision to be obedient to him and his government, were fully in accord with Christ's own words concerning the respective spheres of God and Caesar. They were also in accord with the example the Christian Saviour had given of how to behave towards Casear. It was this example which by and large Christians had followed during the centuries before the conversion of Constantine, and it had been reaffirmed in the writings and actions of Orthodox theologians during the Byzantine period. It implied an understanding that the State is responsible for the whole political and economic side of life and in this respect must be obeyed; while, for its own internal affairs, the Church itself, expressing itself

through its pastors and teachers, and through patristic traditions, written and unwritten, is entirely responsible, and the
State has no right to try to take them out of its hands.

It is against the background of this understanding, especially
as it had been elaborated in the Byzantine period, that the
actions and reactions of the great Church at Constantinople
during the years of the *Tourkokratia* must be set if they are to be
seen in their historical perspective and judged accordingly. In
particular it is only against this background that the policy of
the Patriarch, during the years leading up to the Greek War
of Independence and the subsequent emergence of the Greek
state, becomes intelligible. What confused the situation was not
that the Church recognised and accepted the Sultan as the
temporal power and agreed to be obedient to him, because this,
as we have seen, was quite consistent with the Byzantine tradition. What confused the situation was that the Sultan invested
the Patriarch himself with a large measure of temporal power,
so that he became, in fact, not only the spiritual but also the
secular ruler of the Orthodox Christian peoples in the Sultan's
territories. This meant that any attempt on the part of one
element of these peoples to establish its own secular autonomy
was bound to lead it into conflict with a Patriarch in whose
office the spiritual and the secular were now so radically inter-
twined. It is precisely this that happened where the Greeks are
concerned at the time of the War of Independence. But again
it must be emphasised that the section of the Church in Greece
which allied itself with the Revolution and which subsequently
agreed or contributed to the Church settlement in the new
Greek state, as well as those who prepared this settlement
itself, were not motivated merely by political expediency. They
were acting in accordance with a new conception of things – a
new conception of the function of the state and of the relationship between the Church and the State; and their actions only
become understandable when viewed in the light of this new
conception.

To grasp the significance of this new conception (new when
compared with the traditional Byzantine conception) attention
must be shifted from Byzantium and its religio-political structure and directed to western Europe. This shift of attention has
to be made when trying to understand almost any of the ideas,

political, social or intellectual, which promoted the War of Independence. In this case, the ideas of Church–State relationships entertained by people like Adamantios Korais, or Pharmakidis, the chief Orthodox advisor on Church affairs to the Greek state during the years in which the Church settlement was being prepared, or Georg von Maurer, architect of this settlement itself – these ideas only become intelligible when referred to certain changes in the conception of Church–State relationships that took place in western Europe in the late mediaeval and post-mediaeval world.

Here it must first be said that in the western mediaeval period the Church's own idea of its rôle in this connection was, or became, very different from that of the Byzantine Church. Theoretically, it might be held that there were two sovereign powers, a kind of dyarchy of the *regnum* and *sacerdotium*, each with its own rights over the individual, and that in this respect the pattern was similar to that of Byzantium. As a citizen, the individual was subject to the *regnum*, the political state which demanded his obedience. But he was also a member of the Church and as a member of the Church he was subject to the priestly power, the *sacerdotium*, instituted by Christ with the duty of ruling over every baptised person and directing him towards salvation. Ideally, these two powers were meant to work in harmony. Men's souls were to be in the keeping of the Church, their bodies in the keeping of the State. But in practice, both in Byzantium and in western Europe, this harmony was often disrupted. In western Europe, this disruption became particularly marked in the later Middle Ages when the Church, not content with being one of the two sovereign powers or an *imperium in imperio*, began to put forward what amounted to imperial claims in its own right.

The Hildebrandine movement in the eleventh and early twelfth centuries, and then the canonist pope, Innocent IV, and the canonists and philosopher-publicists who came after him, established a doctrine according to which the two powers of Church and State, *sacerdotium* and *regnum*, were not equal in dignity or even complementary. The one, it was claimed, was superior to the other and, in a way, included the other within it. This superior power was the Church – or, rather, the papacy, since the Church in western Europe was governed by the papacy. Briefly, the papalist argument was that since spiritual or religious ends are superior to temporal or secular ends, and the latter are a means to the former, it follows that the pope as spiritual authority is superior to the temporal power. The pope, that is to say, is the supreme ruler and judge over all men in both temporal and spiritual affairs. He need not exercise his authority directly. He might well delegate it to the secular ruler. But the plenitude of both spiritual and temporal power is vested in him, and the secular ruler only exercises his power in so far as it is delegated to him by the pope.

If this new papal theory is compared with the traditional Byzantine arrangement, it might be said that the papacy is claiming an authority vis-à-vis the secular ruler which the Church in Byzantium could not claim vis-à-vis the emperor. The papacy is claiming an authority which in Byzantium was regarded as belonging to the emperor and as conferred on the emperor not by the Church but directly by God. That the papacy was able to do this could, in part, be attributed to the fact that for several centuries during which the complex relationships between Church and emperor were being determined in Byzantium, there was no comparable secular ruler in western Europe. Indeed, the papacy, centred on Rome, was the one supra-national power in western Europe capable of exercising an individual authority. Then with Charlemagne and subsequently when there was an emperor in western Europe, this emperor might claim that his authority was derived from Caesar (an authority which, as Dante was to point out in his *de Monarchia*, did not derive from St. Peter); but he could not claim, as the Byzantine emperor after Constantine could claim, that his authority derived directly from Christ independently of the formal institution of the Church. Thirdly, the papacy was able to appeal to the *Donatio Constantini*. This document, believed to be entirely genuine both in eastern and western Europe until the fifteenth century, had, in fact, been forged probably in the late eighth century; and it set forth how Constantine the Great decided to transfer his capital to Constantinople after being cured of leprosy by Pope Sylvester, so that he could bequeath to the pope and his successors his sovereignty over Italy (a bequest which Dante again regarded as one of the most disastrous events in history, although, he added, it was completely illegal, since the emperor could not alienate, nor could the pope receive, temporal power). Finally, one has to remember that the Church in western Europe had become emphatically a clerically controlled body: the laity had no voice in doctrinal decisions, in legislation or in administration or discipline. 'Church' and 'clergy' became convertible terms, and it tended to be forgotten that the clergy were also members of the state, and that the laity were also members of the Church.

These factors, together with others, may explain why, in western Europe, the papacy began to claim the powers and assume the rôle which in Byzantium were recognised as belonging to the holy emperor, Christ's Vice-regent on earth. Moreover, it is the pope's claim to combine and confuse in his single office the powers and rights of both St. Peter and Caesar, *sacerdotium* and *regnum*, and to be the undivided and absolute authority in a hierocratic state system; it is this claim which in its turn may explain why, when secular rulers and the apologists for the temporal state began to affirm what they conceived to be their just titles, they came into head-on collision with the papacy. So great was the confusion provoked by papal claims that the only effective method of counteracting them appeared to be to reverse the situation altogether and to maintain that the Church, as an institution, is subject to the State. In other words, supporters of the *regnum* now had to maintain that the plentitude of all power resides not in the papacy but in the State.

At this point it is relevant to introduce a figure who might be regarded as the presiding genius of the Greek War of Independence and of the state which emerged from it. His right to occupy this position is based on the fact that most of the ideas, social, political and intellectual, of which this War and subsequent constitutional and other developments were an expression, can be traced back in one way or another to his work. The importance of Padua as a forging-house of the new philosophies which were to be the forerunners of modern natural science and political theory, and as the centre from which these philosophies were diffused through the Greek world has often been emphasised. But it also played an important rôle in connection with the challenge to papal claims and with the whole development of a conception of the relationship between Church and State which practically reversed the papal position. It played this rôle in the person of one of the most important theoreticians of the anti-papal movement and, therefore, one of the most imposing mediaeval rebels, Marsiglio of Padua.[7] And Marsiglio might be regarded as the presiding genius of the Greek War of Independence and the modern Greek state not simply because of his link with Padua, but also because when he was excommunicated in 1326 after the publication of his great work, *Defensor Pacis*, he fled for refuge to the court of the Emperor Ludwig of Bavaria, and became one of his most influential advisors. In this way he may be said to have penetrated into Greece not only through Padua but also through Bavaria. He may be seen as one of the intellectual ancestors of the regent, Georg von Maurer.

Briefly, Marsiglio regarded the secular state as the only cohesive and coercive force capable of creating a civilised life for man on earth. It must be remembered that Marsiglio was writing within a perspective in which Aristotelian standards were deeply respected; and according to these standards society is a human and not a divine institution, and it exists not for the immortal but for the mortal welfare of the individual. Man is said to be a social animal and his *summum bonum* is first self-preservation and second the full realisation of human happiness on earth through the pursuit of social, political and economic self-sufficiency. Moreover, the State itself can provide this 'sufficient life', and it can provide it, according to Marsiglio and others of his line of thought, without any intervention on the part of the Church. In other words, Marsiglio had forsaken those standards effective for the world of mediaeval Christendom or even for the Christian tradition itself. For him, the State is omnipotent, self-sufficient and entirely responsible for supplying the needs of its people and of the present life.

Yet, although in Marsiglio's system the State is accorded this exalted position, it is said to derive its authority, not of course from the papacy or other spiritual authority or even directly from God, but from the people. For Marsiglio it is really the people that become the ultimate authority in and custodian of religious as well as secular values. With this republican thesis – with the idealisation of that ambiguous entity, the people, and the attribution to the people of a kind of infallibility and plenitude of power associated with the papacy – Marsiglio shifts the whole form of the traditional mediaeval Church–State debate. That debate, as we have seen, had been between two different centres of authority, representing different values and functions: the *regnum* and the *sacerdotium*. Marsiglio subsumes both these centres under a new over-riding authority, a new *universitas*. This new sovereign power is the whole body of the citizens, the people. The body of the people is both secular and religious, both *civilis* and *fidelis*, State and Church; and it is equally infallible in both spheres. In addition, he bases the people's authority in the religious sphere on the same principle as its authority in the political sphere: its freedom and its volitional and intellectual superiority over all its 'parts', including the priesthood.

Although in Marsiglio's system the supreme sovereignty in both spiritual and temporal matters resides in the people, yet it is the government or 'ruling part' which it elects that acts as the executive and coercive agent of the people in all things, in both the religious and the secular sphere. This is the beginning of the fiction which has been so persuasive in later centuries to the effect that an elected government is or can be representative of the people and carries out its will. What it means in the context here under discussion is that the State is accorded complete control over the Church. The Church must direct thought and action on the next world. In this world it can claim no rights, no property, no jurisdiction except what the state sees fit to delegate to it. The clergy, equally with laymen, must be subject to all state law. It can claim no right to tithes or other emoluments unless the State grants them. All officers of the Church, from popes and bishops downwards, receive their offices from the civil rulers. At the same time, the Church itself is said to consist of and to be constituted by the whole people, the whole body of believers (*universitas fidelium*), which controls all the institutional aspects of religion. The Church is merely the citizen-body organised as simply as possible for other-worldly purposes.

What Marsiglio does in effect is to turn the whole doctrine of the papal plenitude of power upside down. The papal hierocratic conception of society is translated into secular form, with the people, this mythical entity, exercising its sovereignty through the State. The State itself is now to have a priest-king at its head, taking the place of the pope; and the Christian religion is to provide the unifying bond of belief necessary to secure worldly peace and order. Both the papal system and Marsiglio's system are monistic and absolutist, in spite of the republican basis of Marsiglio's system. The difference is that, while in the papal system the purpose of society is to help man to achieve his supra-terrestrial well-being, in Marsiglio's system it is society as an end in itself which takes precedence over society as a means to a future life or to salvation. The ideal is now to achieve a peace and a unity and a stability of the State so that man may live a self-sufficient life in this world. Marsiglio stands as the forerunner of both democracy and the police-state. The conjunction is not a coincidence. Apologists for systems of absolutism like Bodin and Hobbes, and defenders of the principle of popular rights and the sovereignty of the people, both base their arguments on those of Marsiglio. Idealisation of the people as the sovereign power has resulted in tyrannies as great as any achieved by either monarchical or ecclesiastical forms of government.

In relation to the theme of this essay, however, it is Marsiglio's rôle as forerunner of the doctrine of the ascendancy of the State over the Church (Erastianism) which must be emphasised. In this respect, he stands at the head of the movement of ideas that led not only to the changes of Henry VIII in England, but also to the changes brought about in the relationships between State and Church in Greece immediately after the War of Independence some three hundred years later. Marsiglio provides as it were the intellectual blue-print for these changes in Greece. If the conception of the relationships between Church and State advocated and implemented by Korais and Pharmakidis and von Maurer derived from models established in western Europe as a consequence of the Protestant Reformation as well as from the model provided by the reforms of Peter the Great in Russia (itself a reflection of Protestant models), these models themselves were ultimately inspired largely by the theories of Marsiglio.

So it was that in Greece or in the Greek world at the end of the eighteenth century and during the first half of the nineteenth century two conceptions of Church–State relationships came face to face. The first, represented by the Patriarchate, was inherited from Byzantium. According to this conception, the Church is a kind of *imperium in imperio* or *imperium iuxta imperium*. It owes obedience to the temporal power in all things lawful – that is to say, in all matters which do not violate the explicit tenets of the Christian faith and which may be said to cover the whole political and economic side of life. On the other hand, the Church itself is entirely responsible for its own ecclesiastical government, organisation and law without reference to the temporal power. The second conception was that of the Greek reformers. It derived from western Europe and was originally the product of a reaction against the hierocratic system of the mediaeval papacy which grew out of a non-Orthodox background and had no parallel in the traditional Church–State relationships in Byzantium or for that matter anywhere in the Orthodox world before Peter the Great. According to this conception, the Church is definitely subordinate to the State. It is a department of the State responsible for the religious life of the citizens and as such it is subject to state control in its own internal administration and organisation.

The two groups representing these two conflicting conceptions – the great Church centred at Constantinople on the one hand and the Greek reformers on the other – thought and acted according to the rival and incompatible logics of the rival and incompatible systems each had accepted. The Patriarch in condemning the War of Independence, excommunicating those who took part in it, and in refusing to recognise the new Constitution of the Church in the new Greek state was acting within the traditional Byzantine perspective. This is true in spite of the fact that his own position may have been compromised or confused because he was not only the Patriarch but also the *ethnarch* of the Sultan's Orthodox Christian subjects. In acting as he did he was basing himself firmly on the system of Church–State relationships which had been elaborated in Byzantium from the time of Constantine the Great onwards.

The reformers, on the other hand, in establishing the new Constitution of the Church in Greece were acting within a non-Byzantine and basically Protestant perspective. This, in its turn, is true in spite of the fact that in their desire to erect a national state of west European lines they came into conflict with the

Patriarch, not so much in his spiritual rôle as in his supranational and temporal rôle of *ethnarch* over all the Sultan's Christian subjects. Moreover, not only did the way in which the reformers proceed to enact the new Constitution violate the canons of the Orthodox Church; but also, according to more than one Orthodox theologian, the articles of the Constitution themselves are incompatible with the principles of Orthodox doctrine and so are basically non-Orthodox.

NOTES TO CHAPTER 8

1. Extracts from this text in T. H. Papadopoullos, *Studies and Documents Relating to the History of the Greek Church and People under Turkish Domination* (Brussels, 1952) pp. 143–5.

2. See C. A. Frazee, *The Orthodox Church and Independent Greece 1821–1852* (London, 1969) p. 8.

3. *Ibid.*, p. 28.

4. Adamantios Korais, *Aristotelous politikon ta sozomena* (Paris, 1821) p. 120.

5. Frazee, *The Orthodox Church*, pp. 110–12.

6. *Ibid.*, p. 113.

7. On Marsiglio's thought, see M. J. Wilks, *The Problem of Sovereignty in the Later Middle Ages* (Cambridge, 1963), pp. 96 ff.; and Marcilius of Padua, *The Defender of Peace (the Defensor Pacis)*, introduced and translated by A. Gewirth (New York, 1956).

9 The Other British Philhellenes

ALEXIS DIMARAS

Philhellenism during the War of Independence, and especially its British manifestations, has been adequately investigated in the works of Douglas Dakin and C. M. Woodhouse.[1] There seems, however, to be some confusion in these and other books on the subject, over the use of the term 'philhellene', a certain vagueness as to who qualifies for the title. On the whole the main focus is on the military, who are given greater attention than, say, the doctors, the teachers or the missionaries, who in some instances are omitted altogether. Further, there appears to be no agreement as to whether the philhellenes include both those who had and those who had not set foot on the soil of Greece, while confusion exists over the geographical concept of Greece in this context. There are also doubts of a chronological nature, concerning the beginning and the end of the philhellenic movement. Further difficulties arise when individual cases are taken into consideration. David (later Sir David) Urquhart had fought bravely with the Greeks during the War, but later turned against them, and Dr Julius Millingen appeared devoted to the Greek cause before changing sides and becoming personal physician to the Sultan. And these are not the only ones who changed their allegiance. An individual's philhellenic proclivities, then, cannot in every case be regarded as permanent.

Even more confusing, perhaps, is the fact that a friend of the Greek people may not necessarily be well disposed towards their rulers. Richard Church, George Lee, George Finlay and Thomas Gordon, to mention only some of the best known examples, openly supported in July 1829 the 'Patriot Party' in Greece, which was in opposition to President Kapodistrias' autocratic rule, and demanded a constitution. All four had made a considerable contribution to the effort for Greek independence before the arrival of the President, but it is very doubtful whether they would still be officially considered as philhellenes in 1829.[2]

Be this as it may, in many cases the friends of the insurgent subjects of the Ottoman Empire were, in fact, 'philhellenes', significantly not 'Graecophils', and were primarily motivated by an admiration for ancient Hellas rather than by affection for modern Greece.[3] The contrast between the dreams of the classicist and the reality seen by the visitor to the country often caused disappointment that was strong enough to provoke a change of camp. But on the other hand the Greeks – or at least their cultural leaders – soon realised the benefits they could expect from an exploitation of their 'heritage'. Before developing into a substitute for action (as it often seems to be today) this stressing of the affinity between the ancient and the modern Greeks was considered to be of use in a better cause. It was expected to arouse the sympathy of the rest of the world, and at the same time help the Greeks to regain their national identity. That the fighters of the War of Independence were none other than the sons of the Three Hundred who had died with Leonidas was constantly stressed. Examples of this type of thinking are to be found in the lines of the *Ymnos eis tin Eleftherian* (later to become the Greek national anthem) by Dionysios Solomos, the national poet, or in the preoccupation of Adamantios Korais with the classics and their translation into modern Greek. In a different field, it is known that Rigas Velestinlis, an early promulgator of the idea of independence, wandered around wearing an ancient Greek helmet, a practice followed later by General Theodoros Kolokotronis himself, while teachers urged their pupils to change their Christian names into Hellenic ones.

These attitudes, however, were not without their immediate side effects. The belief that an obligation of gratitude was due to the modern Greeks on account of their ancestors has had a curious psychological impact on the relations of Greece with the rest of the world. It has not only led to expectation of gain without effort but has also created unjustifiably hard feelings when help was not offered as enthusiastically and as disinterestedly as expected. Nevertheless, admiration of ancient Greece was not the only motive behind the philhellenic movement during the War of Independence. The fact that the oppressed were Christians and the oppressors Muslims was also a potent source of sympathy. Thus, when the French *Société de la Morale Chrétienne* decided to offer its assistance to the Greek victims of the war, it proclaimed that it was acting under a moral obligation since

> nous ne pourrons jamais désavouer devant Dieu que nous n'ayons aux Grecs une obligation plus grande encore [than to the others in need] puisque nous leur devons les lumières de l'Evangile.[4]

And it was a British philhellene, Edward Blaquiere, who combined these Hellenic and Christian motives when he told the Greeks that he was helping them because he was 'enthusiastically favoured to Grecian freedom, not less from a sense of religion than of gratitude to their ancestors'.[5]

Still, to the classicists and the Christians, other groups must be added to complete the picture of philhellenism. They include the philanthropists who seem to be generally treated as belonging to a class of their own, not directly related to philhellenism, as well as the adventurers and the speculators.[6] They all contributed to the creation in Europe and America of a philhellenic public opinion, which in this instance demonstrated a remarkable strength. Ultimately, in combination with other factors, they helped in changing governmental attitudes towards the War. In general terms we may agree with the French politician who later put forward the view that 'it is not the governments of Europe who have saved Greece, but public opinion'.[7] Even further, they, or at least the most eminent among them, helped significantly by the pressure they exerted in attempting – in many instances successfully – to unite the disunited Greek forces, and bring an end to factional struggles. In this respect, as in so many others, the Britons deserve special mention; not only the military such as Thomas Gordon, Richard Church, Frank Abney Hastings, or even Thomas Cochrane, but also others who acted in different capacities, such as Lord Byron and George Finlay, and the controversial agents of the London Greek Committee, Leicester Stanhope and Edward Blaquiere. Even the Greek Loans, that complicated example of Anglo-Greek incompetence and speculation, acted as a rallying force for the Greeks at one time.

What is, however, often forgotten is that, at the time, Greece had to face problems not only directly related to the war effort. In addition to the battle for national independence, the Greeks had to fight two more battles: one against misery and poverty, and the other to gain personal freedom. Yet we seem to know far better the extent and nature of foreign contributions on the battle-field than the assistance offered by the 'other philhellenes', who played their part on these other fronts. Occasionally some of them are mentioned in studies of philhellenism. The Swiss millionaire Jean-Gabriel Eynard who contributed financially, the American Samuel Gridley Howe who provided work and protection for the poor, Frederick North, fifth Earl of Guilford who promoted education, as well as politicians like George Canning and writers like Byron, are usually included in relevant surveys. But the dominant place is always reserved for the military, the generals as well as the privates, the sea captains as well as the cooks. This adds, of course, to the confusion regarding the concept of philhellenism referred to above, and distorts its essence.

It is true that there is hardly one philhellene who belongs exclusively to one of the above-mentioned categories, and that classifications of this sort are arbitrary. It is also true that omission is a way of valuing contributions. But it is difficult to believe that in studies on philhellenism omissions of those who helped in a non-violent way are due to such considerations. As our history books are overloaded with battles and massacres, as our squares are embellished with statutes of military men rather than doctors and scholars, so are non-militant philhellenes traditionally considered less important than the military ones. The existence of an article on a philhellene scholar in this or that periodical does not change the balance. The issue becomes more interesting when looked at from the point of view of the efficiency of this military assistance. It seems, indeed, that with a few notable exceptions this contribution was of a rather doubtful order. Among those who went to Greece to fight, there are endless examples of men who, willingly or not, remained idle, who were disappointed or disillusioned and abandoned the effort, who were more interested in adventures than in contributing to a good cause. It is in this respect significant that almost all the early arrivals who really did fight were lost in a single battle, at Peta in 1822. Historians do not seem to be agreed in apportioning responsibility for that defeat, but it is hard to believe that military incompetence did not have something to do with it. Spyridon Trikoupis, the meticulous recorder of the events of the War in which he himself took part, says about these less efficient military types that they were 'sleepwalking' (*oneirovatoun*).[8] Other historians, like Thomas Gordon, formerly a military philhellene himself, are more critical, and Byron, placing the issue on a different basis, would remark that 'all these penniless officers had better have stayed at home'.[9]

These considerations justify an investigation of the other aspects of philhellenism. Foreign contributions to the battle against misery and poverty were indeed much more effective than purely military aid. They were expressed in the activities of doctors, the shipment of relief supplies, and pecuniary assistance. Here the Swiss and the Americans were the most active, while the British helped considerably in the fight for personal freedom which had to be gained in addition to national independence. The outcome of this third battle may seem in retrospect to have been unsuccessful, but, contrary to what has been said about the military, it would not appear fair to attribute this failure to the incompetence of the philhellenes. In this, the London Greek Committee deserves special mention, despite possibly justified criticisms which have been made of some other of its activities.

Founded in 1823, the Committee was able to offer services related to the transformation of the Greeks into citizens of a free state. Its agents, inspired by the ideas of Jeremy Bentham, held progressive views and were committed to the ideal of freedom. Their activities covered all forms of philhellenism and in this they differed from the other European Committees which were usually restricted to its more philanthropic aspects. It had as its 'grand object . . . to give freedom and knowledge to Greece',[10] and it is this association of the concepts of freedom with knowledge which is of particular significance in the present context. A strong belief in the benefits to be expected from education had developed at the time among the Greeks, and they were led to consider it as a shield against any form of tyranny. Advice to this effect was offered through the newspapers:

> Take care . . . of the enlightenment of your minds, and of the enlightenment of your children. Have you not yet understood this? Where ignorance exists, there are to be found in the greatest number the most inhuman demagogues (*laoplanoi*). These demagogues decry enlightenment so that you remain blind, so that they, who have their cunning eyes half open, may manipulate you.[11]

But before analysing the way in which the London Greek Committee endeavoured to help the Greeks to diffuse knowledge and promote education, mention should be made of the philhellenic activities of their spiritual leader, Jeremy Bentham. He is considered to have belonged to those who lacked 'a whole-hearted commitment to philhellenism', among other reasons because his 'generous sympathies were equally engaged on the side of one of the Greeks' bitterest enemies, the pasha of Egypt, Mehmet Ali'.[12] This may be true, but, looked upon from the Greek point of view, the fact that he offered his services in more than one way, and the nature of his assistance suggest that he was motivated by a sincere desire to help the Greeks in building up their independent state. It was, indeed, the Greek Deputies in London who approached him in February 1823 and asked for his comments on the Greek Constitution promulgated in the January of the previous year.[13] Bentham was, apparently, delighted with the idea and immediately approached Samuel Parr, the educationist and classicist, who was also to become a member of the London Greek Committee. He wrote to him:

> Can you sing *Ille ego qui quondam*? Can you sing it in Greek? I want a little batch of good Greek for a useful purpose; and if not in your backhouse, in what other can it be looked for with any reasonable hope? In the days of your youth, you received instruction from Greece in no small quantity. Lo! I will put you in the way to make some return for it.[14]

The reason for this demand, as Bentham explained, was that he wanted to give to the Greeks

in addition to observations on this their Constitutional Code

or Proposed Code, a ditto of my own, with reasons for every
Article and distinguishable part of an Article: the whole as
much compressed as possible.

This Code of his own, however, Bentham did not send to the
Greeks until January 1825. In the meantime apparently, he
supplied them with his comments, brought over by Blaquiere
and Andreas Louriotis in May 1823, another text of an uncertain nature presented by Stanhope a year later, and in
September 1824 with a Code prepared in 1822 by Bernardino
Rivadavia for the Republic of Buenos Aires.[15] His offers were
gratefully acknowledged by the Greek National Assemblies, and
letters of thanks were also sent to him by such distinguished
politicians as Theodoros Negris and Alexandros Mavrokordatos; the latter even received from Bentham a personal letter
with details of his projects.[16] Bentham's emissaries reported that
in Greece 'resolutions were immediately passed for translating
the works [of Bentham]',[17] and that his manuscript was
'received with expressions of deep-felt gratitude' by the Greeks
who promised 'that they would consult it as their wisest oracle,
and act accordingly'.[18]

It is, however, very doubtful whether any of these texts were,
in fact, translated into Greek, either in England or in Greece.
No such translation is recorded in the Greek bibliographies, and
the assertion that the distinguished Greek scholar Adamantios
Korais had undertaken to translate Bentham's Code into
modern Greek rests on particularly doubtful evidence.[19]
Korais was indeed an admirer of Bentham, and as early as 1821
he had advised the Greeks, as part of their preparation for
independence, to study political science, and to this effect
translate relevant foreign treatises 'and especially those of the
wise teacher of Law (*nomodidaskalos*), Bentham'.[20] Of this advice
Bentham was aware, and it is known that Korais had sent him
the book in which it appeared, through another Greek scholar
Nikolaos Pikkolos who drew Bentham's attention to the
relevant passage.[21] Korais seems to have been familiar with
Bentham's works mainly through their French translations, and
he quotes among others from the *Traités de législation civile et
pénale*, and the *Théorie des peines et des récompences*, as well as from
the *Draught of a New Plan for the Organisation of the Judicial*

Establishment in France. It is worth noting that there is more than one direct reference to Bentham in Korais' *Notes* on the Greek Constitution of 1822,[22] 'one of the most brilliant achievements of the neo-hellenic democratic thought'.[23]

The first recorded Greek translation of a work by Bentham was made in 1826, and announced in 1828 but not published until 1834 in Aegina. This was the first volume of E. Dumont's translation *Traités de législation,* referred to above, and translated into Greek by Georgios Athanasiou (the second volume was published in Athens in 1842). Also in 1842 a part of Bentham's *Théorie des peines et des récompences . . .,* translated by A. Petsalis, was published, significantly as an appendix to an edition of Korais' translation of Beccaria's *Dei Delitti e delle Pene.*[24] But a basic idea of Bentham's principles had already been made available in 1824 in a Greek newspaper. For the *Ellinika Khronika,* the newspaper established by the efforts of Stanhope, and directed by the Swiss Johann Jakob Meyer, had published on 30 January 1824 a very short description of the contents of Bentham's *Codification Proposal Addressed to All Nations,* and on 1 October 1824 a long article by Anastasios Polyzoidis, one of Korais' disciples, on *Publicity,* extracted from Bentham's *Tactique des Assemblées Législatives.*

This appears to be a rather limited diffusion of Bentham's ideas, and the small impact that they may have had is also demonstrated by the fact that there are substantial doubts as to the extent to which Greek newspapers and books of the time had a readership of any noteworthy size. Further, there is little evidence of any direct influence exercised by Bentham on the Greek legislators who drafted the second (1823) and third (1827) Constitutions. His advice arrived too late for the former, and the very liberal character of the latter was probably due to a number of different influences, none of which can be singled out.[25] But when philhellenic intentions, rather than results, are taken into consideration, as is usually the case with the 'established' philhellenes, Bentham certainly deserves a place among them.

Moreover, Bentham's philhellenic activities also assumed a more concrete form in his involvement in the scheme to train Greek boys in England as teachers, who would return to Greece to promote education. Here, however, two other Britons played the dominant roles: the distinguished Quaker William Allen, and Edward Blaquiere, the active agent of the London Greek Committee. Allen had visited Greece in 1819 together with his French-American friend Stephen Grellet, as part of a journey which lasted for a year and a half. The tour included Norway, Sweden, Finland, Russia, Turkey, Greece, Malta, Italy, Switzerland and France. At the end of it he came to the conclusion that 'the Greeks are a people eminently worth caring for',[26] and some years later, after the massacre in Chios in 1822, he thought that through his friendship with Tsar Alexander I, he might help the cause of the Greeks, and decided to attend the Congress in Vienna. He went with the Duke of Wellington and while he does not seem to have been successful in his approaches to the Tsar, he did manage to influence the Austrian authorities to adopt a less strict attitude towards the Greek refugees who had become a major concern of the Society of Friends, of which he was the treasurer. To the Duke of Wellington himself he later stated his views on the political future of Greece, suggesting that

> it would be good policy to countenance a Greek empire, if England did not wish to see all that country joined to Russia, which, otherwise in time it assuredly would be.[27]

But Allen's political views, interesting as they may be, are not strictly relevant here. Nor is this the place to deal with the more philanthropic side of his care for the Greeks. What is worth noting is his conviction that 'by proper treatment and management – especially of their youth – the Greeks might be made a fine people'.[28] His beliefs in this respect are characteristic of the deep significance he attributed to education. Writing to the Greek Deputies in London on 29 April 1825, and referring to plans made by the Greek government to promote education he said:

> I love Greece, and I deeply feel that her independence and happiness can only be consolidated by rendering the mass of her population virtuous and intelligent. Let us always bear in mind this great Truth, that a nation without morals may acquire liberty, but without morals they cannot *preserve* it. Be assured, my dear Friends, that I shall deem myself happy if

Divine Providence will permit me to be a humble instrument in His hand to promote so glorious a work as this which your government has so nobly begun.[29]

It is in this direction that Allen exercised his influence, and his interest was mainly related to the spread of the teaching of the Scriptures and the foundation of Lancasterian schools. Although there seems to be no clear evidence of this, it was almost certainly through his initiative that the British and Foreign School Society became directly involved in activities aiming at the promotion of education in Greece. Its assistance took the form of translations and publications of school-manuals, financial assistance to schools, and the training of teachers. It was in this last, and most important, activity that both Allen and Blaquiere were directly involved.

During his second visit to Greece, in 1824, Blaquiere thought that he should act according to

a passage in one of Mr Bowring's letters to Colonel Stanhope, in which he said that the great philanthropist and good man, William Allen, expressed a wish that twenty Greek youths might be sent to England to be educated at a cheap rate.[30]

Of this letter there appears to be no trace today, but it is known that a similar suggestion was made to the Greek authorities by the Greek Deputies in London with whom, as has been said, Allen was in contact. On an other occasion he had written to them:

Si vous voulez dépendre seulement sur nous pour l'éducation de vos jeunes gens, nous vous mettrons en état d'élever tous les enfants de la Grèce, même les plus pauvres, à des frais très modérés.[31]

Allen had talked to the Deputies regarding the education of three Greek boys in England. Bentham had offered to take another two boys under his care. These various suggestions and invitations became rather confused not only as to the number of boys invited, but also regarding the financial arrangements involved. At some time, in July 1824, after Blaquiere had explained the idea to the Greek Legislative Body, the following numbers were considered: two boys invited by Bentham; three by Allen; twenty suggested by the Greek Deputies in London and Blaquiere; and ten to be sent at the expense of the Greek government.[32] Eventually, and after long deliberations, Blaquiere left Greece for England in August 1824 accompanied by only nine boys and an escort, and with the issue of the expenses still not clarified.[33] This confusion and lack of precision may be an example of administrative incompetence on the part of the Greek authorities, and of actions influenced by emotion rather than reason on the part of Blaquiere. But it certainly indicates that under the influence of some philhellenes the belief that education was a pillar of independence and freedom gained additional strength.

Moreover, seven of these boys and their escort were sent to Borough Road School in Southwark run by the British and Foreign School Society, and this brought the total number of Greek boys educated under its auspices up to 1831 to twelve The record of this enterprise must be considered to be very satisfactory by any standard. Of these twelve boys one died in April 1827, but of the rest one (Georgios Tombazis) returned to Greece to become twice a Cabinet Minister; one (Dimitrios Kalliphronas) went to Cambridge and was then ordained in the Anglican Church; one (Georgios Konstantinou or Konstantinidis) returned and directed for over twenty years the only existing State Model Primary School; one (Dimitrios Pieridis) went back to his native Cyprus and established in Larnaka what was perhaps the first Lancasterian school there, and later became a distinguished and respected member of the community; and six others were engaged in teaching for longer or shorter periods after their return to Greece. Expenses for their education were apparently met jointly by the London Greek Committee, the Society of Friends, and the School Society. To this end a special Education Committee was established in Britain and two appeals were issued for the purpose of raising funds.

In all this, another Quaker, besides William Allen, demonstrated particular enthusiasm. This was Robert Forster (1791–1873), who appears to qualify for the title of philhellene, and yet has not found a place in the relevant studies. A member of a well-known Quaker family in Tottenham (to which W. E.

Forster, the initiator of the 1870 Education Act, also belonged), he was a surveyor, but had devoted his energies to the spread of education, and was an active member of the School Society, where he developed a particular interest in its foreign work. He was in touch with some better-known philhellenes such as Edward Masson and James Emerson, took under his personal care some of the Greek boys, and was always ready to advise and help. To Georgios Konstantinou, for instance, who encountered some difficulties when he first returned to Greece, he wrote:

I would have thee keep thyself devoted to the one grand object, the education of thy countrymen. If driven from one place, pursue it in another. If thou canst not collect children by hundreds, be satisfied with tens or twenties.[34]

The experiences of the two boys taken into the care of Bentham are also interesting. They were sent to Hazelwood School in Birmingham, at the time one of the most progressive schools in England. Founded in 1819 by Thomas Wright Hill and his three sons, it seems to have combined Pestalozzian practices with the theories put forward by Richard Lovel and Maria Edgeworth, the progressive educationists of the first decade of the nineteenth century. In common with most non-conformist educationists of the time, the Hills were influenced by the ideas of Bentham, who apparently had taken particular interest in their school.[35] This is how some of the principles and practices followed at the School have been summarised by a modern historian:

The Hills tried to avoid the harsh methods of obtaining class order that were usual in the other schools, and sought to enlist the co-operation of the pupils through interest. Plenty of freedom was allowed the pupils in the choice of subjects for study, and the scheme of self-government adopted was based on a written constitution. Offenders were tried and awarded punishment by the boys themselves and, in order to foster a sense of responsibility, older pupils were allotted important duties in connection with the running of the school.[36]

When the state of education in Greece just before and during the War of Independence is taken into consideration, especially the principles on which it was based and the methods applied, the experience gained by the Greek teachers who had been educated at Hazelwood School must have been particularly valuable. This seems to have been in Bentham's mind. On the other hand, it could be argued that such progressive ideas and revolutionary practices had little relevance to the Greek situation which required educational establishments of a more traditional type. This, however, would be to disregard the fact that, as mentioned above, schools in Greece after the outbreak of the War had to perform the additional task of training the future citizens of the new free state. More significant in the present context is that ideas strongly reminiscent of those dominating Hazelwood School were also held by some teachers in Greece. Indeed, as early as 1825 a teacher in Athens, Neophytos Nikitoplos, who had probably been trained in Paris, was running a school for girls on surprisingly similar lines. In a report regarding his school he says:

> Such a school represents in miniature a whole nation; for this reason it must be organised more or less according to the political system of the nation, so that the pupil will be accustomed from an early age to govern and to be governed according to the laws. I have first suggested to the common assembly of the school that every nation has laws, and according to what the law says the people act; for this reason we, too, in our school must write laws, and proceed according to what they say. Then I proposed and the Assembly elected by vote nine legislators while I am the tenth. And thus we formulated the laws to which all agreed and which were signed by the elected legislators. Then, following elections by the Assembly, I appointed the Governors; they form the Government of our School and, together with myself, sign the reports of the School.

In this organisation the teacher ('a sort of Legislative Body') had to consult learned people and decide on the lessons to be taught in the school and on matters regarding its organisation. Of the pupils, one acted as the 'Executive Body', following the instructions of the teacher, and others had duties equivalent to those of the Minister of the Interior and the Minister of Police. These girls were given many and varied responsibilities regarding the running of the School. The organisation was completed by the establishment of the Judiciary:

When the elected legislators laid down the laws and the Governors were elected, there followed by vote the election of ten Judges (nine pupils and myself). The description of the Court is posted in four places in the School. I have written the four general virtues – Wisdom, Justice, Prudence, Courage – so that Justice was written above the Laws.[37]

It is further interesting to note that this progressive Athenian school was functioning under the auspices of the Philomuse Society (*Philomouson Etairia*), which had been founded long before the War of Independence, in 1813, aiming 'to promote education and spread European civilisation in Greece'.[38] Less than a year after its foundation the list of subscribers to the Society comprised 100 names: there were on the list 21 Athenians and 22 Britons. Among the Athenians were Teresa Makri and Ioannis Marmarotouris, closely associated with Lord Byron; the British Consul in Athens; and Spyridon Trikoupis, who became later an important supporter of the British philhellenes. Among the Britons were John Oliver Hanson, Charles Robert Cockerell and Thomas S. Hughes, as well as entries from Liverpool, Cambridge, Dublin, Forres and Guernsey. Frederick North, Earl of Guilford, was elected honorary President of the Society soon after its foundation. A branch of it was established in Vienna, and it was soon taken over by Kapodistrias, who believed that the idea had been part of an English political scheme. He developed it in accordance with his own particular interests, leaving the original Society in Athens to decline. When, in 1824, Stanhope decided to proceed to the establishment of a 'utilitarian Society for the purpose of spreading knowledge and everything that contributes to good government',[39] the Athenians decided instead to reorganise the Philomuse Society. At one of the first meetings of this revived Society Stanhope was even given the right to vote in the election of its officers. Thus, in both periods of its life, the Philomuse Society, which developed considerable cultural activities, owed much to the initiative or the support of British philhellenes.

There was a second Society with similar aims founded in Greece during the period of the War, the Philanthropic Society in Nafplion, and, interestingly, British philhellenes were also involved in its establishment. Edward Blaquiere was present at its first meeting and although he claims that it had 'originated with the citizens', it is very likely that he had at least encouraged its founders. Indeed, Blaquiere was one of the three members of the Society who presented its statutes to the Legislative Body for approval.[40] The Society addressed a letter to Joseph Hume, William Allen, Jeremy Bentham and John Bowring, inviting them to become its agents and representatives in Great Britain. Further, it nominated Bentham a member of the Society. To these strong British associations another one was added two years later, in 1826, when Edward Masson became involved in its activities.[41]

Edward Masson is among the 'established' philhellenes, but not, apparently, for the reasons for which he is discussed in this paper. He is best known as secretary and interpreter to Lord Cochrane, and, on the Greek side, for his having served in 1834 as Public Prosecutor at the trial of one of the war heroes, Theodoros Kolokotronis, though his behaviour during this trial was obscure. Interestingly he is not remembered for earlier attitudes which had a more 'liberal' character, such as his sympathy with the anti-Kapodistrian party, or his acting for the defence of President Kapodistrias' assassins. These can probably be explained by his fear that Greece was falling under the influence of Russia, of which Kapodistrias was often believed to be an agent. A similar feeling obviously lay behind Masson's involvement in the affair of the Philorthodox Society.[42]

But nothing of all this concerned Masson when he first set off for Greece. He was sent there in August 1824 under the auspices of the London Greek Committee, and settled in Hydra soon after his arrival.[43] He was a good friend of Howe's, who gives the following description of him:

Masson . . . is a gentleman and a scholar; a republican and a philanthropist, enthusiastically attracted to Greece. He has left his country in high hopes of being useful to her, and by his conduct since his arrival [he] has [gained] renown [for] himself to be one of the very few philhellenes, who were not entirely showing themselves off. He first solicited the Government that they would give him the superintendence of establishing a system of schools over the whole country; but finding them rather dilatory, he came to this place [Hydra] . . . Here he gives instruction gratuitously to several young men in the English language and some other studies. He speaks the modern Greek with ease and elegance, and is proficient in the Hellenic. Should he be spared he will be the silent but powerful organ of the distribution of knowledge through this country, and will thus confer the greatest good on her, the greatest honor to himself. The first thing that pleased me in Masson was his liberality of sentiments on all subjects, and his candid, open way of speaking of America towards whom like few Englishmen he entertained feelings of respect and admiration.[44]

Again, if intentions rather than results are considered, Masson appears to have been one of those philhellenes who were willing to help in a non-militant way. His attitude towards the Greeks was described in a short article about him published in a Greek newspaper. It stated that Masson

loves the Greeks very much; he offers them useful and bene-ficial advice; he has a philanthropic consideration for their misfortunes and errors; and knowing as a philosopher, that a nation enslaved for so many centuries especially under the barbarian Turks, the persecutors of any learning and of everything beneficent, cannot be without many and great vices, he endeavours by every means to change the defects caused to the Greeks by slavery into virtues.[45]

In addition to the few activities already referred to above, mention should be made in the present context of the fact that in the early 1840s Masson was appointed Reader in Philosophy, and then Professor of History at the University of Athens; but he did not hold the posts for long. During this period he was also in contact with the 'Christian Knowledge Society' (possibly the Society for Promoting Christian Knowledge), on the subject of the publication of religious books in Greece. It is also of interest to note that the first article printed in the periodical *O Paratiritis*, published by Masson in Nafplion in 1838, is a 'Legislator's Speech' translated, according to the editor, from a manuscript of Jeremy Bentham.

However, what best illustrates Masson's views is perhaps his theory on the way in which ancient Greek should be taught. He has described it himself, and it might explain to some extent Greek reactions to his work – they are reported to have been quite strong at a time – bearing in mind the attitudes in the matter traditionally held by 'established' Greek teachers. Masson, in fact, believed that ancient Greek should not be taught

> as a dead but as a living language; and should not employ the routine system, which requires a length of years to lead to any great proficiency, but should train students to write and speak Hellenic on a plan similar to Ollendorff's approved method of teaching living tongues.[46]

To this presentation of a form of philhellenism that does not seem to have been studied enough, a word should be added about another Briton who helped the Greeks in a different way. There is indeed very little evidence regarding the activities of an Irishman, William Bennet Stevenson, who arrived in Greece probably some time late in 1827.[47] Earlier he had served as secretary to Lord Cochrane in South America, where he had also held other official posts. He speaks of his experiences in a three volume book published in London in 1825, *A Historical and Descriptive Narrative of Twenty Years' Residence in South America*, a book that was translated into at least two languages (Spanish and French). No Greek translation is recorded, though newspapers of the time were reporting at length events in South America. At the beginning he remained apparently idle in Greece, but then, in January 1828, claiming that he was an expert in potato cultivation, he started, under the auspices of Kapodistrias, a plantation of potatoes in Aegina, where he came to employ, according to some accounts, up to 1500 workers a day. His work was considered successful, and some months later he extended it to Argolis. Stevenson, called by Kapodistrias 'a most useful man and admirable for his dedication', was also proposing to plant 'useful' trees around the potato plantation, and along the coastal road in Poros. When in July 1828 he had to leave Greece because his health had been affected by his living in the fields among the workers, he left detailed accounts of his expenses and an inventory of his equipment and livestock.[48]

Stevenson also serves as an example of the way in which foreigners helped to develop tendencies which had already been apparent among the Greeks themselves. As in the case of legislation and education, the initiative in the introduction of new ideas did not belong to foreigners. The Greek Legislative Body had already in 1827 underlined the necessity of spreading the cultivation of potatoes over the country.[49] Interestingly, in this vital question of agricultural development, assistance was also offered by another foreigner, an Italian, Antonio Magno (who, incidentally, was critical of the methods applied by Stevenson), and then by a Greek, Grigorios Palaiologos, who had specialised in France.

To conclude these thoughts on the non-military aspects of philhellenism, and to put them into the right perspective, it should be remembered that they manifested themselves when Greece, despite tremendous internal and external difficulties, was striving to build up all the characteristics of a free state. In politics this period saw the promulgation of a markedly liberal constitution. Culturally it was the time when a great number of scholars and teachers were active in the liberated parts of the country, as they had rallied to the cause from abroad and from the regions still under Turkish rule. In literature these years are marked by the activity of two great poets, Dionysios Solomos and Andreas Kalvos. Finally Korais exercised from Paris, both directly and indirectly, his seemingly very considerable influence on political and educational developments. And if many felt that salvation would come from a revival of ancient values, there were few who, like the anonymous correspondent of a Greek newspaper in 1826, wanted to remind their compatriots that the Greek of the time had not been 're-born', as was generally asserted, but he had simply been 'born', and because of this he had quite different needs.[50]

It appears that a very useful foreign contribution was offered to the Greeks in this spirit. Still, reactions to this type of assistance were not unanimously enthusiastic in England, even before the involvement of the London Greek Committee in the affair of the Loans. It is, perhaps, possible to detect in this negative attitude some further reasons for the place generally given in Greek history to non-military philhellenism. Admiration of Lord Byron, who was sceptical about some of the more liberalising and enlightening activities of the 'progressive' philhellenes and critical of Jeremy Bentham and his followers, may also have contributed to the playing down of the importance of their assistance. Political reasons should also be taken into account, and especially the fact that almost all the Members of Parliament belonging to the London Greek Committee were Whigs, Radicals or Independents. Contemporary objections to the type of help offered to the Greeks were strongly expressed, for instance, in the *Quarterly Review*. As early as 1823, referring to Greece, it stated that

> to give at once complete freedom to a people with whom slavery, in its most odious and dreadful form, has been long familiar, is not to confer a blessing; it is to offer to them a temptation to disorder; it is to stimulate them to violence.[51]

In 1827 it attacked even more explicitly the 'liberalising' character of the help that was being offered. It criticised the London Greek Committee and its agents for wanting to introduce

> printing presses for a nation that cannot read! Constitutions for a country, the purest patriots of which are *klephtai*, i.e. robbers! Mathematical instruments for a people who do not know one cipher from another! And whirligig schools for youth who have hardly a village in which they can rest for a moment without the expectation of having the scymitar at their throats.[52]

Mention is often made of the view expressed by Korais, that the Greeks were intellectually unprepared, not so much for the War of Independence, as for the freedom which would follow. This belief he shared with others no less eminent, like Frederick North and Grigorios Konstantas, the enlightened scholar who was given wide responsibilities in education during the War. It was for this reason that, unlike others, they intensified their efforts to spread knowledge among the Greeks, and it was exactly in making up for this want of political and intellectual preparation that the assistance of the 'other philhellenes', the non-military ones, was particularly important. Many aspects of this cultural philhellenism have been left out of this survey, such as the contribution of the British through the Ionian

Islands, or the work done by the missionaries, all of whom would qualify as philhellenes.[53] Still, the nature of their help did not differ in spirit from that discussed here, and it is by looking closely at some small matters that we can often understand the bigger issues – by looking at what was about to begin we can judge the harm done when that beginning was not allowed to develop and come to fruition.

NOTES TO CHAPTER 9

The issues discussed in this paper are directly related to the subject of a Ph.D. thesis (*Foreign, and Particularly English, Influences on Educational Policies in Greece During the War of Independence and Their Development under Capodistrias, 1821–1831*), submitted by the author to the University of London.

1. D. Dakin, *British and American Philhellenes during the War of Greek Independence, 1821–1833* (Thessaloniki, 1955); C. M. Woodhouse, *The Philhellenes* (London, 1969). As for the philhellenic movement in other countries, Stephen A. Larrabee's *Hellas Observed, The American Experience of Greece, 1775–1865* (New York, 1957), deserves special mention for its comprehensiveness. Many other relevant studies (none of which can be singled out) are mentioned by Odysseas Dimitrakopoulos in his introduction to the second edition of the Greek translation of Samuel Gridley Howe's *Letters and Journals: Samuel Howe, Imerologio apo ton Agona, 1825–1829* (Athens, 1971).

Since this paper was first read at the School of Slavonic and East European Studies, a third important English book on philhellenism has been published: William St. Clair, *That Greece Might Still Be Free, The Philhellenes in the War of Independence* (London, 1972); it is, however, less scholarly than the studies of Dakin and Woodhouse.

2. Dictionary definitions are also vague in this respect. It must be remembered, moreover, that the term *philellin*, was used by the Ancient Greeks to designate the followers of Greek culture. It is interesting to note that the term is still used for present-day friends of Greece (its people and/or its rulers), and even with a wider meaning, as in P. K. Persianis, 'Church and State in the Development of Education in Cyprus, 1878–1960', in *Educational Policy and the Mission Schools, Case Studies from the British Empire*, ed. B. Holmes (London, 1967) p. 249 where reference is made to the English 'liberal minded governors [of Cyprus], known also as philhellenes'. Cf., in this context, T. J. B. Spencer, *Fair Greece, Sad Relic, Literary Philhellenism from Shakespeare to Byron* (London, 1954).

3. It is perhaps significant of the emotional element involved, that there is a lexical opposite to a philhellene, i.e., a 'mishellene', while there is no similar equivalent for, say, a francophil or a turcophil. For an emotional approach to the subject of philhellenism see, for instance, Anastasios Lignadis, *To Proton Daneion tis Anexartisias* (Athens, 1970).

4. *Journal de la Morale Chrétienne*, II (1823) 349.

5. E. Blaquiere, *Narrative of a Second Visit to Greece* (London, 1825) p. 116.

6. A striking example of this is the study *Amerikanoi Philellines ethelontes sto Eikosiena* by Th. Vagenas and E. Dimitrakopoulou (Athens, 1949), which sharply divides the Americans who were active in Greece during the War of Independence into two groups, the philhellenes and the philanthropists, the former being the military, and the latter all the others. It is significant in the present context that the section on the philanthropists has not yet been published.

7. E. Chapuisat, *La Restauration Hellénique d'après la Correspondance de Jean-Gabriel Eynard* (Paris-Genève, 1924) p. 11.

8. Spyridon Trikoupis, *Istoria tis Ellinikis Epanastaseos* (3rd ed.; Athens, 1888) III, p. 92.

9. Quoted by Virginia Penn, 'Philhellenism in England, 1821–1827', *The Slavonic and East European Review*, XIV (1935–6) 363 ff. and 647 ff. For Thomas Gordon's criticisms see, for instance, his *History of the Greek Revolution* (2nd ed.; London, 1844) I, pp. 315–16.

10. L. Stanhope, *Greece in 1823 and 1824, A New Edition . . . Greece in 1825* (London, 1825) p. 6.

11. Published anonymously in *Ellinika Khronika*, 28 January, 1825.

12. Woodhouse, *The Philhellenes*, pp. 90–1.

13. See the letter signed by Andreas Louriotis among the *Bentham Mss* at University College, London (XII, 100); a quotation from it has been published by K. Lipstein, 'Bentham, Foreign Law and Foreign Lawyers', in *Jeremy Bentham and the Law, A Symposium*, eds. G. W. Keeton and G. Schwarzenberger (London, 1948) pp. 211 ff. This study, however, must be approached very cautiously since it makes no use of other sources except the *Bentham Mss*, and reveals poor knowledge of Greek matters. Similarly, the following studies on Bentham and Greece do not give an accurate and comprehensive picture of the topic: K. Triantaphyllopoulos, 'Ypomnima tou Bentham peri tou protou Ellinikou Politevmatos', *Praktika tis Akadimias Athinon*, XXXVII (1962) 80 ff.; Ap. Daskalakis, *Oi Topikoi Organismoi tis Epanastaseos tou 1821 kai to Politevma tis Epidavrou* (Athens, 1966) p. 211 ff.; E. G. Vallianatos, 'Jeremy Bentham's Constitutional Reform Proposals to the Greek Provisional Government, 1823–1825', *Balkan Studies*, X (1969) 325 ff. See also D. Petrakakos, *Koinovouleftiki Istoria tis Ellados* (Athens, 1935) I, p. 359 ff. For his assistance with my research on Bentham I am deeply indebted to Mr. Philippos Iliou, who is preparing a study on the matter.

14. J. Bowring (ed.), *The Works of Jeremy Bentham* (Edinburgh, 1841 etc.) X, p. 534 ff.

15. Of these texts apparently only a version of Bentham's comments on the Greek Constitution has survived among his papers at University College (various papers in Boxes XXI and CVI); the staff of the Bentham Committee are now in the process of deciphering and studying it. So far the content of these texts has been assumed from the relevant correspondence of Bentham with the London Greek Committee and with Greek politicians. I am grateful to Dr. F. Rosen for helping me to study the *Bentham Mss*, and

to the Librarian of University College, London, for allowing me to quote from unpublished material.

16. Bowring (ed.), *Works*, IV, p. 589 ff.; this letter was also published by Petrakakos (*Koinovouleftiki Istoria*, I, p. 361 ff.), who seems to have ignored its earlier inclusion among the *Works*.

17. E. Blaquiere in a letter dated Tripolitsa, 16 May 1823, quoted by Lipstein, in *Bentham and the Law*, p. 212.

18. Stanhope, *Greece*, pp. 196-7.

19. This assertion made by Lipstein in *Bentham and the Law*, p. 213, is based on a reference in the draft of a letter by Bentham to Korais (*Bentham Mss*, XII, 304), where J. Bowring is mentioned as the source of this information. There is no proof that the letter was ever sent (it does not seem to have been found among Korais' papers), and there is apparently no mention of such a project in any of his writings.

20. Korais, *Aristotelous Politikon ta Sozomena* (Paris, 1821) p. rma.

21. See Pikkolos' letter to Bentham (27 January 1822) in *Bentham Mss* (XII, 47). Cf. Bentham's letter to Parr referred to above (Bowring (ed.), *Works*, X, 535).

22. *Simeioseis eis to Prosorinon Politevma tis Ellados tou 1822 etous*. The work, written in 1823, was only published in 1933 (in Athens) by Th. Volidis. Regarding Korais' respect for Bentham it is worth noting that the Greek Deputies' initiative to ask Bentham's advice on the Greek Constitution may well have originated from Korais. For it is known that one of them, Andreas Louriotis, who wrote the letter to Bentham had, before reaching London, been to Paris where Korais was resident. Despite the fact that there seems to be no record of their having met on this occasion, there is mention of an intention of such a meeting (in a letter by Bentham to Blaquiere, 2 March 1823, *Bentham Mss*, XII, 103), and it is known that soon after their arrival in London the Deputies frequently corresponded with Korais to whom they showed a deep respect.

23. Philippos Iliou, 'Anekdota kai Xekhasmena Grammata apo tin Allilographia tou Korai' in *Eranos eis Adamantion Korain* (Athens, 1965) p. 128.

24. Kharilaos P. Sophianopoulos, *O Vekkarias tou Korai, Ekdosis Deftera tou 1823* (Athens, 1842).

25. These remarks are made despite the fact that specialists underline the importance of Bentham's influence on the Greek legislators, without, however, offering any proof of their assertions. See, for instance, A. Svolos, 'Ta Prota Ellinika Politevmata kai i epidrasis tis Gallikis Epanastaseos', *Ephimeris ton Ellinon Nomikon*, II (1935) 737 ff.; P. Zepos, 'Synoptiki Istoria tis Nomikis Skholis', *Nea Estia*, XXII (1937) 1786 ff.

26. *Life of William Allen with Selections from his Correspondence* (London, 1846) II, p. 107.

27. Quoted by Helena Hall, *William Allen, 1770-1843, Member of the Society of Friends* (Haywards Heath, 1953) p. 112.

28. Quoted *ibid.*, p. 105.

29. The letter is among the papers of the *Arkheion Lourioti* (XI, 87) at the *Kentron Neoellinikon Erevnon* of the *Ethnikon Idryma Erevnon*. I am grateful to the

Directorate of the *Kentron* for allowing me to quote from their unpublished material, and particularly to Mrs. L. Droulia for assisting me in my research.

30. Blaquiere, *Narrative*, pp. 110–11.

31. The letter is dated 27 April 1824; *Arkheion Lourioti*, VI', 92.

32. Some misunderstanding led the Greeks to believe that Bentham had invited three and not two boys, but there is no doubt as to the right number (see his letter to the Greek Legislative Body, 28 January 1825, in Bowring (ed.), *Works*, IV, 588).

33. Bentham in his letter to the Greek Legislative Body (referred to in note 32 above) says that Blaquiere had taken with him ten boys, one of whom 'died on the passage'. This information, however, does not seem to be confirmed by other sources.

34. The letter is dated 24 October 1825, *Library of the Society of Friends, Temp. Mss* 7/16; I am grateful to the Society's Library Committee for allowing me to quote from their archives.

35. See particularly, J. L. Dobson, 'The Hill Family and Educational Change in the Early Nineteenth Century', *The Durham Research Review*, II (1959) 261 ff.; III (1960–1) 1 ff. and 74 ff.

36. S. J. Curtis, *History of Education in Great Britain* (7th ed.; London, 1967) pp. 142–3.

37. The Report, first published in the *Ephimeris ton Athinon* (nos. 15 and 17), was also published in a separate pamphlet in 1826.

38. D. G. Kambouroglou, *Mnimeia tis Istorias ton Athinon* (2nd ed.; Athens, 1891) I, p. 216 ff. On the Philomuse Society in general see E. G. Protopsaltis, 'Nea Stoikheia peri tis en Athinais Etaireias ton Philomouson', *Athina*, LXI (1957) 253 ff.; and E. Koukkou, *O Kapodistrias kai i Paideia 1803–1822, A. I Philomousos Etaireia tis Viennis* (Athens, 1958).

39. Stanhope, *Greece*, p. 71.

40. Blaquiere, *Narrative*, p. 148 ff., has printed the statutes of the Society in English translation.

41. It is interesting to note that the *Philekpaideftiki Etairia*, which was founded in Athens in 1836 and could be considered as the 'successor' of the two Societies mentioned above, may have also originated from the initiative of another friend of Greece, the American missionary Jonas King. This can be gathered from an entry in his Journal for 2 May 1836 (*Missionary Herald*, 1836, 421), and reinforced by the active role played in the Society by some of his friends such as Kh. Philadelphefs.

42. On the Philorthodox Society in general, and Edward Masson's involvement in its affair in particular, see J. A. Petropulos, *Politics and Statecraft in the Kingdom of Greece, 1833–1843* (Princeton, 1968), the relevant sections of which draw mainly on unpublished material. Regarding Masson's place among the philhellenes, it is worth noting that he has not gained a mention in St. Clair's *That Greece Might Still Be Free*, where William Allen is also ignored, and Bentham is mentioned, not on his own merits as a philhellene, but as the spiritual leader of the London Greek Committee.

43. That Masson went to Greece under the auspices of the Committee and the exact date of his arrival are deduced from indirect information in various sources, and particularly in a manuscript record of some activities

of the London Greek Committee to be found in the *Bentham Mss* (CX, 40).

44. This page of Howe's journal (for 17 June 1825), has only been pub-lished in translation by O. Dimitrakopoulos in his introduction to *Samuel Howe, Imerologio*, p. iz. To the courtesy of Mr. Dimitrakopoulos I owe the transcript of the original English text used here.

45. *Geniki Ephimeris tis Ellados*, 3 July 1826.

46. *Testimonials in Favour of Mr Edward Masson*, Second Series (Edinburgh, 1852) p. iv.

47. The sources refer to him without his first names; that he was indeed William Bennet has been deduced from reports published in the *Geniki Ephimeris tis Ellados* (e.g., 1 February 1828), according to which he was well-known for his book 'on Brazil' (see below).

48. For some information about Stevenson, consisting mainly of relevant extracts from Kapodistrias' correspondence, but ignoring other sources such as Greek newspapers of the time, see S. and K. Vovolinis, *Mega Ellinikon Viographikon Lexikon* (Athens, n.d.) 1, pp. 22, 24 and 27.

49. See, for instance, D. Zographos, *Istoria tis Ellinikis Georgias* (Athens, 1921) 1, p. 267.

50. *Geniki Ephimeris tis Ellados*, 20 February 1826.

51. *Quarterly Review*, xxvIII (1822–3) 475.

52. *Ibid.*, xxv (1827) 227. Cf. the following view expressed by another sceptical British visitor to Greece: referring to her inhabitants he says that 'the only key to their affections is the *loan*. They ask neither for our counsels, nor our hospitals, nor our officers, nor our Lancasterian schools'. (G. Waddington, *A Visit to Greece in 1823 and 1824* (2nd ed.; London, 1825) p. 154.

53. It is characteristic that the school established in Syra by agents of the Church Missionary Society was often called 'philhellenic', and so were the missionary presses in Athens, Tinos, etc.

10 Byron in Nineteenth-century Greek Literature

ROBIN FLETCHER

'To the Greeks he was a poet, a hero, and a god.' So writes C. M. Woodhouse of Byron in his agreeable book *The Philhellenes*.[1] The title of this paper represents an attempt to trace the form of the recognition by the Greeks of Byron as a poet, that is to say when and through what channels it originated, which poems were particularly influential and which Greek poets were most subject to that influence. It might reasonably be assumed that modern Greek literary criticism would conveniently provide the material for the theme, which may perhaps be termed 'Greece and Byron' as the counterpart of the well-established and well-documented *Byron and Greece*.[2] Yet it is apparent that no study in detail has yet been made of the influence of Byron's poetry on nineteenth-century Greek poets. Most critics have been content to use the vague term *Vyronismos* to describe the romantic extravagance of their subjects as and where it has seemed suitable. They have tended to avoid a clear definition of its meaning. Moreover, it is scarcely possible to separate the Greek view of Byron as a poet from the Greek recognition of Byron as a hero, if not a god.

The apparent neglect of the critics can find an excuse in the fact that most of their subjects are lacking much literary merit. It may, therefore, not be thought important how well versed they were in Byron's poetry or how they reflect his influence in their works. I shall myself claim the same excuse in this short paper and shall limit myself to the more obvious examples of Byronic influence. In doing so, it will become clear that I wish to provoke others to disprove my assumption that, while it is undeniable that the name of Byron has from the day of his death been a household word among the Greeks, it is dangerous to conclude that his influence on Greek authors has always been deep and his poetry widely read in Greece.

When Byron went on that fateful first journey to Greece in the years 1809–11 – from that moment onward every move that Byron made was somehow fateful – he went without political and with small literary reputation. It was not to be expected that the Greeks would receive him any differently from those other strange young noblemen to whom they were by now becoming accustomed. Those who became better acquainted with him may have sensed that this milord was unusually affected by the grandeur of the natural scenery, and they must have been surprised and flattered by the interest which he took in themselves and their language. But his Greek acquaintances were limited and their appears to be no record of any Greek source which later boasted reminiscence or anecdote from those two years. Teresa Makri seems to have been too modest to give any but the briefest answer to those who sought her opinion in later years – or was it that she really had but little recollection of the guest who had lodged in her mother's apartment? After all, she was only thirteen that winter of 1810–11, feminine emancipation in Greece was not far advanced, and Byron's stay there was only of ten weeks' duration. Andreas Londos, whom Byron met in Patras, has not given us his impressions of the man with whom he spent a wild evening in advance celebration of *eleftheria* or of the aptitude of the pupil to learn the patriotic songs he is reputed to have taught him. Possibly his 'Romaic master' Marmarotouris would have liked to write something about him, but he was without the means to publish. Likewise Athanasios Psalidas, the schoolmaster at Ioannina with some pretension to scholarly learning, might have had interesting things to say of his conversation with Byron, but he published nothing in Greece. From his own observations on the state of Greek letters (of which, considering the brevity of his stay and the claims of other interests, he was by no means ill-informed), Byron himself would not have expected mention in Greek literary works, for he writes in the notes to *Childe Harold:*

A Greek must not write on politics, and cannot touch on

science for want of instruction; if he doubts, he is excommunicated and damned; therefore his countrymen are not poisoned
with modern philosophy: and as to morals, thanks to the
Turks! There are no such things. What then is left him, if he
has a turn for scribbling? Religion and holy biography: and it
is natural enough that those who have so little in this life
should look to the next. It is no great wonder then that in a
catalogue now before me of fifty-five Greek writers, many of
whom were lately living, not above fifteen should have
touched on anything but religion.[3]

If the better off, like Londos, and the learned, like Psalidas,
have said nothing, it is not surprising that those who lived 'full
on the coast of Suli's shore' or those who 'wield the slavish sickle,
not the sword' should have failed to hand down any written
monument to posterity. It might have been different if Byron
had chanced to meet either of the two most interesting Greek
poets of the time, both of whom were also active supporters of
the demotic language as the medium of writing. Athanasios
Khristopoulos was presumably at Constantinople in the summer
months of 1810 which Byron spent there – the furthest point of
his *Gyro*. Ioannis Vilaras might have crossed his path either at
Ali Paşa's court at Ioannina or with Veli Paşa in the Peloponnese, since Vilaras generally accompanied Veli on his tours.
History, however, provides no evidence that either side lived at
this time in anything but perfect ignorance of the other.

When we turn to the years between 1811 and the outbreak of
the Greek War of Independence in 1821, we need to remind
ourselves that in no area of southern Greece did there exist
anything which can be described as a centre of creative literature. However many of Byron's volumes the Hellenic travellers
of the day may have taken with them, it is very unlikely that the
Greeks in that area understood from them more than that they
were honoured to find a mention in them, or that they caught
more than a whiff of the meteoric rise of Byron's reputation
throughout Europe. On the other hand, it may be assumed that
the Phanariot circles in Constantinople, in the Balkans, and
particularly in the European centres, were better informed.
However, those in these circles with intellectual leanings, and
particularly the scholars among them, were engrossed rather in

the problem of how to educate the nation in order to befit it for the freedom to come than in discussion of the trends in contemporary European literature. Thus, in the voluminous correspondence of Adamantios Korais during these years, no reference to Byron is to be found, despite Byron's spirited defence of Korais in the notes to *Childe Harold* on receipt in Athens of a number of the *Edinburgh Review* containing a review of the French translation of Strabo's *Geography*.[4] Some of the works of Byron may well have been introduced into the rare atmosphere of the small literary groups within the Phanariot circles, probably through French translations, but their interest in poetry and their own efforts to compose poetry were for their own exclusive pleasure more than for promulgation and publication. What was published tended to lack distinction and was mainly influenced by French and Italian literature. In a survey of translations of the time, all that Björje Knös can find to say is that

> vers la fin de l'époque on resent l'influence de Young, d'Ossian et de Byron, qui ont contribué beaucoup au développement du romantisme grec au siècle suivant.[5]

Of concrete examples, it is Young who influences Georgias Sakellarios in his *Poiemata* published in Vienna in 1817.[6]

If we are left with a question to be resolved concerning the interest in Byron among Phanariot literary circles, what of the situation in the Ionian islands where there was a strong connection with the intellectual life of Italy? Here we are in a field which has been more thoroughly explored and the problem centres round the two poets who were to herald the dawn of the later development of modern Greek literature, Dionysios Solomos and Andreas Kalvos. Both were young men studying in Italy in the first half of the ten years under discussion, Solomos returning to his home in the island of Zante in 1818 and Kalvos following Ugo Phoscolo to Switzerland in 1816 and then accompanying him to London, whence he returned to Switzerland in 1820. Neither of them published poems in Greek before 1821 or, as far as can be ascertained, are recorded as making any reference to Byron before then. Undeniably, both were acquainted with circles in Italy where radical ideas were rife and where the seeds of romanticism were being sown. But Kalvos was primarily concerned with the classics and Solomos is not known (at least at that time) to have had a command of English, while he is known to have been well versed in Italian literature from Dante onwards. Romilly Jenkins wrote that Solomos might have met Byron in Milan in 1816, although he concluded that without evidence of such a meeting it is to be assumed that 'Byron and Solomos . . . met one another only when it was too late'[7] – a macabre allusion to the presence of Solomos among the crowd at Zante when Byron's coffin arrived there from Mesolonghi. However, we do know that by 1822 Solomos had some knowledge of English poets, for Spyridon Trikoupis states that on his first visit to Solomos in Zante

> accompanied by Lekatsas, I went to his country-house and he gave me a warm welcome thanks to my conversation with him about English poets, whom he admired as I did too.[8]

As we shall see later, Byron must have been included among them. For the moment, we shall leave the delicate question of Byronic influence on Solomos and conclude that there is as little evidence from the Ionian islands as from elsewhere to suggest that any but a few Greeks knew much more than the name of Byron before the Revolution and that it would have been hard to find one among them truly conversant with his works. As an illustration of the extent of general knowledge, an extract may be quoted from a letter of Alexandros Mavro-kordatos from Pisa to a bookseller in Geneva, which is dated July 1820. Referring to the receipt of some books, he says of those which were included for a certain Mr. Vlakhoutzis:

> Mr. Vlahoutzy étant parti depuis longtemps d'ici, je ne me trouve plus à même de m'acquitter de votre commission, je retiendra cependant pour moi le choix des poésies de Byron que vous avez envoyé pour lui.[9]

The outbreak of the War of Independence naturally disrupted the intellectual life of the Greeks in lands occupied by the Turks. Only the Greeks in Europe and in the Ionian islands could lead relatively normal lives and pay attention to their literary interests. These obviously tended to embrace concepts of liberty and heroism as they watched the struggle with anxious hearts. For such themes Byron, among others, could provide a source of inspiration. But it does not seem that he came close to Greek hearts before it became known that he was thinking of returning to Greece. At this point the influential Greeks, engaged in attempting to plead their cause and raise funds for it in England, clearly became interested. The maximum advantage must be gained from the sympathy and the purse of so rich an aristocrat of European fame and noted liberal views. When he finally made up his mind to take an active part, the rumour of milord's impending visit doubtless evoked hope and wonder in Greece. But as he himself wished, or stated that he wished, it was the man of action whom they awaited. Amongst those who coaxed him on his way from Italy with flattering words, one or two at least were a trifle apprehensive of how he might react in the event. The metropolitan Ignatios, who may have known Byron personally at Pisa, wrote thus to Mavrokordatos at the end of July 1823:

> I have recommended Lord Byron to you, who ought to have arrived at Zante by now. Do what you can to see that he is pleased, not so much because he can provide funds and be of practical assistance, but rather because if he is displeased he will do more harm than you can imagine. Let the government show every sign of a good welcome and honour to the man, because good references and good testimony from him are of essential importance.[10]

In similar vein, Orlandos wrote to Mavrokordatos in Mesolonghi from Cephallonia on 1 November 1823, following a meeting with Byron (in quarantine at the time):

> Byron desires, as he told me, to meet you. Before you meet him, I have time to tell you a few things about his character. The noble Lord is a philhellene; although perhaps he himself wants to be a benefactor of Greece, others too, however, have influence on his will. From this, perhaps, springs the instability and change of mind in his decisions.[11]

The metropolitan may have been well enough informed to know that Byron had written: 'Indeed, a more abandoned race of miscreants cannot exist than the lower orders of the Greek clergy.' Clearly all mistrusted his vacillation, but it is nice to record that Ignatios was perfectly satisfied in the event and

wrote in the early months of 1824 to both Louriotis and Kapodistrias to express his satisfaction at Byron's material help and
his efforts to put an end to disarray.[12]

It would be agreeable to learn that the days of sojourn in
Cephallonia, and particuarly those of waiting – or inspired pro-
crastination – at Metaxata, provided an occasional opportunity
for literary discussion with the literati of the Ionian islands. Had
his poetry really been well-known to them, it is difficult not to
believe that some of them would have tried to contact him,
despite his profession of lack of interest in the muse now that he
had taken on the new mantle of action. The record of his stay is
well attested and makes no reference to any such attempt.
Solomos must have been aware that he was there, but he may
have been indulging in one of his moods of retreat. Anyway,
nothing appears to have resulted from the efforts of Edward
Blaquiere to make arrangements for him to be received and
entertained by 'a distinguished young poet' of the Ionian
islands.[13]

The only surviving testimony comes from Andreas Laskaratos,
Count Delladecima's nephew, then eleven or twelve years old
and later to become famous as poet and satirist, but the
recollection is disappointing:

> In my uncle's house at that time I had the luck to see Lord
> Byron who used to come there, and sometimes I had the
> honour of sitting at table with him. One day my uncle was
> not ready to receive him and suggested that I should ask him
> to go into the sitting-room and keep him company until he
> arrived himself. However, Byron did not want to go in at
> once on the excuse that his boots were wet and would dirty
> the carpet. 'Let's walk here,' he said 'until your uncle's
> ready.' And in fact we walked a little at the entrance.
>
> He never stopped talking to me, but I had no idea of the
> importance of the person with whom I was conversing.[14]

The story of Byron's active participation in the war is very
well known. Its effect on the attitude of philhellenes abroad and
on foreign government policy has been treated fully by
historians. There is no doubt of the interest shown in his arrival
in Greece not only locally at Mesolonghi (despite the apprehen-
sion of Ignatios and others that he might not be suitably

welcomed), but throughout the country. The confused times, as well as the scarcity of printing presses in Greece at the time, make it hardly a matter of surprise that Greek records of the event are scanty. But the Greeks somehow divined, as Byron divined, that his setting foot on Greek earth was an act of destiny. From this moment the 'Byronic myth' begins with tales of the rich prince of the West come to share in the Greek ordeal with supreme faith in the justice of the cause.

It was always possible that the myth would explode while Byron was alive. It was his death which gave it immortality. More than most peoples, perhaps, the Greeks are apt to belittle the achievements of the living and compensate for it by an exaggerated eulogy of the dead. In Byron's case they recognised that no eulogy could be exaggerated. The symbol of sacrifice was the more significant for the choice of place, heroic Mesolonghi already once besieged, and of time, the Greek Easter, which made almost more than natural Byron's expressed sense of destiny:

> Seek out – less often sought than found –
>   A soldier's grave, for thee the best;
> Then look around, and choose thy ground,
>   And take thy Rest.

Reactions of Greek emotions, rather than of political or business matters of fact, are revealed for the first time immediately after Byron passed away. An edition of *Ellinika Khronika* (itself financed by Byron), with suitable black frame, contains an article written on the same evening of his death. If, in the grief of the moment, it fails to realise the symbol of immortality, it makes the other points which were to become the embodiment of the myth:

Greece mourns inconsolably this joyful Eastertide, for suddenly there slips from her embrace her valued benefactor, the illustrious Lord Byron . . . His zeal on behalf of the true freedom of Greece gave us great encouragement and the fairest hopes for the nation . . . The people of Greece, deprived of such a father and benefactor is smitten with bitter heartfelt grief . . . The hopes of our nation in him have not been realised, and nothing remains to us than to lament inconsolably a death so harsh for us . . .[15]

Apart from the thirty-seven rounds of cannon fire and the funeral service, the outward signs of mourning demanded of the people of Mesolonghi were not likely to be forgotten. Their Easter Day had been one of anxious prayer; now everything was to be closed for three days except food and chemist shops, there were to be no musical games, none of the usual Easter dances, no drinking in the *phagopotia*, no other kind of merry-making, twenty-one days of *penthophoria*. In May, orders from the central government decreed a further day's mourning throughout Greece with similar official marks of grief and esteem.

The most immediate response to Byron's death which may reasonably be considered under the heading of literature was the funeral speech delivered by Spyridon Trikoupis at the impressive ceremony at Mesolonghi on the day following Byron's death. It is stated by contemporary sources to have been composed within a period of three or four hours.[16] If this is true, it not only shows the excellence of its rhetoric to be remarkable but also suggests that the expressions in it are Trikoupis' own. In it he not only demonstrates that he has grasped the meaning of the 'myth' for both Greece and Europe, as well as recognising Byron's own presentiment of his destiny, but he also marks Byron's position as the revolutionary poet:

> He has given his name to the age in which we live. The breadth of his intellect and the height of his imagination did not allow him to follow the splendid but beaten path of the literary glory of those before him: he seized a new road, a road which ancient prejudice has tried and is still trying to shut in learned Europe, but as long as his writings live (and they will live as long as the world exists) this road will always remain open since, like the other, it is a road of true glory.

Here, then, in Trikoupis there is proof of a Greek with insight into the Byronic revolution in poetry and the extent of its spread into Europe.

Moreover, in the next passage of the speech, Trikoupis makes clear that he has himself read and been inspired by Byron's writings. Nor need this be thought surprising. He was born in 1788 and moved from his home at Mesolonghi to Patras for further education. There he learnt Italian, French and English and took employment in the British Consulate. He became secretary to Lord Guilford in Corfu and was sent by Guilford on a scholarship to Europe. He studied literature and philosophy at Rome and Paris from, it seems, 1815 until the outbreak of the war. During this time he frequently visited Guilford in England. In addition he was himself quite a respectable poet. There was thus every reason for him to come into contact with, and to become attracted to, the works of Byron and his knowledge of English would have allowed him to read them in the original.

I will come back to the funeral speech and Trikoupis. Let us for the moment return to Solomos, in certain of whose works of this time Byronic borrowings and Byronic influence have been traced. They have recently been discussed by Byron Raizis,[17] whose general conclusion has been that it is facile to assume with Jenkins that 'it is probable that next to those of Dante, Byron's works were most profoundly studied by Solomos'. The first of these works, the *Hymn to Liberty*, was completed before Byron's death, probably in May 1823, but not published until after it (a second edition was published in the same year, 1825, in Paris). The only apparent influence of Byron is found in stanzas LXXXIII–LXXXV, but it is certain and acknowledged by the poet himself in his notes.[18] It is necessary to go into this in some detail since Professor Raizis appears to have misinterpreted in attributing the influence solely to stanza XXX of the third canto of *Don Juan*, beginning 'And further on a group of Grecian girls,' and concluding from this that Solomos has only echoed Byron.

The three stanzas of Solomos run as follows:

Στὴ σκιὰ χεροπιασμένες,
Στὴ σκιὰ βλέπω κι' ἐγὼ
Κρινοδάκτυλες παρθένες
'Οπού κάνουνε χορό·

Στὸ χορὸ γλυκογυρίζουν
'Ωραῖα μάτια ἐρωτικά,
Καὶ εἰς τὴν αὔρα κυματίζουν
Μαῦρα, ὁλόχρυσα μαλλιά.

Ἡ ψυχή μου ἀναγαλλιάζει
Πῶς ὁ κόρφος καθεμιᾶς
Γλυκοβύζαστο ἑτοιμάζει
Γάλα ἀνδρείας καὶ ἐλευθεριᾶς.

[Their hands clasped in the shade, in the shade I too see
maidens with lily-white fingers dancing;
In the dance beautiful eyes turn sweetly and lovingly,
and in the breeze waves black and golden hair.
My soul rejoices that the breast of each is making ready
the milk which will sweetly suckle courage and freedom.]

It is clear that *kheropiasmenes* and *krinodaktyles parthenes* dancing
represents 'were strung together like a row of pearls, link'd
hand in hand, and dancing' of stanza XXX of *Don Juan*, while
for *kymatizoun mavra, olokhrysa mallia* we may sense 'down her
white neck long floating auburn curls' from the same stanza.
For the rest, however, it is, along with the note, the *Isles of
Greece* which is in question. The poet of the note is the bard at
Juan and Haidee's banquet and his song that which

> Thus sung, or would, or could, or should have sung,
>   The modern Greek, in tolerable verse . . .

and the particular verses Solomos had before him here must
surely have been those of stanza LXXXVI 15:

> Fill high the bowl with Samian wine!
>   Our virgins dance beneath the shade –
> I see their glorious black eyes shine;
>   But gazing on each glowing maid,
> My own the burning tear-drop laves,
> To think such breasts must suckle slaves.

This certainly amounts to borrowing, more so than is
apparent in any of the 166 stanzas of the *Lyrical Poem on the
Death of Lord Byron*, of which he is said to have composed the
first verse on receiving a letter from Trikoupis reporting
Byron's death. It took him a year to finish it, neither he nor
anyone else was ever pleased with the result, and it was not
published until after his death in 1857.[19] The myth is fully
represented in it: Byron's destiny as the bard of liberty, his
demand for unity, his sacrifice in person, the affirmation of the

survival of Greece. In the notes he reveals some knowledge of Byron's life history and quotes a passage from Byron's letter of 2 December 1823 to Mavrokordatos. The notes also show that he knew of Byron's project for visiting America, a theme which he introduces into one stanza of the poem. The three stanzas which precede it are presented as a lament by Byron on the lack of freedom everywhere except in America. They are reminiscent of Byron's passage on America and freedom in his *Ode on Venice*, but they lack the similarity of imagery and epithet of the borrowing in the *Hymn to Liberty*. It could be reasonable to assume that they are a précis from Solomos' reading of Byron's poem, but the laconic note 'see his lyric odes'[20] is so vague that it suggests that Solomos was unaware just how much he was asking of his readers and that he knew the gist of the reference rather than the text itself.

Solomos sketched out his *Lambros* as early as 1823. It was worked over later, but remained fragmentary until after his death. Jenkins (whose translations carry a Byronic ring hardly justified by the style of the original text) maintained that many passages were directly inspired by Byron,[21] but gave no chapter and verse. Almost all critics have labelled it 'Byronic', but there seem no obvious parallels to justify Jenkins' assertion. The poem certainly has a romantic flavour, but it is about this time that we come up against the problem of the spread of the romantic breeze in Europe which makes pin-pointing of specific influence very difficult. It is safer to conclude that Solomos was swayed by the breeze.

The borrowings in the *Hymn to Liberty*, however, do require more explanation. It is to be remarked that in the funeral speech of Trikoupis there is a passage which reads:

> Then [i.e., in the Blessed Hour of Freedom] with garlands of flowers the Maidens of Greece, of whose magic beauty our glorious fellow-citizen Byron sang in many of his poems, then will our fair children, fearing no longer stain from the rapacious hands of our tyrants, set up their dance round his grave and sing of the beauty of our land, which the poet of our age sang with such grace and truth.

Clearly the imagery of this passage is in part taken from the stanzas in *Don Juan* to which I have referred in discussion of the

Hymn to Liberty. Is it too daring to suggest that it was Trikoupis who was responsible for introducing Byron's poetry, or some small part of it, to Solomos at first hand? Cantos III, IV and V of *Don Juan* were published in 1821. Trikoupis could have brought them back with him or had them sent out from Europe and discussed them with Solomos on that first visit to him in 1822. The particular stanzas with their core *The Isles of Greece* would have been of special attraction. Trikoupis may even have translated them for Solomos (a translation by him of the poem '*Tis time this heart should be unmoved* appeared, together with the English text, in the edition of *Ellinika Khronika* for 11 February 1825). And, if one is right to discern the influence of Trikoupis, it is not impossible that Trikoupis' speech was later studied by Solomos during composition of the *Lyrical Ode on the Death of Lord Byron*. There is a good deal of similar expression and three images are common to both – the reverse arms at the funeral, the last thoughts 'Greece' and 'My daughter', and the concept of that daughter's receipt of the poet's mortal remains.

If the premise is correct, it is not difficult to explain the Byronic elements in the three poems of Solomos which we have discussed. The passages in the *Hymn to Liberty* derive from immediate contact with passages from *Don Juan*, discussed with and, perhaps, translated by Trikoupis. The information about Byron revealed in the *Lyrical Ode* is culled mainly from Greek sources, read and heard. Behind this, and particularly strong in the *Lambros* (and perhaps also in the later poems) is what Solomos had learnt in Italy and afterwards about the nature of romantic poetry, including the nature of Byron's poetry.

Solomos was not alone in commemorating Byron's death in verse. Such odes, if on a rather less ambitious scale, became quite the rage, playing their part in the consolidation of the myth. Adamantios Korais, in a letter of July 1824 to Iakovos Rotas, refers to *stikhous typomenous epitaphious eis ton Byron*, sent to him via a third party by Angelica Bartolomeo, née Pallis, who resided in Italy.[22] His interest was not aroused. All he asked of his correspondent was whether he could or should answer her. But Korais never showed much enthusiasm for Byron, whom he appears to have held responsible for flattering Mavrokordatos with the unrepublican title of Prince. He was, however, gracious enough in 1825 to send out in his regular parcels of books from Paris one copy of Gamba's *A Narrative of Lord Byron's Last Journey to Greece*, despite expressing his opinion in the same year to Neophytos Vamvas that 'the death of B. is not all that great a loss to Greece, as neither would be the loss of many others such'.[23] The metropolitan Ignatios evidently remained sceptical of Byron's poetry. While he wrote to his friends in England (in much the same terms as he had written to Byron himself)[24] that Byron's death had deprived 'letters of the closest friend of the Muses and Apollo' he wrote to Koundouriotis in Greece that Byron was '*elaphromyalos* as a poet and that it was not improbable that he would have left in displeasure and by writing against the Greeks done more harm than he had done good . . .'[25] But in Mesolonghi *Ellinika Khronika* was more receptive and published a poem including verses on Byron in the latter half of December 1824. Without merit, it marks, like Solomos' *Lyrical Ode*, the association of Byron with the hero Markos Botzaris, who was killed in action before Byron had time to meet him. It was again a feminine hand which wrote it, 'a girl born far from Greece and brought up in another nation's language'.[26] Probably it was also from outside Greece that Thomas Moore received at about the same time 'a modern Greek song upon Byron's death (with the music), *Odi pros ton Lord Byron*. Hallam and I made out the words between us, but they are nothing remarkable.'[27]

The best of the commemorative poems comes from the Greek who had been with Phoscolo in England, and who was inspired by Byron's example to go back to Greece in 1826. *The Britannic Muse* of Andreas Kalvos is the first in his second book of odes, published in Paris in 1826. Kalvos pictures Byron leaving the shores of England for the last time, his sunset to lead to a star of hope. He laments the Muse that sang so well and will sing no more and then calls upon Byron to rise from sleep, sing again to Europe and receive the crown with which Greece is waiting to adorn him as poet, liberal and benefactor. In vain!

Αἴ! τῶν θνητῶν οἱ ἐλπίδες
ὡς ἐλαφρὰ διαλύονται
ὄνειρα βρέφους· χάνονται
ὡς λεπτὸν βόλι εἰς ἄπειρον
βάθος πελάγου.

'Ο Βύρων κεῖται ὡς κρίνος
ὑπὸ τὸ βαρὺ κάλυμμα
ἀθλίας νυκτός· ἡ αἰώνιος,
ὦ λύπη, τὸν ἐσκέπασε
μοῖρα θανάτου.

[Alas! the hopes of mortals disperse like the light dreams of a child, are lost like a tiny shot in the boundless depths of the sea.

Byron lies like a lily beneath the heavy covering of night's wretchedness; grief! the eternal fate of death has covered him.]

But it is on a note of hope that the poem ends:

"Ότι, ἀν φθαρτὸν τὸ σῶμα
πέσῃ, καὶ τ' ἄϋλον πνεῦμα
τῶν ἀγαθῶν καὶ ἡ φήμη
νικήσουν ὡς ἡ ἀλήθεια
τὸ ἀένναον μέλλον.

[For though the body falls and perishes, the immaterial spirit of good will, like the truth, conquer the everlasting future.]

And not only will spirit and fame survive, but the mortals who mourn will be led through their mourning to the path of virtue.[28]

Despite an underlying romantic strain, the odes of Kalvos are far from Byronic in style. He returned to the Ionian islands but published no more poetry. Solomos turned to other channels for his inspiration and created his own idiom and for all the British mandate and Lord Guilford's academy his contemporaries were too much overawed by his influence to strike out on their own. Only in Aristotelis Valaoritis some thirty years later, are played in the Ionian islands the full chords of romanticism and the main source of his inspiration is Victor Hugo.

The literary climate of the first years of the new kingdom was that brought by the Phanariots who came to settle there. Their best known representatives are the brothers Panagiotis and Alexandros Soutsos. To the former belongs a drama which achieved remarkable popularity both in book form and on the stage. It was first published in 1831 and is entitled *Odoiporos*. It is certain that it owes something to Byron. He says in the prologue to one of the editions: 'What sort of a man does the *odoiporos* represent in the play? A soldier of the Greek struggle like Byron, and like Byron melancholic and full of imagination . . .'; while in the play itself one of the lesser characters says to the hero:

> Ἐγκλείει κόσμους ἰδεῶν τὸ μέγα μέτωπόν σου
> τὸ ἦθος σου τὸ ἄγριον καὶ μελαγχολικόν σου·
> μ᾽ ἀνακαλεῖ τὸν Βύρωνα, ὁπόταν τοῦ Ὑψίστου
> τὸ βλέμμα φεύγων μ᾽ ἄνοιγε τὸν Ἅδην τῆς ψυχῆς του.
> Τῆς δόξης πῶς, καθὼς αὐτός, πῶς δὲν κτυπᾶς τὰς θύρας;

[Your great forehead, your wild and melancholy nature, contains worlds of ideas; it reminds me of Byron, when, fleeing the look of the Almighty, he opened up the Hell of his soul to me. How do you not knock, like him, on the doors of glory?][29]

The passage is not very illuminating (the gates of glory, alas, are not so easily opened) but we can assume that Soutsos thought he was creating his own *Manfred*, and he must have known Byron's drama because there are a number of obvious similarities. To match the Alps and Mont Blanc 'On a throne of rocks, in a robe of clouds with a diadem of snow', we have:

> Κρυσταλλωμένη Ἄθωνα! τὸ ὕψος σου θαυμάζω . .

[Athos of crystal! I wonder at your heights][30]

and the shores of Athos surrounded by snow-covered rocks. There is the same concept that the hero will fall off the precipice, the same theme of lover meeting lost heroine (though Rallou, unlike Astarte, is more flesh than spirit and thus most incongruous in her Athonite surroundings), and the same ultimate disappearance in equally, though differently, enigmatic fashion. In one case:

> He's gone – his soul hath ta'en its earthless flight;
> Whither? I dread to think – but he is gone.

In the other:

> Καθ᾽ ἣν στιγμὴν ἀνοίγεται ἡ οὐρανία θύρα,
> τὸν ἀληθῆ του ὁ θνητὸς λαμβάνει χαρακτῆρα.

[At the moment when the heavenly door is opened, mortal man takes on his true character][31]

However, it is doubtful whether Soutsos was more than passingly familiar with *Manfred*. There are no passages of obvious borrowing and the work contains borrowings from many sources. Herein lies the difficulty of tracing Byronic influence through the romantic mania, of which the first example is the Athenian School, which gripped Greek poets in the period 1830–80. They derive their inspiration from countless snatches of other people's plums which they mix in a spontaneous stew. Without the secret of the subjective element, they carry all the trappings of the romantic movement: spurned heroes, disillusioned lovers, death and the grave, ghostly meetings. Not unnaturally they make special play with ancient Greek references and, above all, with the theme of freedom and patriotism as represented by their own recent heroes of the War of Independence.

Much of the spirit of it, it may be claimed, derives from Byron. However, the predominant foreign influence of the Athenian Phanariots is French literature. Thus, it is the French romantics, particularly Victor Hugo and Béranger, whom Panagiotis Soutsos' brother Alexandros so fervently admires. And it was French rather than English with which these poets were generally familiar. The *Periplanomenos* of Alexandros Soutsos may take the form of *Childe Harold* (the first three cantos were published in 1839), but the resemblance is superficial only. Similar titles like *Loiplanos*, *Kodoniatis*, *Exotistos*, and *Alphredos* carry as little conviction. References to Byron, often in association with the heroes of Mesolonghi, reflect the myth and not necessarily any close acquaintance with his poetry.

For the first twenty years of independence, interest in literature in Greece was very limited. In giving what at first sight looks an imposing list of periodicals Professor Sakhinis says that

> the capital assets of Greek intellectual thought in writers, literary or scholarly, were generally insufficient to preserve a periodical. In the same way, it seems that the reading public too was insufficient to give economic strength to the different periodical editions.[32]

The periodicals themselves were comparatively weak in literary content. Around 1850, however, there are signs of a growing interest in literature. This is helped by the decision of Amvrosios Rallis to finance an annual poetry competition, which not only

encouraged poetry but also literary criticism. It is further helped
by the appearance of two new periodicals, *Euterpe* which ran
from 1847 to 1855 and *Pandora* which ran from 1850 to
1872.

Traces of Byronic influence or references to Byron are sparse
in the pages of the periodicals. *Euterpe* contains a number of
biographies, but Byron does not seem to be included among
them. *Pandora* was not so much concerned with poetry, but in
the detailed analysis which Professor Sakhinis gives of this and
other contemporary periodicals only one reference to Byron is
found, and that remote, in a translation of a passage of Washington Irving's *Newstead Abbey*.[33] On the other hand, an impetus
was given to the publication of translations. From what is
seemingly a first start in 1836 in Smyrna with the translation of
The Bride of Abydos in 1837 by K. Lambryllos, and with that of
the same work and *The Curse of Minerva* in 1837 in Athens by
N. Mandrikaris, the 1850s witnessed translations, in Edward
Masson's *Philellinika* (1852), of *The Siege of Corinth* by O. S.
Pylarinos (1855), of *The Giaour* by Aikaterini Dosios (1857)
whose husband Konstantinos translated *Lara* and *The Corsair*,
and in the *Ios* of Angelos Vlakhos, who himself translated
Mazeppa. In 1864 Eric Green published a translation of
Manfred in Patras and in 1865 Khristos Anastasiadis (writing
under the name Parmenides) one of *Sardanapalus* in Athens.

By this time, and the output of translations was to be
continued, it must have been possible for those Greeks who so
wished to become genuinely conversant with Byron's poetry.
Some had already made the effort. Stephanos Koumanoudis
admits that his *Stratis Kalopikheiros* of 1851 owes a debt to
Byron (a long poem, K. Th. Dimaras says of it,[34] in iambic
trimeters, monotonous and without any attraction for the
modern reader). In 1860 Dimitrios Vernardakis, acting as
spokesman for the panel in the annual poetry competition, gave
an outline sketch of the personality of the author of *Don Juan*,
and in the same year Karasoutsas published a poem on Byron
which recalls his stay at the Capuchin convent by the monument
of Lysicrates on his first visit to Greece and one passage of which
could be interpreted as inferring knowledge of one of those
stanzas in *Childe Harold* less flattering to Greek pride. The height
of Greek imitation of classical elegance was reached by Philippos

Ioannou in a lament in hexameters stated to have been composed soon after Byron's death and revised later.[35]

The most extreme expression of romantic passion, grief and patriotism reached its apogee in the poetry of Akhillefs Paraskhos and it is generally considered among the most 'Byronic'. His star was at its height the same moment that reaction to romanticism began to set in among Greek intellectuals. Paraskhos achieved an astonishing popularity, but his art was the art of the showman rather than of the poet. His personality and oratorical prowess enabled him to move his uncritical audience to share the passion of his moods. Proclaimed by him, the words that flowed from his lips were magic. Subjected to cold scrutiny, they showed up laughable and meaningless. Unschooled, he needed only to know enough of his heroes to fire his imagination; his own talents would supply the rest. Among his heroes was Byron, but it was still the idolised Byron of the myth whom from his youth (he was born in 1838) he wished to emulate. Snatches of Byron in translation he may have known (it is said to have been from prose translations), of the secret of Byron's poetry very little. Nonetheless, it was fitting that this exponent of the last word in *Vyronismos* should recite a poem on Byron when his statue was unveiled at Mesolonghi in 1881. A better poet, however much he might have improved upon the expression of it, would not have revealed so clearly the power of the myth. Who else could have so fearlessly written, as the shade of Byron rises before his erstwhile comrade-in-arms now weighed down by wounds and years:

"Ἄχ, νᾶτος, εἶπε· εἶν' αὐτός· χαρᾶς δὲν εἶναι πλάνη·
Νὰ τὰ σγουρὰ του τὰ μαλλιὰ καὶ νὰ τὸ μέτωπό του,
Συννεφιασμένος οὐρανὸς κι' ὁλάργυρο ἀστέρι·
Νὰ τὸ πικρὸ χαμόγελο, τὸ φιλτισένιο χέρι,
Ποὺ μὲ ταὶς χούφταις μοίραζε φλουριὰ στὰ παλικάρια
Κ' ἔδιδε δρόμο στὸν ἀϊτὸ καὶ νύχι στὰ λιοντάρια! . .
Καλῶς τὴ λύρα, ποὺ κανεὶς δὲν ἔπιασε ἀκόμα·
Τῆς Λευθεριᾶς τ' ἀέρισμα, τῆς δάφνης τὸ λουλούδι·
Καλῶς τὴν ἄφθαρτη καρδιά, τὸ πικραμένο στόμα,
Ποὺ ἔβγανε τὸ στεναγμὸ μαζὶ μὲ τὸ τραγούδι·
Καλῶς τὰ μάτια, πῶκλεισαν τὰ δάκρυα κι' ὄχι μνῆμα,
Τὸ θυμωμένο πέλαγος μὲ τ' ἀσημένιο κῦμα!

['Ah! look,' he said: "Tis he, not joy's deception;
Behold his curly hair, behold his brow,
A clouded heaven and a silver star;
Behold the bitter smile, the ivory hand,
Whose palms dealt shillings to the pallikars,
Gave flight to the eagle and claw to the lion! . . .
Hail to the lyre, on which none has yet laid hold;
Hail the pure air of Freedom, hail the laurel's flower;
Hail to the immortal heart, the bitter lips,
Which sihned as well as sang;
Hail to the eyes, closed by tears and not the grave,
Hail to the angry sea with the silver wave!'][36]

The continued popularity of the myth is vouched for by travellers' tales and folklore in the nineteenth century. It is still there for all to see in the statue in the Zappeion garden of the naked Byron sheltered by mother Greece and at their feet the figure of slavery. But the new literary movement of the 1880s blew away the cobwebs and permitted a more objective view. The passage of the myth to reality was marked by none more clearly than the principal representative of the new movement, Kostis Palamas. Had he not been brought up in Mesolonghi, steeped himself in its heroic traditions? Had he not been taken to tea with Mrs. Black and been rowed across the lagoon by old Kazis, the same boatman who had ferried Byron (and of whom Patrick Leigh Fermor tells such an amusing tale with regard to Byron's slippers)? Had not *Manfred* (in Eric Green's translation) been one of his first loves and did he not absorb, again in translation, the 'golden words of that great genius' as he read the fourth canto of Byron's *Childe Harold* 'in the midst of complete silence and solitude, stretched out under the columns of the Erechtheium'[37] the first year of his student life in Athens? The thoughtful critic of later years would approach the subject of Byron with more balanced judgement.[38] But the poet who meets Pegasus still riderless from the day of Byron's death still reflects something of the magic of the myth as he makes Pegasus tell of their former rides together:

> Τὰ φρενιασμένα τὰ ταξίδια μας τὰ ὡραῖα!
> Ψηλὰ ἀπὸ τ' ἀλπικὰ βουνὰ
> κι ὡς κάτου στὰ βενέτικα παλάτια,

Πήγασος, εἶχα τὰ φτερά,
κ' ἐκεῖνος, ἄνθρωπος, τὰ μάτια.
Σᾶς γγίξαμε, κορφὲς τῶν ἰδεῶν,
κ' ἤπιαμε μέσα στῶν παθῶν ἀχόρταγα τὰ βάθη·
μὰ καβαλλάρης μέσ' στοὺς καβαλλάρηδες
ποιός ἄλλος ξαναστάθη;
Τὸν ξέρει ὁ Ρῆνος ὁ περήφανος
διαφεντευτὴς ξεδιψαστὴς πλατὺς
κάστρων, ψυχῶν καὶ τόπων·
καί, λίμνη Ἑλβετική, κ' ἐσύ,
ὅσο γλυκειά, τόσο βαθιὰ ζωγραφιστὴ
στοὺς πόθους τῶν ἀνθρώπων
καὶ πιὸ βαθιὰ στοὺς ἔρωτες τῶν ποιητῶν, κ' ἐσεῖς
δρυμοὶ τευτονικοὶ καὶ ἰταλικὰ ἀκρογιάλια,
καὶ πύργοι ἐσεῖς ρωμαντικοὶ κ' ἐρείπια στοιχιωμένα
κι ὁ ἀδιάντροπος ξεφαντωτής, κ' ἐσύ, δειλὴ παρθένα.
Τῆς ἁμαρτίας τοὺς ἄγριους τοὺς ἀνθοὺς
ἀπόκοτα τοὺς ἔκοβε καὶ στόλιζε μ' αὐτοὺς
καὶ φόρτωνε τὰ σύμμετρα τῆς τέχνης του ἀνθογυάλια
Ἑλληνολάτρης βάρβαρος, ροβόλησε
μακρυάθε καὶ γονάτισε στὸ δοξασμένο χῶμα·
τῆς Ἀττικῆς οἱ μέλισσες δὲν τὸ καταφρονέσανε
τὸ σκυθικό του στόμα.
Τῆς θείας τῆς γῆς διαλαλητής,
μὰ καὶ κρίτης,
τῆς ἔφερε τὴ λύρα του καὶ τὸ σπαθί του ἀντάμα,
κ' ἦρθε, καὶ σβεῖ στὴ ματωμένη λιμνοθάλασσα
τὴ φλόγα τῆς ζωῆς του καὶ τὸ δράμα.

[Our frenzied wonderful journeys!
High up on the mountains of the Alps,
and down to the Venetian palaces,
I, Pegasus, had the wings,
and he, a man, the vision.
Peaks of ideas, you we touched,
and drank in the insatiable depths of passion;
what other has risen up
as horseman among horsemen?
The proud Rhine knows him,
the broad thirst-quenching defender

of castles, souls and lands;
you, too, Swiss lake,
sweetly and deeply painted in the desires of man
and more deeply in the loves of poets,
and you, German forests and Italian shores,
romantic forts and haunted ruins,
shameless reveller, and shy maid.
Daringly he plucked the wild flowers of sin,
with them adorned and filled the measured vases of his art.
Worshipper of Greece from barbarian lands,
he came down from afar, knelt on the famed soil;
the bees of Attica did not spurn
his northern lips.
Herald of the divine earth,
but critic too,
he brought to her both lyre and sword,
and came, and in the blood-stained sea-lake
extinguishes the flame and drama of his life.][39]

NOTES TO CHAPTER 10

1. C. M. Woodhouse, *The Philhellenes* (London, 1969), 92–3.
2. The title of a book by Harold Spender (London, 1924). For another example see the chapter 'Byron's Poetical Inheritance' in Terence Spencer's *Fair Greece, Sad Relic* (London, 1954).
3. Contained in the appendix to *Childe Harold's Pilgrimage* (4th ed.; London, 1812) p. 268.
4. *Ibid.*, pp. 181–3.
5. Björje Knös, *L'histoire de la littérature néo-grecque* (Uppsala, 1962) p. 610.
6. *Ibid.*, p. 611.
7. Romilly Jenkins, *Dionysius Solomos* (Cambridge, 1940) p. 89.
8. My translation of part of a letter from Spyridon Trikoupis to Polylas written in 1859, taken from its reproduction in K. Kairophylas, *I zoi kai to ergo tou Solomou* (Athens, n.d.) pp. 15–19. It was first published in *Ekthesis ton pepragmenon apo tis Kentrikis Epitropis epi tis ekatontaetiridos tou Solomou* (Zakynthos, 1902) p. 221, to which I have not access. Jenkins (54) translates the last few words '. . . whom he admired no less than I, and understood a great deal better.'
9. *Istorikon Arkheion Alexandrou Mavrokordatou* (Athens, 1963) 21 (*Mnimeia tis Ellinikis Istorias*, v, i).
10. *Ignatios Mitropolitis Oungrovlakhias* (Athens, 1961) 162 (*Mnimeia tis Ellinikis Istorias* IV, ii),

11. *Istorikon Arkheion Alexandrou Mavrokordatou*, v, iii (Athens, 1968) 569.

12. *Ignatios Mitropolitis* 189 and 185.

13. Quoted by William St. Clair in *That Greece Might Still Be Free* (London, 1972), p. 152. I have assumed that the reference is to Solomos.

14. Andreas Laskaratos, *Aftoviographia* (Athens, n.d.) p. 11 (translated from the Italian by Kharilaos Antonatos).

15. *Ellinika Khronika*, 9 April 1824. The article is dated 7 (19) April 1824.

16. Editor's note to the text of the speech, described as *aftoskhediasmenos kai ekphonimenos*, in the edition of *Ellinika Khronika* for 16 April 1824.

17. Byron Raizis, 'Solomos and the Britannic Muses', *Neo-Hellenika*, 1 (1970) 94–121.

18. Solomos, *Apanta*, ed. L. Politis, 1 (Athens, 1948) p. 98. The note reads in translation:

> Lord Byron, in the third canto of Don Juan,
> presents a Greek poet who, in despair and
> complaint over the slavery of his country, has
> before him a cup of wine, and amongst others says
> the following words: '. . . our women dance beneath
> the shade; I see the charms of their eyes; but when
> I consider that they will give birth to slaves, my
> eyes fill with tears' . . .

For the problems of the dates of the editions of the *Hymn to Liberty* see Politis, pp. 335–6.

19. Politis, pp. 101–35.

20. *Ibid.*, p. 133.

21. Jenkins, *Solomos*, p. 134.

22. G. Valetas, *Korais* II, ii (Athens, 1965) p. 407.

23. *Ibid.*, p. 438.

24. *Ignatios Mitropolitis Oungrovlakhias*, 190.

25. Letter from Pisa 7/19 May 1824, in *Arkheia Koundourioti* II (Athens, 1921) pp. 275–6.

26. *Ellinika Khronika*, 17 December 1824.

27. Thomas Moore's diary for 30 December 1824, *Memoirs, Journal, and Correspondence of Thomas Moore*, IV (London, 1853) p. 264.

28. G. Th. Zoras, *Kalvou odai* (Athens, 1962) pp. 87–91.

29. *Vasiki Vivliothiki* 12, ed. K. Th. Dimaras (Athens, 1954) p. 82.

30. *Ibid.*, p. 77.

31. *Ibid.*, p. 111.

32. Prof. Sakhinis, *Symvouli stin Istoria tis Pandoras* (Athens, 1964) p. 15.

33. *Ibid.*, p. 157.

34. K. Th. Dimaras, *Istoria tis neoellinikis Logotekhnias* II (Athens, 1949) p. 74.

35. For this and a selection of other relevant poems see the volume marking the centenary of Byron's death, entitled *Ellas kai Vyron* (Athens, 1924).

36. *Ibid.*, pp. 85–6.

37. Letter to his cousin Masinga dated 3 December 1875, K. S. Konstas, *Anekdota Palamika Keimena* in *Nea Estia* (1952) p. 291.

38. See article *Vyronolatreia* in *Kosti Palama Apanta* (Athens, n.d.) pp. 185–220.

39. *Kosti Palama Apanta*, v (Athens, n.d.) pp. 224–5.

Index